Dharma, Color, and Culture

NEW VOICES IN WESTERN BUDDHISM

EDITED BY

Hilda Gutiérrez Baldoquín

PARALLAX PRESS
BERKELEY, CALIFORNIA

Parallax Press
P.O. Box 7355
Berkeley, California 94707
www.parallax.org

Parallax Press is the publishing division of Unified Buddhist Church, Inc.

Cover and text design by Gopa and Ted 2, Inc.
Author photo © Jen Randolph
Illustrations © Mayumi Oda. Please do not photocopy or otherwise
reproduce them without permission.

"Reading the Eightfold Path" reprinted with the permission of Scribner, an
imprint of Simon & Schuster Adult Publishing Group, from *Turning the
Wheel* by Charles Johnson. Copyright © 2003 by Charles Johnson.

"Fire" reprinted with the permission of Alfred A. Knopf, a division of
Random House, Inc., from *The Fifth Book of Peace* by Maxine Hong
Kingston. Copyright © 2003 by Maxine Hong Kingston.

"Don't Waste Time" and "This Was Not an Area of Large Plantations"
reprinted with permission from *Turning Wheel, The Journal of Socially
Engaged Buddhism.* Copyright © 2003 Hilda Gutiérrez Baldoquín and
copyright © 2003 Alice Walker.

Library of Congress Cataloging-in-Publication Data

Dharma, color, and culture : new voices in Western Buddhism / edited by
Hilda Gutiérrez Baldoquín.
    p. cm.
  ISBN 1-888375-42-6 (pbk.)
  1. Religious life—Buddhism. 2. Buddhism—Doctrines. 3. Four Noble
Truths. I. Baldoquín, Hilda Gutiérrez.

BQ4302.D5 2004
294.3'4442—dc22

                                                            2004018209

1 2 3 4 5 / 08 07 06 05 04

One who sees suffering also sees the origin of suffering, also sees the cessation of suffering, also sees the way leading to the cessation of suffering.
—SAMYUTTA NIKAYA 56.30 (10)

The dharma is nobody's property. It belongs to whoever is interested.
—TIBETAN PROVERB

DEDICATION

Abuela Margót por las enseñanzas.

Xiomara por ser la razón.

Lola por el gran ejemplo.

Berta Baldoquín Marrero por su decisión.

Abuela Margót for the teachings.

Xiomara for being the reason.

Lola for the great example.

Berta Baldoquín Marrero for the decision.

DHARMA, COLOR, AND CULTURE

Pañña: Wisdom
    Right understanding
    Right intention

Sila: Ethical Conduct
    Right Speech
    Right action / conduct
    Right livelihood

Samadhi - Concentration
    Right effort
    Right mindfulness   sati
    Right Concentration

Table of Contents

HARITI (KISHIBOJIN)

Foreword

KAMALA MASTERS

Then I was standing on the highest mountain of them all, and round about beneath me was the whole hoop of the world. And while I stood there I saw more than I can tell and I understood more than I saw; for I was seeing in a sacred manner the shapes of all things in the spirit, and the shape of all shapes as they must live together like one being. And I saw the sacred hoop of my people was one of the many hoops that made one circle, wide as daylight and as starlight...and I saw that it was holy. —Black Elk, Oglala Sioux (1863–1950)

D*HARMA, COLOR, AND CULTURE* is a crucial book at this significant time in the history of the spread of the teachings of the Buddha. We are bearing witness to horizons that are lifting and expanding to include a greater diversity of people and possibilities than ever before. We are also bearing witness to the profound pain that we have felt and carried individually and collectively. As we walk a noble path toward the end of suffering, our hearts grow bigger with compassion and wisdom. We can become a vital source of inspiration, hope, and guidance for our younger ones, our sisters and brothers, and even our elders. Our individual and collective growing pains are not in vain.

I sometimes wonder what the growing pains were like for those who lived during the time of the Buddha, and the centuries after his death when the Dharma was brought into other cultures. Siddhartha Gautama, who became Shakyamuni Buddha, was a person of color living in the north of India. He turned the wheel of the Dharma more than 2,500 years ago when he offered the teachings on the Four Noble Truths. He gave more than 84,000 down-to-earth and profound teachings in the forty-five years after his enlightenment. He taught to all those who were interested, regardless of their caste or clan.

In the centuries after his death, the seeds of the Buddhadharma took root in the hearts of many people of color as it migrated to Sri Lanka, Burma, Cambodia, Laos, Thailand, China, Korea, Japan, Tibet, and Vietnam. No doubt each of these cultures had their own unique challenges and their own openings to the truth of suffering.

From these countries, the Dharma moved outward along trade and travel routes, carried by tradespeople, scholars, yogis, spiritual seekers, and adventurers. It touched the hearts of people all over the world. They too recognized and embraced this genuine path to liberation.

Eventually, the seeds of transformative wisdom were brought into this land of the Native American people, Turtle Island, as Eduardo Duran calls it. This land whose population includes the rich and growing diversity of numerous people of color from Africa, Asia, and the rest of the Americas. The Dharma is coming full circle. It is coming back to the ears, hearts, and hands of people of color, where it began many centuries and generations ago in the time of the Buddha. This is a crucial pivoting point.

Each story in *Dharma, Color, and Culture* is a sacred re-connection. Between the words there is a palpable feeling of the author's own innate wisdom and compassion. These stories helped me transform some of my despair into faith that the cause of our individual and collective pain can be truly healed.

I felt electrified and awakened by the honesty and courage it took each story teller to confront the layers of heartache, to meet the inner barrier of anger, frustration, hopelessness, resentment, and bitterness with tender awareness and piercing intelligence. Some stories pulled me deeper into my own heart, moving me to tears. Others opened me to bigger perspectives.

This book is an inspiring act of love. With hands together at my heart, I bow in deep respect and gratitude to Hilda Ryūmon and each of the authors for sharing their journeys and for giving us the opportunity to bear witness to the individual and collective transformation taking place at this significant time in history.

KANNON AND DEER

Introduction

DHARMA, COLOR, AND CULTURE brings together a community of Native American, African, Asian, and Latina/o heritage teachers, practitioners, and lovers of the Dharma to share their insights on the Buddha's seminal teaching, the Four Noble Truths. These writers can be seen as contemporary versions of the students of ancient times who are "locking eyebrows" with their teachers of old. Resembling an elegant, yet earthy and informal five-course dinner, each writer has given us the fruit of their practice for us to savor. You will find twenty-five vibrant expressions of the Buddha's basic teachings to lock eyebrows with, regardless of who you are; whether you call yourself a Buddhist or not; whether you are just discovering the path or have been walking it for miles; whether you are just looking for a bit of inspiration and support; even if you just want to look at the beautiful art found within these pages. Causes and conditions arise, something manifests, and eventually it will disappear. What is left, if we are fortunate and aware, is experience.

Why these writers? Why these truths? I can answer this best by sharing a few stories of my own path from AfroCuban immigrant to Zen priest.

Before I learned how to read, I learned how to pray. Sharing a bed with my grandmother and younger sister in the small town of Victoria de las Tunas in Cuba, I would listen to my grandmother pray out loud. I don't recall at what point she began to slow down her recitation and encourage us to repeat after her. Together, our voices formed an intergenerational triad petitioning for protection, peace, happiness, and well-being for all people. My grandmother was my first Dharma teacher. Perhaps she knew of something greater than the gunshots, running bootsteps, and cries right outside our bedroom windows——incidents that often made me and my sister hide under our grandmother's bed. It was the late fifties in eastern Cuba and the times were changing.

On my sixth birthday, the 1959 Cuban Revolution was only five days old. As I was preparing to enter first grade, my life would take an irrevocable turn. In 1962, my sister and I were sent to the United States less than two months before the October missile crisis, the showdown between John F. Kennedy and Nikita Khrushchev and what at that time appeared to be an imminent nuclear war. The Buddha Shakyamuni said it well: *There is Suffering.* This is the First Noble Truth.

Though not officially, my exodus from Cuba was part of a larger, historical event. In *Operación Pedro Pan,* thousands of Cuban children were sent away from the island by parents fearful that the new Socialist Revolutionary government would take away parental rights or, in the worst case, take away their children. Vividly, I recall hearing, *"Los rebeldes barbudos nos van a cortar en pedazitos, y enlatarnos para darle de comer a los niños Rusos."* The bearded rebels are going to cut us up into little pieces, can us, and send us to feed hungry Russian children. The Buddha Shakyamuni said it well: *The causes of Suffering are greed, aversion, and delusion.* This is the Second Noble Truth.

Many of the children sent from Cuba went to strange places, both in the United States and abroad: orphanages, foster homes, and religious institutions. I was fortunate and privileged. Unaware that almost twenty-five years would pass before I would see my mother again, I came to live with my grandmother, aunts, and uncles in New York City on La Salle Street and Broadway, right where Oscar Hijuelos's mambo kings played their songs of love. I adored my grandmother, who had left Cuba a few months prior to my arrival in New York. For a nine-year-old little girl, being with her *abuela,* who never said "no," meant great happiness. The Buddha Shakyamuni said it well: *There is an end to Suffering.* This is the Third Noble Truth.

Almost to the day of my first anniversary in the United States, Reverend Dr. Martin Luther King, Jr. spoke of his dream at the Lincoln Memorial. And a couple of years later, at the threshold of my adolescence, I recall Malcolm X being assassinated in the midst of the community where I was growing up. The wheel of *samsara* is endless.

His Holiness the Dalai Lama continuously reminds us that each of us wants to be happy, and that each of us seeks not to suffer. After leaving my Harlem Elementary School for a Catholic school near Columbia University, happiness for me meant doing what the boys did. Attired in white robes, they helped the priests (white, male priests, of course) with the water and wine, spent time in the sacristy among the colorful vestments, rang bells, and walked in the procession, carrying Jesus on the cross. Little did I know at the time that some of these young boys might have been carrying their own crosses of deep suffering caused at the hand of God's representatives on Earth.

Pre-puberty, I did not want to be a girl or a boy. I wanted to be a priest. And

I said so, very proudly and emphatically, to the tall, handsome young Spaniard in Sunday green and gold vestments who ministered to the parishioners who did not speak English. I never forgot his outright laughter, a mixture of disbelief and amusement, his green eyes opening wide, or his holy gesture of patting my head full of kinky curls. In the dismissive act of one who is entitled to smash dreams, he said: *"Que dulce, pero las niñas no nacieron para ser curas."* How sweet, but girls were not born to be priests. However, even more powerful than his dismissal is the memory of my own response, a silent thought in my native language, *Este hombre no conoce a mi abuela.* This man doesn't know my grandmother. From her I learned a fundamental teaching: you can do anything you set your mind to do. As an adolescent, brown-skinned, immigrant girl, I set my mind to be free in this very lifetime. From that point on, it was only a matter of time and place before I fulfilled one of my heart's deepest desires by shaving my head, putting on the robes of a Soto Zen priest, receiving the eating bowls, and committing my life to practicing the Bodhisattva Vows.

I came to Zen not knowing that such a thing as Buddhism existed. I came to Zen knowing that only in silence and stillness would I intimately know the mind that is inherently free and luminous. I came to Zen because the causes and conditions of my life brought me here. The Buddha Shakyamuni said it well: *There is a path to the end of Suffering.* This is the Fourth Noble Truth.

Buddha Shakyamuni discovered how to be free in this lifetime. He did this without becoming a god, an anointed one, or a bigger-than-life superhero. At the moment of his most difficult challenge, when many forces tried to tempt him away from his practice, he touched the earth as the witness to his effort. Upon enlightenment, the Buddha ("the awakened one") said: "All beings are, in their essence, Buddha. They just don't know it, and thus, continually drown in a sea of suffering."

THE FOUR NOBLE TRUTHS AND THEIR SIGNIFICANCE FOR PEOPLE OF COLOR

Originally beginning its turning in India, the Dharma traveled south to Sri Lanka, and on to Burma, Cambodia, Laos, and Thailand. Traveling north, the teachings reached China, Korea, Japan, Tibet, and Vietnam. Centuries later, the Dharma made its way to Europe and North America. When speaking of the history of Western Buddhism in general—and its presence in the United States, in particular—it is imperative that the point of origin not be located in a white,

European American context. The story of how the Dharma reached the shores of the United States is embedded in the history of immigrants of color.

The Chinese were actually the first Buddhists to reach America, whether the date is marked by the legendary party of monks who accompanied Hui Shan in the fourth century or by the immigrants of the 1860s. The next significant wave of Asian, including Tibetan and Theravada, Buddhists would not occur in significant numbers in the United States until the late 1950s and on through the 1970s.

When we speak of Buddhism in the United States, we are speaking of a cultural movement that has brought to this continent ancient Indian, East and Southeast Asian, and Tibetan spiritual teachings and practices. For the first time in history, these teachings have arrived in a land that is racially heterogeneous. At the same time, they are taking root in a society that was founded, by a white majority, on the unwholesome seeds of colonialism, genocide, and slavery. In this meeting, the values of community, interdependence, and collaboration come face-to-face with the values of the pursuit of individualism, self-interest, and competition. Deep bow meets handshake. The cultural encounter is not only East meeting West, it is the spiritual encounter of heart meeting mind.

Today, we are able to speak of the Dharma due to the generosity and compassion of an ordinary man who woke up. When Shakyamuni Buddha set the wheel of the Dharma rolling, he was not giving us instructions for the modern day, highly acclaimed practice of self-improvement. When the Buddha spoke to the ascetics who had previously practiced with him, he offered the teachings of liberation itself. In the ancient tradition of the healer administering to the sick, the Buddha gave us a diagnosis and a prescription. He identified the disease and its cause, gave us a pronouncement on whether it can be cured, and a prescription for the medicine.

When people from groups who have historically found themselves socially, economically, and politically outside the margins, hear that the Buddha taught liberation, nothing more needs to be said. There is no need to proselytize or seduce. All our lives we thirst for freedom, and when we recognize the path that will lead us there, our hearts validate that recognition. To wake up is the task at hand. Not wishing that our lives are better, nor different, we wake up to the reality of our lives, just as they are.

To see this reality clearly is the first step to freedom. Such is the significance of the Four Noble Truths to the racially and culturally excluded people living today in the United States. Teachings of liberation heard clearly in a culture driven by ignorance, fear, anger, and hate is like the breaking of chains after centuries of subjugation. This is the gift the Buddha Shakyamuni gave us.

The five sections at the heart of *Dharma, Color, and Culture* speak to the teachings of the Four Noble Truths and to a fifth truth, the truth of Bringing the Teachings Home. Each section is illustrated by the beautiful art of Mayumi Oda. Her paintings shine the way as we walk through these pages. Each painting brings the spiritual and the feminine quality of these truths to light.

The essays in the first section focus on the truth of suffering. Maxine Hong Kingston looks at the painful reality of situations completely outside of our control. In the midst of the loss of loved ones, home, and treasured possessions, the heart surrenders to the truth of impermanence and change. Marlene Jones and Eduardo Duran come from two different cultures and worldviews, but each reminds us of the pain of invisibility and exclusion. And Earthlyn Marselean Manuel's lyrical and raw description of her experiences in the Dharma pulls us close to the suffering caused by sexual violence and oppression, while simultaneously enveloping us in her steady search for healing and liberation. Rounding out the first section, elder Vipassana teacher José Luis Reissig invites us to pay close attention to the cages we build in an effort to avoid suffering. Reissig challenges us to stay connected to the here and now, even in the midst of profound suffering.

For people who throughout history have been subjected to the systemic experience of oppression, finding a place to call home is the search of a lifetime. Opening section two, the teachings of Venerable Zen Master Thich Nhat Hanh shine as a brilliant morning sun. He asks us, "In your true home, is there any suffering?" He takes our hand and we learn to embrace the suffering; for without it, we cannot learn compassion.

Recalling painful discoveries he made while practicing as an ordained monk in Burma and Thailand, Ralph Steele writes about external and internal suffering and the relationship between the two. Michele Benzamin-Miki remembers her ancestors as core to her practice of gratitude. She reminds us that there is hope and choice and always the possibility of freedom. Drawing from his experience working with inner city male adolescents, George T. Mumford acknowledges the unpleasant feelings of anger and outrage that arise when we are mistreated. By applying the teachings of the Buddha, he says, we are able to lessen suffering and begin the practice of letting go. And in the last essay for this section, Sala Steinbach reveals how the stories that shape us are also footsteps on the path to compassion and wisdom. With grace and honesty, she shares her journey.

During my long years of practice, I have often thought that such was the wisdom of the Buddha that he did not just leave us with naming the illness and telling us the cause. Fortunately for us, he assured us that there is indeed an end to the suffering. The experiences shared by the contributors in section three speak to the cessation of suffering. Gaylon Ferguson, an *acharya* in the Shambhala tradition, talks about developing a deep friendship with ourselves, cultivating the compassion to truly embrace our life in both the good times and when things are rough.

In a voice as clear as Basho's pond, Soto Zen Dharma lineage holder Merle Kodo Boyd remembers those that came before her as she taps into her early life experiences as a child of the Jim Crow era. Envisioning the Buddha as a spiritual freedom fighter, Viveka Chen writes of the moment he launched a spiritual movement empowering people to end slavery, teaching that "even in oppressive conditions, freedom can be had by freeing the mind." Infused with present-day humor arising within teachings of old, Mushim Ikeda-Nash vividly describes the two moments in her life when she experienced the end of suffering and dissatisfaction. And Sister Chan Chau Nghiem's essay on coming home is a journey of self-discovery enveloped in a mantle of healing. We walk with her as she allows an opening of the heart as the path for touching our ancestors.

The writers in the fourth section look at the last of the Buddha's original Truths—the path to the cessation of suffering. Charles Johnson lays out the road map given to us by the Buddha. According to Johnson, we can go to the mountaintop with "this time-tested guide for spiritual and moral progress." Bonnie Duran walks this road in her journey from Native American mixed race child to university professor to social activist. Larry Yang's essay on the practice of right concentration is one beautiful flower in a bouquet. Writing on the last element of the Noble Eightfold Path, Yang offers us a way to cultivate a non-distracted mind. Reverend Kenneth Kenshin Tanaka explores the element of conduct or right action, reminding us that "the aim of the Dharma is to know oneself." This modern exchange of questions and answers could very well be a direct Dharma descendant of age-old master-student existential inquiries. In the final essay for this section, I hope to pass on a bit of my personal journey of discovering how to dig deep and work on that which matters most.

For the past two and a half millennia, in every land where the winds of change have brought Dharma seeds, indigenous manifestations of the teachings have arisen closely woven to the cultural context of the times. In the last section of this anthology, truth speakers accentuate the personal connection to the Dharma and how they have integrated it into the realities of their lives. These essays stretch the Dharma path wide and deep to include multiple approaches to practice—a necessary requirement if Buddhism is going to survive in this hetero-racial, twenty-first century Western land.

With her unmistakable directness, Alice Walker takes us into the heart of suffering as a door to reclaiming our place; a place Buddha also claimed in trusting himself to the earth. Collaborating in the public sphere, as well as moving in the world as life partners, Lourdes Argüelles and Anne Rivero bring us close to their vulnerable selves as they reflect upon their work in India on behalf of animal beings. Rosa Zubizarreta questions what appears to be a basic tenet of Western convert Buddhist practice as we know it—sitting meditation— and handing us a spiritual gauntlet, forcing us and requiring us to grapple with what exactly it means to be a Buddhist. And having met kindness at the pivotal age of adolescence, Julia Sagebien invites us to walk with her side by side as she hikes into self-discovery.

Growing up with my paternal grandmother, profound teachings fell from her lips just as the sweat fell from her brown skin as she toiled over a hot stove in a small, overcrowded West Harlem apartment. One of the things *abuela* always said was how important it was to mark endings, whether it was to a long conversation, a succulent meal, or a dearly loved relationship. She would refer to this as the importance of *cerrar con broche del oro*, to close with a golden broach. And this indeed is what Professor Jan Willis does in her essay. Bringing the anthology to a close, Professor Willis engages us in critical inquiry motivated by a question posed to her by a young black woman at the end of a conference: "Was there anything left out as Buddhism made its way to the West?" With laser-like accuracy, she gives us a dose of reality, mixed with an inquisitiveness of purpose, shaken through cultural assumptions, and served with precision. She gently holds the door open for us to experience the Buddhist teachings of freedom while simultaneously remaining true to our familial history and faith roots.

It is our birthright to be free and it's our responsibility to wake up to that freedom. The writers in this anthology have made a commitment to do just that. Individually and collectively, we are swimming to the other shore and discovering the sweetness and grace of liberation. Each essay here speaks to

the basic teachings given to us all by Gautama Buddha out of his deep compassion for all beings. Each essay reflects the writer's heritage and Buddhist
lineage. Together, they represent various ages, classes, sexual orientations, cultures, genders, languages, immigrant statuses, physical abilities, and they weave
a beautiful tapestry, bringing the teachings alive for our times. With this
anthology, the Dharma wheel continues to turn in the West and specifically
among those who physically resemble most closely the original practitioners
who followed the Buddha Shakyamuni.

This book is an experience of love, kindness, trust, and support by Dharma
sisters and brothers, friends and strangers alike. It is a work of profound *Ache*.[1]

May the merits of these labors benefit all beings, in all directions, in all
realms, and may all beings be happy, protected, peaceful, and free from
suffering.

Ryūmon Zenji
(Hilda Gutiérrez Baldoquín)
The Sea Ranch Lodge, California,
Summer 2004

NOTES

1 *Ache* is from the Yoruban word for divine power. In Santeria/Lukumi and related traditions, Ache is life force. It is invoked as both gratitude and blessing.

Red Fudo

The Truth of Suffering

Fire

MAXINE HONG KINGSTON

I F A WOMAN is going to write a Book of Peace, it is given her to know devastation. I have lost my book—156 good pages. A firestorm blew over the Oakland-Berkeley hills in October of 1991, and took my house, things, neighborhood, and other neighborhoods, and forests. And the lives of twenty-five people.

I almost reached my manuscript, typescript, printouts, and disks in time. I was driving home from funeral ceremonies for my father. I have lost my father. He's gone less than a month; we were having the full-month ceremony early, Sunday day off. Never before had I driven by myself away from Stockton and my parents' house. I turned on public radio for the intelligent voices, and heard that the hills were burning, toward Moraga, toward Walnut Creek. It's not my poor sense of direction, I told myself, but the newscasters' in confusion. The perimeters of the fire were different from station to station, from taped news to live news. North of the Caldecott Tunnel, south of the Caldecott Tunnel, east, west of the Warren Freeway. I pictured wildfire far up in the hills—ridgelines of flame spilling down, then running up sere-grass slopes. I have seen it at night—red gashes zigzagging the black. Impossible that it cross ten lanes of freeway and take over settled, established, built city.

Behind me, my sister-in-law Cindy was chasing me at ninety miles per hour. My family believed that I didn't know about the fire, and would drive into it, and not be able to find my way out on the altered, burning streets. Like all the Chinese members of our family, I have an instinct that left is right and vice versa. Too easily lost. Cindy, who is not Chinese but Arkie, ran out of gas at Tracy.

In a half-hour, halfway there, forty miles to go, I was speeding over the Altamont Pass (where there be ghosts and accidents; it is the ground upon which the stabbing happened at the Rolling Stones concert, after Woodstock), and through the windfarms. Some windmills turned, and some were still. Here the winds and all seemed normal; I had no evidence that hurricanes of fire were storming on the other side of these hills but for the radio. "Forty-five houses have gone up in flames." "About a hundred homes." "A hundred and fifty structures have burned." The numbers would keep going up—nine hundred degrees, the temperature of molten lava; twenty-one hundred degrees, the temperature of kilns; thirty-five hundred houses. "Winds of forty-five miles per hour . . ." ". . . sixty-five-mile-per-hour firewind . . ." ". . . record heat and winds . . ." "Foehn winds." "Northeast winds . . ." I would have to look up "foehn," which sounds like "wind" in Chinese, as in "typhoon." "The fire has jumped the junction of Highway Twenty-four and Highway Thirteen." It's blown over and through ten lanes. Ten lanes are not wide enough firebreak. It's on our side of the freeway. ". . . dynamite College Avenue." ". . . draw the line at College Avenue." ". . . helicopters and available cropdusters chemical-drop the Claremont Hotel." "If the Claremont Hotel goes, explodes, the fire will burn to the Bay." "No cars have been trapped in the Caldecott Tunnel." Once, a propane truck had exploded inside the tunnel—a giant flamethrower pointed at Oakland.

NO TANK TRUCKS
WITH HAZARDOUS MATERIALS
ALLOWED IN CALDECOTT TUNNEL

A police car was parked sideways across my exit, Broadway Terrace. I drove fast to the next exit, which was blocked by a Highway Patrol car and flares. They are setting up the roadblocks moments ahead of me, I thought. If only I had driven faster, I might have saved the book, and my mother's jewelry, and my father's watch, and his spectacles, which fit my eyes, and his draft card, which I had taken from his wallet. "This card is to be carried on your person at all times." He carried it safely for over fifty years.

When I got off the freeway, I was somewhere in downtown Oakland, and driving too slowly through complicated traffic. It was the middle of the afternoon, about two o'clock. Too late. Too late. The sky was black. The sun was red. Leaves of burned black paper wafted high and low among the buildings. Ashes from a forest fire were falling and blowing in downtown Oakland.

In the middle of my U-turn, the radio said that Broadway and/or Broadway Terrace was on fire, and that there was looting on Ostrander Street. Parallel streets—big Broadway Terrace for cars, little Broadway Terrace for walking—eucalyptus and pine trees and apple trees between them—a tree-high, two-street-thick wall of flame. Mass fire. I said out loud, "No. No. No. No." Ostrander is—was?—a one-way road through a small woods on a hill. On my walks to and from the Village Market, families of quail would surprise me. They walked ahead just so far, as if leading me, or as if I were giving chase, then took off running into the bushes, and flying up into the lower branches of the oaks and pines. Once, on Ostrander, I stood amazed at the center of a storm of birds—hundreds of robins, jays, and chickadees—flying touch-and-go, on and off treetops and roofs and grass, circling and crisscrossing singly and in schools, and never bumping into one another—better than the Blue Angels. I love looking out at Oakland and seeing a crane extend itself over the city. So—their flyway can sweep this far west, and they rest at Lake Merritt or Lake Anza or Temescal. Anne Frank saw cranes out the sky window. Another time, riding BART, as the train came up out of the Bay into Oakland, I saw twelve angels wheeling in the sun, rays of white wings and gold light. "Swans!" I said loudly; the other passengers had to see them too. "Look. Swans."

It can't be too late. All I want is a minute inside the house—run to the far end of the living room, to the alcove where my book is in a wine box, take one more breath, and run upstairs for the gold and jade that my ancestresses had been able to keep safe through wars in China and world wars and journeys across oceans and continents.

Where Broadway meets the start of College Avenue, at the California College of Arts and Crafts (where Wittman kissed Taña; but I'll get to that), only a few feet from the sign pointing up to Broadway Terrace, the police were herding cars down and away to College Avenue. I stopped at the light, left the car, and ran over to talk them into letting me through. Even though the light turned green, the line of cars I'd blocked did not honk; nobody yelled. I wished for a hand gesture to communicate "Sorry," to use in traffic situations. Sorry. Thank you. I asked a policeman, "Are you absolutely sure I can't drive up there?" He answered that no cars were allowed past this point. I thought, May I go to my house on foot, then? I got back in the car, drove diagonally across the intersection, and parked in the red-curb stop for the College Avenue bus. The police shouldn't write tickets on this terrible day. Twenty-eight dollars, worth it. Have mercy on this car that could very well have been left here by someone who had escaped the fire and was getting a drink of water, parking as close as she could to home.

I stood at the curb plotting how I was going to fade past the police, and got in step with an African American family with many children crossing the street. I told them I lived on Golden Gate Avenue and was trying to go up there; where did they live? They lived on Brookside, which winds around Golden Gate. I asked, "Were you officially evacuated? Has our area been officially evacuated yet?" They didn't know, but they had been back to their house. The father said, "The police will escort you home if you tell them you have a life-and-death situation." The mother said, "They drove us to our house." I asked, "What was the life-and-death situation you told them?" "We couldn't find our son. Our son was missing." The kids, all about junior-high age, were smiling and safe; I couldn't tell which was the one lost and now found. An unfinished book is nothing as important as a child. I told the family that I was trying to save the manuscript of a book I was writing. Said out loud in the open to actual people, who did not get excited, my plight did not seem to have enormity. "I've been working on it for years," I said. About one and a half to two years of pure writing, not counting thinking and imagining. Is one and a half to two years much? It depends on which years. Didn't Rilke write *The Duino Elegies* in six months? Or was it six hours one wide-awake night? He did it about ten years before his death at fifty-one. The happy family and I wished each other Good luck and Take care.

While the policemen—the Oakland cops aren't as big as during the Viet Nam demonstrations—were busy, I walked through the barricades into the defined fire area. Householders were staying, hosing down roofs and dry lawns. A flare of fire fell out of the sky and landed behind a man intent on watering his property. I motioned to him that he should look to his rear, but he stared at me as if I were a crazy woman, pointing at my own butt. I didn't try to shout over the helicopters; they chopped up sound and the air, and whupped up heartbeats. Anyway, only now, as I write, am I coming up with words for the things that were making wild appearances and disappearances. That flame went out; another fell out of nowhere onto his roof. Even if he saw it, he couldn't have reached it with the spray from his garden hose. I ran on.

I felt afraid when there was not a person in sight. I ran up the center of the street, between the houses, locked up tight. I wanted to run faster, through and out of this deserted place. But I was trying to breathe shallowly. The car radio had said that poison oak was burning; I coughed, thinking of breathing poison-oak smoke, which must blister lungs. The air smelled poisonous—toxic polymers, space-age plastics, petrochemicals, refrigerants, Freon, radon. I am breathing carcinogens, I will die of lung cancer. I held my long white hair as a filter over my nose and mouth and ran at a pace that allowed me to control my wind. I passed side streets without deciding to turn left into one. Many streets end in culs-de-sac, or loop around. I would lose time backtracking out. I wished for a photographic memory to recall the map of this area in the Thomas Guide. But the Thomas Guide only blurredly indicates the snarl of these streets, lanes, paths, and steps; they curl around boulders and oak trees and Lake Temescal and hills. From now on, wherever I live, I will pay attention to which streets go through exactly where. Pages of ash were floating high up, and also skimming along curbs. I did not stop to try to read them. Someone once told me about a child who lived at the time of the burning of a great library. He caught pages of burned paper, and read Latin words. At Margarido, a long, wide street, I turned left toward the heat and fire. I hoped that I would see again the enormous old ginkgo tree that fountains up and up—wings, gold, autumn. I passed a man and a woman leaving their house, and a home-owner on his rooftop wetting it down. None of them could answer me: whether or not this street was officially evacuated. I arrived at the edge of the golf course, which was lined by a row of eucalyptus trees. Their tops were on fire. This is crown fire, and flames jumped from tree to tree. I imagined myself running under the eucalyptus trees, but, before I reached the open field, the trees dropping fire on my head, and me exploding. More eucalyptus trees lined the other side. (My husband, who should be at my side helping me, would tease, You're always afraid that things will explode. " 'Be careful,' " Earll mim-ics me. " 'Watch out. It's going to explode.' " But I have seen and/or heard for myself the explosions of an automobile motor, a sewing-machine motor, my electric typewriter [a cat pissed in it], a toilet, mother spiders, tules. In Phoenix Park in Dublin, I made Earll get away before a dead cow, its big stomach expanding, blew up.) Eucalyptus trees have big wood-cells filled with euca-lyptus oil. The bangs I was hearing were houses, cars, and trees blowing up. If I made it across the golf course (Private Robert E. Lee Prewitt, the hero of *From Here to Eternity*, was killed on a golf course), I would come out at the corner of Broadway Terrace and Ostrander, amidst the fire and the looters. I turned about. Is this retreat, then, and am I giving up on my book? I let the possibility that the book was gone—my book gone—enter my ken. I did not feel bad; I did not believe it was lost. I had not stopped trying to rescue it. The same men were still watering down their houses, which their wives and chil-dren must have evacuated. The sky was darker now, and the air hotter. The sun was ugly red. ("Ugly red" are Judy Foosaner's words; she's a painter, we're "friends since girls." She was down in the flatlands, and watched the cars exploding up on the hills. I'd thought until she said "ugly red" that to a painter all colors were beautiful.)

Gravity sped me downhill, back to crowds and industrial-strength buildings. I found my red car—no ticket—and drove down College to Chabot Road, which was barricaded. Chabot Road was my familiar turn home. It was not right that it be an impasse. I left the car there, surprised at the free parking. Again, I became invisible to the police, and walked for home. This way seemed almost normal. I should have come up these known streets in the first place. As always, there was a stillness at St. Albert's College; either the monks had evacuated the seminary, or they were staying hidden. You hardly ever see them in the garden or out on the tennis courts anyway. The atmosphere feels full of prayer. The row of elm trees—grandmother tree, grandfather tree—stood unharmed. This was the first tree seen by me as a child, and is more magnificent each time I find another one. Some people call them Chinese elms, some call them American elms. Here was a stand of nine elms, here before I was here, and meant to outlast me. I do not remember touching them, each one, the elephant bark, the horned-toad bark, the crocogator bark, as I usually do; I must have rushed past. Their jigjag leaves were a strong green, though October was ending, and my fiftieth year was ending.

The strange shifting light—the winds were blowing the weather and the time of day crazily up and down the street—stilled at St. Albert's and started up again at Chabot Elementary, shadows swinging across the asphalt and through the cyclone fences, backstop, and jungle-gym bars. Why do we raise children on ground barren of trees and grass? We are teaching them to endure a world like a cage, a jail.

Chabot Road tails up and off into hills and forests, and Golden Gate Avenue, my street, starts to its right. This corner—I am traveling northeast—is a natural border between man-built city and wildland. Flats and hills, chapparal and forest also meet here. All influenced by underground rivers, and by fault lines. The wind changes its blowing; the climate turns. At such a place, you enter and leave ecosystems. Leina-a-ka-'uhane. I was at a border of the fire, the built city behind me, and ahead black ground. I walked onto it. I could disappear, I thought. If I had continued walking northeast, up the hill, I would've come to the place where the fire killed nineteen people. The slopes on either side of me had just burned. The ivy, dill, vetch, pampas plumes, and coyote bushes do not exist anymore, except in my mind.

I have been at controlled burns. Farmers weed fields by burning them down to fertile ash and black earth. The harvest fires in the cane fields run at you, and suddenly stop. The burning kansaa, the prairie grass of Kansas, smells like baking bread. The Forest Service clear-cuts trees, then napalms, then seeds. Storms of wildfire are as normal as timely rain. The reason for this fire is five years of drought.

Golden Gate, my street, begins with a small cement bridge marked "Narrow Bridge," which goes under a steel bridge for the BART train. It's a wonderful surprise when, overhead, up in the air, the train appears out of the trees. The Concord line was not running today, the radio had said. The girders were smoking. Were they usually this red? Was the bridge rusty, or red hot? I stood still and thought about whether I should go under it. The metal could melt or crumble, the loosened structure break apart, drop, and hit me on the head. I only worried for my head, had not a thought for other parts of my body. The head looks out for itself. I needed to see around a bend to look for my house. I didn't see any houses on the other side of the bridges, but wasn't sure if you ever could from here anyway. I threw myself straight forward, and felt the heat from above. I ran through a gigantic kiln, which has since recurred in nightmares: I am flying up into the hot ceiling, and can't wake up. The concrete walls that support the trains and the freeways boxed me in. I was a long time under the BART rails, then under Highway 24 West, then Highway 24 East, then Broadway—immense wide slabs of concrete and steel that could fall and squash me entirely, like the Cypress Freeway, which "pancaked" thirty-five cars and the people inside them during the earthquake two Octobers ago.

I came out into a changed world. Its color had gone out. Its dimensions had stretched away here, shrunk there. New mountains and canyons vistaed as far as I could see. To my left, close beside me, a mountain appeared, terraced with streets on which burning cars sat on every level. To my right, below, opened a canyon; I could see its entire contours—a black, defoliated wedge. The canyon contains just the College Prep School, has held it from harm. Clean two-by-fours at roof angles poked up to the canyon's rim, where I was standing. The frame of the gym or auditorium they were putting up had not burned; they could keep on building it. Suppose I were to go on, take myself farther into the fire scene—might I see my house, earn it, cause it to be, after all, there? What with the tricky distances, beyond the next turn could very well be my house. Walking in the center of the street, I stepped over power lines. I was entering a black, negative dimension, where things disappeared, and I might disappear. The only movement and color were flames. I sidestepped burning logs that had flown here; they must have been chunks from houses. The houses cast off logs before falling into ashes. Suddenly, I saw a whole two-story house with high-peaked roof—I have never seen this house before, not from this side; I was looking at it through invisible, gone houses—an enormous house standing squarely inside a flame. A red-orange diamond enhoused the house, the crystal within a crystal. So—a house can burn all at once, not simply be eaten away corner by corner.

I kept looking down at my feet to puzzle my way through the tangles of power lines, and looking up at a wavery, flickering, blinking scene. What I wanted to see, what used to be, popped in and out of sight, alternated with the real. The hot ground was reeking mirages that cheated the eye with blear illusions. A thing would appear—a chimney, an oldened wrought-iron gate, a ceramic pot—but it did not cue the next thing, the thing that should be attached to it (house, fence), to appear. Things were out of the order that was in my mind. Memory was off.

If only I had paid better attention—I have to be more awake—I would not be losing the detailed world. One more bend, and yet one more bend, but my cedar-shake roof did not rise into sight.

I came upon and recognized a tiny white house with wood siding, which looked water-stained or chemical-stained. The poorest house in the neighborhood has survived. I hadn't met its latest owners; it was always changing hands. This small house on a corner lot was affordable entry into our good neighborhood and the housing market. The houses to the side of it and in back of it were gone, and it now seemed to have a huge yard. Happiness rushed back and forth between it and me. The tiny house nicely fit its place in my mind, and gave me my bearings. My house, the next smallest, should be at the other end of this curving, winding block, with only the crest of the hill in the way.

A fireman was puttering with a long yellow fire truck, parked beside the stone retaining wall that held an upswooping street and a hillside of houses. I could not see if any houses were still up there. The fireman did not warn me from stepping through the mess of wires and cables and flat hoses, black serpents and white serpents that had fought, and lay slain. I tiptoed amongst them. Jackstraws—one touch, misstep, trip, and be zapped. I made it across the street—a wire did not wake up and jump me—to say Hi to the fireman. It takes this much upheaval for me to get over shyness. I thought of saying but didn't say, "What a mess, huh?" or ask, "How're things going? Is your truck broken? Where are the other firefighters? Do you know where the main fire is? Why are you here all by yourself?" He might feel embarrassed. I did not bother him with inquiry after my address either. We stood quiet together awhile. I asked, "Which direction did you come from?" He said, "It came down that way, very fast," pointing northeast, up at the hills. "And blew back up, then down again from over there." At my house. The firefighters had taken a stand at my intersection. The fire almost surrounded them, fire in back, then in front of them. They retreated to this rampart. We were standing at the wall of our devastated city. "We didn't get water up here."

The fireman did not stop me. I went on. A bicyclist got off his bicycle to walk alongside me. We hesitated at a maze and thicket of power lines, some piled waist-high and others dangling eye-high. Where to straddle over, where to limbo under? The street was webbed in knots and nets of lines. I remembered learning in Latin class that the triton-and-net was the most dangerous weapon, the one to choose for war games and war. In dreams where I try to fly, I am halted by electrical lines, which shoot ahead of me and cut off the free sky. Where had such a plethora of lines dropped from? Our utilities weren't buried underground, but the sky had never seemed hatchmarked and crisscrossed. Through the knot, I saw Mrs. Fessler's Karmann Ghia. Its paint had been seared from red to white. Tears of melted glass hung from the windows, the eyeholes of a baboon skull. Cables draped like black hair over its low forehead and weeping eyes; the interior was a black hollow. The tires were gone, burned off. Where is Mrs. Fessler? She is all right, please. She was at church; or her son came for her, and they drove off in his car. The simmering ground was flat, no mound of ashes that could be a small human body. There—another recognizable house: the house-in-the-gully—how many lots away from mine is it?— crouched under the flames, and had made it, alive. So—firewinds blow over the top of the earth. You can see why people lived in tunnels in Viet Nam and Okinawa. (But months ago we bulldozed the desert sand into the trenches, and buried Iraqi soldiers alive. I had read an impossible number—seventy thousand. "A turkey shoot.")

The fire had reached from the foot to the armpits of the phone poles; crossbars were hanging by a burning arm. Atop its white metal flagpole, higher than the utility poles and away from trees, on a mound in a clearing, was the American flag, limp and singed, but still there. Its primary colors (which don't occur much in nature) had dulled, scorched in the dark air. The wind stopped; I might have been in the eye of its swirl.

I have ambivalence about the Flag. It is a battle flag, a war flag, and I don't like being patriotically roused and led to war. The Red, White, and Blue stands

for competition and nationalism. I want it to stand for peace and coopera-
tion. I get scared of my fellow Americans' going crazy as it waves. Because of
that dramatic unburned American flag, our part of the fire would keep appearing in the news. A CNN reporter called our area a "picturesque burnscape." A
reporter for a college paper interviewed me, and translated my burbling: "So,
you saw the Flag, and realized that you transcended the fire." I was dismayed—
he was a writer, yet locked inside the Flag symbol: You have the Flag, you win.

I did not have a sudden moment of knowing that my house and all that was
in it were no more. I stood there reasoning, If I can see that flag from here, then
I am also looking through the place where my house was. I was laying eyes on
it without registering which piece of blackened land amidst all this blackened
land was exactly my piece. The landscape was utterly changed. I had come to
the ash moon of a planet that passes through the sun.

I had flown a flag too, a white dove on a sky-blue silk field, UN colors plus
orange beak, green leaves, brown branch, brown eye. I appliquéd and embroi-
dered two peace flags at the beginning of my country's continuing war against
Iraq, and hung one out the upstairs front window, the other out the side,
toward the peaceful neighbor, to hearten her. Christina Simoni was the only
other neighbor who put up peace signs, made on her home computer: across
the top of the picture window, every soldier is somebody's son; and across the
bottom, or daughter. She was answering President Bush, who made a speech—
"our boys"? "our sons"? "our side"?—that didn't make sense, wasn't true, so I
forget it. He kept ejaculating, "Euphoria!" On another day of our country's
mad fit, Christina hand-lettered a new poster—war is not an energy policy. We
were two households with such ideas, amidst neighbors who tied the trees and
poles and gates with yellow ribbons. The giant eucalyptus tree at our cross-
roads was tied. Some middle of the night, it was untied (not by me), and never
retied.

My Book of Peace is gone.

Suddenly, I felt rushing at me—this fire movie is about to run in reverse;
smoky ghosts will hurry backward into rising houses and trees, refill them,
and pull them upright—I felt coming into me—oh, but here all along inside
chest and stomach and all around me and out of the smoking ground—Idea.
Idea has weight and life; I can feel it. Ideas are pervious to firebombs, which
shoot through them without harming them. Americans own too many things.
I can feel Idea because I am thingless, and because of my education, thinking,
reading, meditation. I heard the monk and teacher Thich Nhat Hanh say the

Five Wonderful Precepts, which are the moral foundation of Buddhism. Having ethics, even intentions and aspirations, turns you in the right direction, toward some lasting idea about good. I am a manifestation of Idea, food that makes blood, bones, muscles, body, self. I stood alive in the fire, and felt ideas pour into me.

I know why this fire. God is showing us Iraq. It is wrong to kill, and refuse to look at what we've done. (Count the children killed, in "sanctions": 150,000, 360,000, 750,000. "Collateral damage." The counts go up with each new report. We killed more children than soldiers. Some of the children were soldiers.) For refusing to be conscious of the suffering we caused—the camera-eye on the bomb went out as it hit the door or roof at the center of the crosshairs—no journalists allowed, no witnesses—we are given this sight of our city in ashes. God is teaching us, showing us this scene that is like war.

I'm not crazy; I'm not unpatriotic. People who've been there, who saw Hiroshima and Nagasaki after the A-bombs, the Ong Plain and Huê after the firefights, compared our fire to war. Oakland Fire Captain Ray Gatchalian, Asian American, Green Beret, Viet Nam vet, Panama vet, said, "When I went up in the helicopter the day after the fire, I couldn't even film, I was so stunned. You have to remember, I went to Mexico City after the earthquake where hundreds and thousands of people were displaced, but when you see your own environment, people you know, whose homes were burned to the ground, I was stunned, in total shock. That day, one house burned every five seconds. Seeing it the next morning, it brought me back to the shock and horror of Vietnam. When I looked down on the devastation that day, I thought what an opportunity this would be to bring busloads of people and busloads of children and tell them when we, as a country, decide to go to war against somebody, this is what we are going to get. When we decide to send our military and our bombs into a country, this is what we're deciding to do."

My Book of Peace is gone. And my father is gone. Fatherless. And thingless. But not Idea-less.

not sure I agree in this cause/effect

Bearing Up in the Wild Winds

EARTHLYN MARSELEAN MANUEL

WHAT IS THE SUFFERING often felt by people of color? There is no one answer. But I suspect that we have been taught to love everyone and then have felt betrayed and angered when that love was not returned. We have been deeply wounded by this betrayal and have searched out ways to recover the loving people that we know ourselves to be. We have created names for ourselves, such as "people of color" in order to label the pain. We have created sanctuaries to heal and still have yet to emerge from those sanctuaries for fear of being hurt once again. What happens to a hurt people? We forget that we are butterflies bearing up in the wild winds. We forget that we are tender from the suffering.

My spiritual practice has never been a task at hand. It has always been a journey of unburying pain, an unfolding of surprises, and a search for relief. I have not been alone in this journey. The loud voices of anguish among the descendants of African slaves have been heard throughout the centuries.

As a child, I witnessed my parents befriend hope, resistance, and faith. They engaged in a lifelong pursuit of the promises of wellness and a good American life. They worked harder than necessary and remained close to God. They worked against dehumanization to ensure that their three daughters would not suffer as they had. As I grew into adulthood, it occurred to me that my family, as well as other black folks, had simply learned how to cope with an unfulfilled life. We had not learned how to alleviate suffering. We did not know how to acknowledge feelings of limitation and lack. Although Christianity offered God as a liberator and a community to ease the pain of isolation felt by displaced Africans, we had not learned how to eliminate a sense of inferiority that pervaded our bodies. Social movements gave us a political ideology of equality while education taught us how to assimilate. But we had not healed the wounds often expressed through our music, dance, and written words.

The need to understand and heal such suffering led me through Christianity and Yoruba to Buddhism. In 1988, through Nichiren Buddhism, I started chanting *Nam-Myoho-Renge-Kyo,* one of the names of the Lotus Sutra.[1] I began to reflect on my own life and realized that the knots in my throat and the tears spilling from the corners of my eyes indicated feelings of being unloved and invisible. The teachings of Shakyamuni Buddha offered a different kind of liberation: one that brought forth an innate wisdom that in the past I had sought from God and later from the African Orisha. Although I still carried the basic teachings of love by Jesus Christ and the 8,000 year-old messages of Orisha in my bones, Buddhism became the path in which I could come away from being weary, drained, and suicidal, to being filled with life.

Eleven years prior to being introduced to Buddhist chanting, I had been raped at gunpoint on a street in Los Angeles. The women in my family, my mother and sisters, were afraid to have any in-depth conversations with me about my tragedy. They feared for their own lives. My father had murder in his eyes when he heard what had happened to me. My father had lost a leg to arteriosclerosis and he was in a wheelchair. His rage quickly dwindled into great sadness. There was nothing he could do. A psychotherapist assigned to me fell asleep while I was telling her the gruesome story of my rape. I kept the experience buried for years, waiting for someone to save me. Chanting helped it all resurface and provided a path for healing.

While chanting I expected the pain to dissipate, but instead it increased. Chanting brought memories of the rape and every other dehumanizing act I had experienced. There were times when I simply sat on the floor in front of my altar and cried. I was afraid that I would not be able to bear the pain that was being excavated. I contemplated suicide. However, my teacher encouraged me to continue and to develop an intimacy with who I was in the pain. Living in the Buddha's teachings, there was no fixing the pain. At first, it felt like torture. I needed to understand the nature of my life *as it was.* The path of Dharma became a simple question, *how was I going to live with myself?* I had no recourse other than to continue chanting.

My sister once asked me, "What does Buddhism have to do with black people anyway?" Although Shakyamuni Buddha's teachings came from the earth of ancient India, Buddhism has everything to do with me and with every other suffering living being. There is suffering and something can be done about it, just by being humane enough to feel and understand the pain on the planet, without imposing religious sanctions or political correctness. Intuitively, I knew this. However, Nichiren Buddhism, founded by Nichiren Daishonin in thirteenth-century Japan, helped me to further understand the nature of suffering, which was to begin ending it.

Nichiren Daishonin was ordained as a priest at age sixteen in the Pure Land school of Buddhism. After ten years of travel and further study in Pure Land as well as Zen, he changed his name to Nichiren and declared that the scriptures of the *Lotus Sutra*, which emphasize that everyone can attain enlightenment, held the essence of Shakyamuni Buddha's teachings on suffering. He felt that if Buddhism had truly reached the people of Japan, they would not be suffering the tragedies of war, famine, plagues, and corrupt samurai governments. Nichiren set out to make Buddhism more accessible to ordinary people. He pointed out that if one person followed the teachings, then that person would become a *bodhisattva* of the Earth, or a spiritual warrior who hears the cries of the world and works to end all suffering. He encouraged a simple practice of chanting *Nam* (or *Namu* in some Nichiren schools)-*Myoho-Renge-Kyo*, along with reciting Buddhist sutras and sharing the practice with others as a show of faith and compassion.

Centuries later, Nichiren Buddhism proved satisfying to many Japanese in the 1940s when atomic bombs were dropped on Hiroshima and Nagasaki by the United States at the end of World War II. The surviving war widows and widowers preserved this practice out of the need to stay spiritually alive. They brought the practice to the United States in the early 1950s and 1960s, where they built temples and created lay organizations.

I came to Nichiren Buddhism through the lay organization called the Soka Gakkai International. In most Buddhist schools, the First Noble Truth of suffering includes several aspects including the path to end suffering. Nichiren simplified the Buddha's teachings on suffering to what he called the four sufferings: birth, illness, old age, and death. Also, he claimed that these four sufferings are caused by the idea that the self exists independently of nature and the universe. In other words, the four sufferings derived from the idea: "I am the absolute being."

After about two years of chanting with overwhelming pain, I realized that I am *not* the absolute being; my suffering over my rape and past hurts was tightly woven into a larger world of suffering. Once I understood that no living being exists independently, I understood how I suffered—how I felt isolated in a dark body. I was awakened to an innate wisdom. This wisdom said that there was no separation between me and all other living beings; that I was worthy of a place in the world like any other life. But I had lost track of such wisdom by living in a world that thrived on individualism, making social intimacy among us feel impossible. As I chanted, I understood that I was part of the world, that despite internally and externally imposed separation, I belonged. With that wisdom, I would not be an accomplice to my own disappearance.

At the start, Buddhism seemed to focus on the individual without any mention of discrimination or any communal effort to end it. But as I understood the nature of suffering among living beings, my role in resolving suffering in the world became clear. To be awake and to feel—that was the journey of Buddhism. Before I could have compassion for the rest of the world, including, one day, the man who raped me, I needed to feel my own pain and suffering. I also needed to be aware of what I have done with my life because of that pain and suffering. There was no need to analyze the mentality of the man, but rather I needed to be aware of the terror caused by cruelty and still invite intimacy into my life. My part in ending all suffering was to pay attention to what happens in life as it is happening. This was the path toward liberation from the delusions of oppression and life in a dark body.

I continue to learn about such liberation each day as I return to silence through *zazen*, a Zen Buddhist way of sitting still, receiving, and releasing. As I return to silence, I am learning to pay attention to where I am. Am I awake? This awareness is not a selfish agenda for happiness but rather an honest response to suffering in the world. However deep the suffering, however deep the waters that still run from my ancestors to this life, I respond awake.

NOTES

1 The meaning of Nam-Myoho-Renge-Kyo: *Nam or Namu*—means to have devotion to or to take refuge in the teachings, *Myoho*—the oneness of the law and mystical everyday life, *Renge*—the principle of cause and effect, and *Kyo*—sutra or teachings (Dharma).

Moving toward an End to Suffering

MARLENE JONES

If you let go a little, you will have a little peace.
If you let go a lot, you will have a lot of peace.
If you let go completely, you will have complete peace.
—Ajahn Chah, Forest Buddhist Master
in twentieth-century Thailand

As AN AFRICAN AMERICAN WOMAN who teaches and practices Buddhist meditation in the Theravada tradition, I am often asked why there are not more people of color practicing in the United States. Over the years, I have watched people of color go in and out of meditation centers. Although there are many people of color who practice, there are also those who have not been able to find their place in predominantly white Sanghas or Buddhist communities. Many centers are developing new strategies toward creating a sense of multiculturalism where all are welcome. Creating these new strategies is critical to finding Buddhism's true home in the West and ending the suffering of all people.

Historical domination, colonization, slavery, and oppression of people of color by Europeans have been the rule worldwide for many centuries. In my own community experience I have felt marginalized, invisible, and conspicuous all at the same time. Besides the stares that I have received in my early visits to the meditation hall, I was awkwardly ignored and bypassed, or approached by several people who made comments inncluding, "What would a black person be doing at a meditation center? I thought that you liked Baptist churches and dancing." I felt that I had to leave myself at the door and assimilate in order to fit in. And even then, I couldn't change the way that I looked. I ended up feeling the same sense of isolation and alienation that I experience in mainstream society. Yet I knew Buddhism was my spiritual home.

I was introduced to meditation in 1970. At the time I was very involved in the church. The conflict was overwhelming, so I gave up sitting meditation. Twenty years later, after not fitting in at church, not finding peace, I began to sit again in the privacy of my home. At home I was safe, safer than I had ever been in a church environment. As much as I loved Jesus, I didn't feel protected by Christianity.

People harm each other. But we can use the unwanted and unfavorable circumstances of our lives as the material of our own awakening. It is all an opportunity for practice. The Buddha's First Noble Truth teaches us that suffering is part of the human experience.

Many of us use attachment to struggle as a survival tactic. We struggle with work, finances, bills, relationships, tragic situations, and just running late to work or a meeting. When things are not going well, when confusion erupts, we feel irritated and upset. The result is more suffering.

We need to look at the difference between seeing that harm has been done and blaming. Blame and shame are big parts of life that can be addressed in our daily practice. When we blame, we are pointing the finger at others. This is usually followed by anger and hatred.

From moment to moment, circumstances change. All of us are subject to these changes. Anything can happen, anytime. This fact alone reminds us not to hold on. It is so ordinary, we don't even notice it. As we notice this quality of the mind, we can see the impermanence of all things. We can witness the coming and going of thought, speech, and action.

There are two kinds of suffering: the suffering that leads to more suffering and the suffering that leads to the end of suffering. Suffering held correctly can be an enormous cathartic opportunity in practice. The more we accept change, the more we relax the mind, and the more we are able to let go of many of our attachments.

One important way to cultivate moments of knowledge during our daily lives is by knowing our own true nature. Seeking our authentic self is one of the first important steps that we can take on a daily basis. This is known as taking refuge in the Buddha. The second step is taking refuge in the Dharma, the 2,500-year-old teachings of the Buddha that direct our living. Finally, we can take refuge in the Sangha, our spiritual communities. These communities might be large centers, small sitting groups, or our own family practice.

For many years, I sought therapy in order to sustain myself while coping with the racism I felt all around me. Although therapy helped to some degree, it is my practice that has made the greatest difference in my life and my work as a Dharma teacher. Finding both silence and stillness through practice has been a healing refuge.

Everything is practice, a very sacred and personal experience. There is freedom in the silence of practice, in the stillness as well as in the movement of the practice of life. The greatest teaching for me has been practicing compassion, first for myself, then for other individuals, and for all beings in all directions. It is here that I have found true freedom. Ache.

Buddhism in the Land
of the Redface

EDUARDO DURAN

I DID NOT SET OUT to study the Dharma. I grew up in a family in which alcohol and violence prevailed and I enlisted in the military at age seventeen. During a time when most of the American Buddhist teachers were studying in Asia, I was also in Asia but in the Vietnam war. It was after the dissonance created by the war that I embarked on studying psychology and ended up working at a Native American clinic in the mountains of central California.

It was during this time I visited an old man for what I thought was to be a mental health consultation. The old man became my teacher, although I didn't know this at the time. My Root Teacher, Clarence, was an Aboriginal person from Turtle Island (the original name of North America).

My years of daily meditation and mindfulness in the Vipassana Buddhist tradition have been augmented by Aboriginal ceremonial practice. Through the integration of intense ceremonial practice and Vipassana practice, I have discovered what our great great grandpa the Buddha taught: The Dharma was already here in the so-called West long before we had that name for it. The ceremonial practices of the many tribal groups that were here have, as a core quality, the ability to bring strong levels of concentration to the participants, which is similar to the sitting practice of Asia in which *samadhi* is also a result. Aboriginal Dharma can be experienced as ceremonial meditation.

Many tribal people in the world subscribe to a certain etiquette of giving and receiving that would easily fall within the teachings of right view and right action as taught by the Buddha. A clear example of this type of etiquette is the story of what happened when Padmasambhava brought the Dharma to Tibet in the eighth century. In gratitude for the teachings, the King of Tibet offered Padmasambhava the gift of Mount Meru. Truly, the king understood the preciousness of the teachings and also the natural law about "gifting" in order to remain in harmony with the organic process. One way of bringing the teachings to more people without proselytizing is by visiting people in their homes, bringing a gift, and asking permission to tell a story.

By the time the Dharma reached the shores of the Redface, it was, in many ways, at least twice removed from the original teaching and direct experience. Dharma is truth, but it is also compassion and understanding. I believe that this has karmic implications, especially if we cause suffering to people while propagating Dharma. With the same sword we can either cut through people's hearts and cause them suffering or cut through our own ignorance and be the cause of emerging love and compassion. There is always the gap between the purity of the Dharma and the inexactness of expressing it.

Why is any of this important? Because Buddhism is about awakening through love and compassion, we must bring this love and compassion to our practice. For me, the actual Dharma practice happens off of the meditation cushion and in the world where suffering is encountered. In my work with aboriginal people it has become apparent that this practice can be a profound gift to people who are suffering with very few places to turn. Most of the time all I can do is offer silent *metta* (loving kindness) and lately I have been taking the risk to the ego of practicing *tonglen* (taking in the suffering) as I work with patients who are suffering from mental and physcial pain.

The Buddha traveled all over, sharing the way out of suffering in a close and personal way. The goal of meditation in a retreat is not to recover just enough to re-engage with consumerism once the retreat is over. The Dharma must have the cultural competence that will make sense to the worldview of people of color. Cultural competence is the ability to move across cultural boundaries and offer a relevant experience, teaching, and understanding to a person of a culture different from your own. Trying to force a different cultural norm on someone is an act of violence, clearly not the Buddha's idea of skillful teaching.

I say these words with the purpose of relieving suffering. There is only one truth, but in order to make it tasty to the palate of Turtle Island folks, that truth needs to be treated with the correct metaphor. The Buddha would no doubt enjoy a big bowl of blue corn mush with much gusto and in a most mindful way if he were around today.

It's very simple. We just need to watch our intention and make sure that our actions do not cause suffering to others. Much suffering has been caused by the exclusive manner in which the Dharma has been brought into the land of the original people of Turtle Island. If our practice is moving towards the bodhisattva vow of making every moment of each lifetime fully committed to the freedom from suffering of all sentient beings, we must begin to see clearly deep into the suffering of people of color and not shy away from it.

Our practice must involve commitment to working for the happiness of all beings, both on and off the zafu. I can only ask that we practice in such a way to help the mind dissolve into unconditional love and compassion in every moment. *Mitakuye Oyasin.* All are my relations.

What Are We to Do with Our Enclosures?

JOSÉ LUIS REISSIG

JOURNEYING OUTWARDLY

I USED TO LIVE on the Upper West Side of New York City and jog in River-side Park. One day, as I entered the park, I came upon a couple sitting next to a cage with the door open and a bird inside. They told me that they wanted to give the bird its freedom. As I came back from my run thirty minutes later, they were still trying to persuade the bird to fly away. I couldn't get the image of that bird out of my mind. I had lived a lot of my life as that bird, unwilling to even acknowledge my confinement, unaware that my condition was unsatisfactory, blind to what the Buddha called the First Noble Truth.

I had lived largely within the confines of a variety of enclosures. Some were inflicted upon me, such as the cell I was jailed in for a week in Argentina because of my political activities as a high school student. But far more significant were the enclosures I confined myself in because it felt unsafe to be free. I grew up in Buenos Aires in a barrio of modest and substandard houses. Our two-story house towered over all the others in the neighborhood. The outward appearance of our home, and the fact that we had a live-in maid, placed us in the well-to-do category even though we were actually not affluent. Furthermore, my father's status as a writer and educator made him a member of the intelligentsia. The neighborhood kids played soccer on the street. I was not allowed to join them and had no earnest wish to do so.

At age nineteen I was sent to the U.S. to study. I returned to Argentina in the early fifties with a Ph.D. in molecular biology from Cal Tech —now a member of the intelligentsia in my own right. Shortly before returning I dreamt that I was back in the barrio where I had grown up. I was walking along my old street and turned into an intersecting dirt road that I had avoided assiduously in real life. In the dream, I found myself facing a cluster of shanties and meeting with a young man who lived there. I tried to explain to him the importance of what I had just learned and was bringing back home. Upon waking up I was struck by my yearning to transcend the boundaries of class and culture that separated me from the kids in my neighborhood.

It took a long time for me to be able—or even willing—to actually break out of such enclosures. I spent the next five years in Buenos Aires at a research institution led by a biochemist who would eventually receive the Nobel Prize. The laboratory had nothing in common with the social or economic environment surrounding it. The themes we worked on, the bulk of our funding, and the journals we published in were all part of an international enterprise, and I was happy for that. I still longed to connect with my dream-friend from the shantytown, and took a few ineffectual steps in solidarity with people like him, but my commitment was feeble.

In the late '60s, while I was a professor at the University of Buenos Aires, the university fell into the hands of the military after a coup. We left, my wife, three small children, and I, for the safer shores of the U.S.A. There, in Long Island, academia, family, and friends came together as a supporting structure for my life.

I have no gut recollection of being the target of discrimination by race, language, or culture in this country. I have been insulted—my Michigan landlord called me "South American monkey" before kicking me out—but I do not recall feeling hurt. Instead, I took the insult as a sign of ignorance. Or perhaps I was just trying not to be affected by the insults, first by feeling superior, then by forgetting about them. At Long Island University, the chairman of my department persisted in greeting me by chanting "José can you see," a reference to an ethnic joke about a man from Latin America who goes to a baseball game, gets a seat way back in the bleachers, and thinks everyone is singing to him "José can you see?" I had been invited to teach at Long Island by the chancellor of the University, who took no notice of the wishes of the department. In chanting the chairman of the department was proclaiming that I'd be a fool to think that I was liked by my colleagues.

Talking about this with my oldest daughter recently, she said: "For me, it's quite different. Kids can be very direct; they punch you in the face." How did she know that there was a connection between the punches and her nationality? "Well," she said, "they called us spics while they punched." What is extraordinary here is that my children's plight did not seem to have registered in my mind until now. I am overwhelmed by the realization of how much concealment was required for me to inhabit the enclaves of my choice.

The Wake-up Call

My shifting allegiances allowed me to negotiate life with the required flexibility to inhabit enclaves that felt safe, even at the cost of ignoring the systems of oppression surrounding me. But there was one enclave I could not make good by deception, and that was my marriage. Its failure eventually brought down the whole project of my life.

Among the variety of undertakings I embarked on to try to assuage the pain of separation was a spiritual search. This was a surprising twist in the career of someone for whom "Enlightenment" had been the movement that enthroned rationalism in eighteenth-century France, not the journey of the Buddha. I was looking for refuge, but I didn't count on Buddhism's ability to open the mind and heart to the reality of suffering, which made further pretense unworkable for me. I came in touch with much that I had shooed away by pretending to be superior to it. It was a harrowing time. I was face to face with the long suppressed suffering that life kept presenting to me and that I had kept avoiding. In the end, I can only thank the breakdown of my marriage, and my encounter with the Dharma, for the long delayed wake-up call that finally knocked at my door.

Prince Siddhartha Gautama's journey to become the Buddha was also marked by a wake-up call. Siddhartha was living in the luxury of his father's palace. In spite of all the pleasures that were available to him, he felt dissatisfied in that enclosure. He yearned to come in contact with the reality of things, and when he managed to venture out of the palace he came upon the Four Heavenly Messengers: a very old person, a sick person, a corpse, and a wandering mendicant. The first three brought him face to face with the suffering that accompanies living and dying, an encounter that had eluded him in the protected enclave of the palace. That was his wake-up call. The Buddha called it the First Noble Truth.

Journeying Inwardly

The Fourth Heavenly Messenger gave Siddhartha the cue for what to do next. At age twenty-nine he became a mendicant and devoted himself to looking inward. His practice came to fruition six years later when he became the Buddha, the Enlightened One.

For me, the Fourth Heavenly Messenger was Christopher, my teacher. He taught me how to turn inward and open directly to the experience of each moment. Through meditation practice I became aware of how my mind would fashion an identity for myself by giving solidity to the enclosures I found myself in. I was a husband, a father, a teacher, a scientist, a recipient of research grants, a Latin American, a U.S. citizen. Whenever any of the critical structures supporting my identity were threatened, I had a sense of excruciating doom. I came to know directly how this attachment contributed to my misery. From that insight came the possibility to transform my inner experience and move towards freedom. The suffering was still there, but so was the breath, the sounds, the silence, and the bodily sensations of each moment. Felt in this way, that very suffering brought with it an intimation of how to end it. I discovered I could let go of the enclosures I had used to define myself. An uncanny sense of freedom began to permeate my life.

Would this turning inward mean the abandonment of the outer world? The temptation to do so was there, but the teachings kept pointing to a nondual understanding of the world.

Journeying Nondualistically

Right after his enlightenment, while feasting in the sublime peace of nirvana, the Buddha wondered what to do with his discovery. He wanted to share it, but was skeptical about the feasibility of doing so. Initially his mind was inclined to inaction. Then the god Brahma appeared and pleaded with him to teach because there were "beings with little dust in their eyes who are wasting through not hearing the Dharma."[1] The Buddha agreed and eventually went on to teach. But before that there was a hiatus of perplexity—a hiatus between knowing and acting, between bliss and engagement. The Buddha's archetypical story highlights the fact that the transition across such a hiatus is not automatic, but needs to be guided wisely.

The radical change that the Dharma has brought into my life has eventually led to the full acknowledgment of my own journey from one enclosure to another, from one identity to the next. My longing to connect with my friend in the shantytown in Buenos Aires, and all the frustrated longings for connection in my journey are not now discarded but transformed. They have taught me to accept who I was and what I am, as well as what others are, and to consider action not in denial and reactivity, but in the awareness of what is and what could be. At the end of a sitting, I bow down in full acceptance of what is, and get back up again to do what needs to be done.

The revolution heralded by the Buddha was not limited to his mind. It was also directed to the world around him. He defied the conventions of his time by creating a community where all segments of society were welcomed: kings and beggars, brahmans and outcastes, ascetics and householders, law-abiding fellows and criminals, and, eventually, women as well. Surely it is in our hands to give support to a similar development within the circumstances of our lives. We need to do so, not by redrawing the apartheid lines according to the new political correctness—as is now the fashion in the corporate "diversity" programs—but by challenging the contemporary hierarchies of domination wherever we encounter them. This challenge is at times best implemented through political action, at times through consciousness raising, and at times by simply and truly opening up to the reality of suffering. My model for the transformation that this opening can bring about is Etty Hillesum.

I learned about Etty by reading her diary and letters written in the last two years of her life.[2] For much of that time she was imprisoned in a Nazi concentration camp. She was gassed at Auschwitz at age twenty-nine. In facing the overwhelming force of a State gone berserk, there was nothing anyone could do to change the situation externally. But in opening fully to the truth of her suffering, Etty radically transformed her experience. Her voice carries immense authority, the authority of someone who repeatedly chose to embrace the enclosures imposed on her rather than escape them. Her words speak to me poignantly about opening our hearts to the truth of suffering:

> *October 8, 1942.* I am not afraid to look suffering straight in the eye.... This morning I said to Jopie, "It still all comes down to the same thing: life is beautiful. And I believe in God. And I want to be there right in the thick of what people call horror and still be able to say: life is beautiful."

> *July 3, 1943.* The misery here is quite terrible; and yet, late at night when the day has slunk away into the depths behind me, I often walk with a spring in my step along the barbed wire. And then time and again, it soars straight from my heart—I can't help it, that's just the way it is, like some elementary force—the feeling that life is glorious and magnificent.

> *July 7, 1943.* We have to rid ourselves of all preconceptions, of all slogans, of all sense of security, find the courage to let go of everything, every standard, every conventional bulwark. Only then will life become infinitely rich and overflowing, even in the suffering it deals out to us.

There is nothing in her diaries that indicates that Etty is familiar with the teachings of the Buddha. Yet, her words are in full harmony with those of the Buddha, who said, "the breakthrough to the Four Noble Truths is accompanied only by happiness and joy."[3]

As Etty's mind roams freely, the enclosures meant to imprison her lose their power. Having become free through the acceptance of her suffering, she has no more need for enemies and she has no misgivings about dealing with the ultimate closure, the great matter of life and death. She wrote:

> Most of us in the West don't understand the art of suffering and experience a thousand fears instead. We cease to be alive, being full of fear, bitterness, hatred and despair. God knows, it's only too easy to understand why. But when we are deprived of our lives, are we really deprived of very much? We have to accept death as part of life, even the most horrible of deaths...I'm in Poland every day...I often see visions of poisonous green smoke; I am with the hungry, with the ill-treated and the dying, every day, but I am also with the jasmine and with that piece of sky beyond my window.

I opened this piece with the story of the bird in a cage in Riverside Park, free to fly away. I'm closing it with Etty, literally imprisoned in a barbed wire enclosure. Paradoxically, it is Etty who is free as a bird, and it is the bird who was unfree in the open cage. Etty's suffering was inexcusable and horrific. But neither her heart and mind, nor ours, can be held captive as long as we are open to see things as they are.

NOTES

1 *Majjhima Nikaya* (26.20), (Boston: Wisdom Publications, 1995).

2 Etty Hillesum, *An Interrupted Life and Letters from Westerbork*, (New York: Henry Holt, 1996).

3 *Samyutta Nikaya* (56.35), (Boston: Wisdom Publications, 2000).

HARITI (KISHIBOJIN)

The Truth of the Origin of Suffering

The Nobility of Suffering

THICH NHAT HANH

IN YOUR TRUE HOME, is there any suffering? You enjoy your true home, but does suffering exist there?

The Buddha spoke about the Four Noble Truths. The First Noble Truth is ill-being, *dukkha*. He encourages us to recognize ill-being, to take a deep look into its nature, and not to try to run away from it. Ill-being is suffering. Why did the Buddha call suffering a Noble Truth? What is so noble about suffering?

The fact is that, thanks to suffering, you have a chance to cultivate your understanding and your compassion. Without suffering there is no way you could learn to be compassionate. This is why suffering is noble. You should not allow suffering to overwhelm you, but if you know how to look deeply into suffering and learn from it, then you have the wisdom of understanding and compassion.

Ill-being can be described in terms of violence, discrimination, hate, jealousy, anger, craving, and especially ignorance. Out of ignorance we do many things that make us and others suffer. The Gospel says: "Lord, forgive them for they know not what they do." Ignorance is the root of ill-being.

What is the root cause of this suffering? The path leading to ill-being is the Second Noble Truth.

The Third Noble Truth is the cessation of ill-being, which means the birth of well-being. When there is darkness there's no light. And when darkness stops, light reveals itself. When a practitioner looks deeply into ill-being and discovers its roots and understands its nature, then suddenly the Fourth Noble Truth reveals itself: the path which leads to the cessation of ill-being.

According to the teaching and the practice, the presence of well-being and the cessation of ill-being are possible with the practice of the noble path. You cannot see the noble path leading to the cessation of ill-being unless you understand ill-being and its nature.

People tend to think of the Kingdom of God as a place where there is no suffering, only happiness. Many Buddhists believe that in the Pure Land of the

Buddha there is no suffering. This is dualistic thinking. It goes against the wisdom of Buddhism, the wisdom of interbeing.

Look at a pen. You call this side the left and this the right. Do you believe that the right is possible without the left? No, without right there is no left. If you are politically on the left, don't wish for the disappearance of the right; if there is no right you cannot exist as the left. You have to wish for the existence of the right in order for you to be on the left. Now turn the pen and we see the above and the below. Do you think that the above can exist without the below? No. Do you think we can grow a lotus flower without the mud? Can we grow a lotus flower on marbles?

A garden should have both garbage and flowers. A gardener knows how to handle the garbage in order for the flower to be protected and grow. In order to grow vegetables, you need compost. If you are an organic gardener you know that you don't need to throw the garbage away. Garbage is organic, and with the garbage you can make compost and nourish the flowers and vegetables. Suffering and happiness are also organic. If you know this you can transform suffering into well-being. This is the Buddha's teaching of nonduality.

There is no lotus flower possible without the mud. There is no understanding and compassion without suffering. I would never want to send my children to a place where there is no suffering, because in such a place they would have no chance to learn how to understand and to be compassionate. It is by touching suffering, understanding suffering, that you have a chance to understand people and their suffering. Because of your own suffering, you begin to know what it means to be compassionate. My definition of the Kingdom of God is not a place where there is no suffering, but a place where we can cultivate understanding and compassion. A place where there is no understanding and compassion is hell.

Even when you see a lot of violence, discrimination, hatred, jealousy, and craving, if you are equipped with understanding and compassion you don't suffer. You are a bodhisattva, a teacher of understanding and compassion, helping people learn how to be more understanding and compassionate. And you are building the Kingdom of God, the Pure Land of the Buddha. How beautiful and meaningful your life is because you have this opportunity. You are the organic gardener. You know how to make use of the garbage in order to nourish the flowers and vegetables.

Understanding and compassion also protect you. Even if there is anger, violence, and discrimination toward you, you don't have to suffer. Because you understand and understanding brings about compassion. In my true home, there is the presence of well-being, understanding, and compassion so I am able to protect myself and other people. I help them to cultivate more understanding and compassion so they won't suffer because of the presence of these negative things.

In this world there is violence, discrimination, hate, and craving, but if you are equipped with Right View, the wisdom of interbeing and nondiscrimination, you don't have to suffer. Pain is inevitable, but suffering is optional. When you are protected by understanding and compassion, you are not anyone's victim anymore. It is they who are the victims of their ignorance and discrimination, and it is they who are the object of your work. You are living in such a way that you can help them remove and transform their ignorance, discrimination, craving, and hatred.

Craving and anger are born from ignorance. You crave to be recognized as superior. You crave power, fame, and wealth. Around us there are many people with plenty of power, wealth, and fame, but they suffer very deeply from loneliness and despair, while people who have a lot of understanding and compassion don't have to suffer at all. They can live happily because they are protected by their wisdom and their compassion.

The Buddha lived in a society that was, and is still, very divided by the caste system. The brahmans believed they were superior. And then there were the outcastes who lived at the bottom of society. The Buddha always addressed the system of caste, and he talked about nobility in terms of thinking, speech, and action, not in terms of blood or race. In the teachings of the Buddha it is very clear that what makes the value of a person is not their race or caste, but their thought, speech, and action. You are noble not because of your race, but because of your way of thinking, your way of speaking, and your way of acting. This teaching of the Buddha is very clear, is the truth, a simple truth that can be recognized. There are many brahmans and others who believe they are noble, but whose life is not noble at all. Their way of thinking, speaking, and acting is ignoble, so there is nothing in them that can be called noble. There are people, no matter what ethnic group they belong to, whose way of thinking is full of understanding and humanity, whose way of speaking is full of hope and confidence, and whose way of acting is full of compassion. People can see the nobility in them.

The Four Nutriments

The Buddha talks about four kinds of nutriments. The first nutriment is called edible food, the kind you take in by way of the mouth. The Buddha urges us to consume only items that bring about lightness, healing, and nourishment in our body and in our mind.

The second kind of nutriment is called sensory impression. It comes in through the eyes, ears, nose, tongue, body, and mind. When you read an article, you consume. That article may contain the toxins of craving, violence, fear, discrimination, hate. When you watch television, you consume; and the TV program may be full of poisons. Western young people often watch television several hours a day because their parents are so busy. While watching television, the seeds of craving and violence in them are being watered. The seeds keep growing and growing, and this is very dangerous. When you drive through the city, you consume, because what you see and hear as advertisements are also items of consumption. Even when you don't want to consume, you are forced to. Driving through the city, you have to see this kind of publicity. Being aware and mindful of what we are seeing can help protect us.

Even conversation may be highly toxic. What the other person says may be full of hate or despair, and after one hour of listening, you may feel paralyzed by all the toxins in the conversation. That is why we shouldn't listen too much to that kind of conversation. Even if you are a psychotherapist, it's not wise to spend your whole day listening to the suffering of others. You have seeds of suffering in you and if you continue to listen, the seed of suffering in you will be watered again and again, and some day you will get sick and you will go to another therapist. The practice of therapy should include hours of walking, sitting, and getting in touch with the wonders of life, so the therapist will have enough strength to do the work of listening to the suffering. You have to know your limit. If your capacity is to listen to six people a day, don't try to do more than six people; you will burn out. Your suffering will increase to the point that you will not be able to continue.

We have six doors to guard, the door of the eyes, the ears, the nose, the tongue, the body, and the mind. This is the practice of mindful consumption. Select the films, articles, music, and conversation that will not bring toxins into you. This is the practice of self-protection, the protection of your family, and of your community. It is very urgent. If you don't guard these doors, then the negative seeds within you will grow very big and tend to push open the door of mind consciousness and come up.

Store consciousness is like the basement and mind consciousness is like the living room. Anything we don't like we put in the basement. We want to keep the living room beautiful. But the blocks of suffering in you don't want to stay in the basement, and if they become too strong they just push the door open and settle in the living room without your invitation. Especially during the night, when you have no means of control, they just push the door open and go into your mind consciousness.

During the day also, the violence, the craving, the hate, the anger are pushing hard, because you have allowed them to grow every day through unmindful consumption. You try to resist, you try to close the door very firmly. You set up a kind of embargo here in the living room and you repress them. You try to fill up mind consciousness with other items, and you do that by consumption. You don't feel well, you feel that something is trying to push its way in. So you play music to keep the mind busy, you pick up the telephone and talk, you take the car and drive somewhere, or you turn on the television. You do everything to keep the living room occupied so that these blocks of pain have no chance to come up. That is the policy that many of us adopt.

And the market outside provides us with many items that we can bring into the living room to fill it up twenty-four hours a day. We consume television shows, novels, and magazines that may also contain a lot of toxins like craving, hate, and violence. While we are consuming these things, the poisons fall down into store consciousness and make the blocks of suffering grow. These blocks of suffering are the fruit of unmindful consumption in the past, and now unmindful consumption in the present moment continues to make them grow stronger, and this is a very dangerous situation. The first step is to stop this kind of unmindful consumption and prevent these seeds that are already too important from growing anymore.

The third nutriment is volition—the deepest desire that motivates a person's life. Often we keep ourselves constantly busy. What is our purpose in living this way? When we are motivated by compassion, happiness fills our lives and we can live simply and relate to people easily.

The fourth nutriment is called consciousness as food. The Buddha said everything comes from consciousness, and when consciousness is taken care of, when wrong perceptions have been removed, consciousness becomes wisdom.

Our ways of thinking and feeling determine everything within and around us. If a person is fearful and angry and shares this fear and anger with other people, then together they will create a collective feeling of fear and anger. When fear and anger have become collective it is extremely dangerous.

The events of September 11, 2001 created a lot of fear and anger at the same time. Not many people help us to understand our fear, our anger. Not many people help us embrace them, and look deeply into their nature. And our government has acted on the foundation of that collective fear and anger. It is very dangerous.

The war on terrorism tries to force us to look for the worst in people. But the Buddha reminds us that everyone has Buddha nature, everybody has the kingdom of peace inside them. I do not underestimate you, you are a Buddha-to-be. That is his message: Everyone has Buddha nature.

The war on terrorism is the opposite of this Buddhist tradition. Every passenger on a plane could be a terrorist. If you have traveled in the last few years, you know what I am talking about. The security guards and the other passengers are not looking for your Buddha nature, they are looking at you as a potential terrorist. And when a culture goes like that, it goes in the wrong direction. We live in a society where we are influenced by the collective consciousness of fear, anger, craving. Not many of us wake up to that reality.

In 1966, I gave a Dharma talk at a church in Minneapolis, and afterward I was very tired. Back then I didn't have any monks or nuns to help me. The organizers of the talk had arranged for a car to take me to the place I would stay that night. But I decided to walk so I could practice walking meditation. I walked slowly so I could enjoy the cold, fragrant night air, so it could nourish me and heal me. While I was walking, taking each step in freedom, a car came up from behind me and, braking loudly, stopped very close to me. Somebody opened the door and shouted: "This is America, this is not China." And after making this statement, the guy drove away. Maybe he had thought, "This is a Chinese person who dares to walk in freedom in America," and he could not bear it. Maybe he thought, "This is America, only white people can live here. And Chinese people, how dare you come here and how dare you walk with such freedom. You have no right to walk in this way. This is America, this is not China."

His words were discrimination against a nation, discrimination against a people, discrimination against all kinds of things. But I was not angry, that was the good thing about it. I thought it was funny. I thought: If he would just pause for a moment, I would tell him, "I agree with you one hundred percent, this is America, this is not China. What you say is very correct. I agree with you. Why do you have to shout at me?"

We know that the seed of discrimination lies in all of us, black people as well as white people. Once in New York, a black woman shouted at me, even though I am also a person of color, only a different color. The oppressed and the oppressors are inside of us. We are not only victims of discrimination. Others also are victims of discrimination. Our practice is to reach to their wisdom of nondiscrimination.

So when somebody calls me Nhat Hanh, I say "yes," and when you call me Bush, I say "yes" because Bush is also my name. If you call me Saddam Hussein I will say "yes." I want these people to be happy and to have freedom. I don't want Mr. Bush or Saddam Hussein to suffer. They are all my beloved ones. I do not have enemies now, because I do not have discrimination in me. I want all of us to have this mind of nondiscrimination, so we can rebuild our lives. You can be free. And we can help young people to reach this freedom and help build up their communities, whatever their color.

THE THREE COMPLEXES

A color has no self. A color is made only of other colors. Looking deeply into one color, you see all the other colors in it. The color white is made of non-white elements. The color brown is made of non-brown elements. The color black is made of non-black elements. We inter-are; that is the fact. You are in me and I am in you, it's silly to discriminate against each other. It is ignorance to think that you are superior to me or that I am superior to you.

In Europe and America many people with mental illness are told by psychotherapists that they have low self-esteem and that's why they suffer. Then they try everything to help you to feel that you are superior. This past winter, the monastics in Deer Park studied the rule of the Benedictine monks together with the Buddhist pratimoksha, doing comparative studies of the two traditions.[1] They found that in the Benedictine tradition the monks try to combat arrogance and a superiority complex with the complex of inferiority: "I am nothing, I am not worthy." Because the feeling that you are superior can bring about a lot of suffering. But feeling inferior is also a complex. You are using a poison to neutralize another poison.

According to the teaching of the Buddha you cannot compare, because there is no self to compare to and nothing to compare with. The right hand and the left hand don't have separate selves.

In Buddhism, all complexes are born from the notion of self. If you think you are superior to others, you are sick, and the ground of your sickness is your illusion of a self that is better. Many of us struggle to prove that we are better, more powerful, and more clever than others. We seek happiness by proving that we are superior. All of our life we try to demonstrate one thing: I am superior to you; our nation is superior to yours; our race is superior to yours. We want to prove that we are the number one power, that we can overpower and militarily defeat any nation.

And when the other side suffers, they want to respond in the same way. They want to say, "We are not nothing! We are something. If you hit us, we can hit you back another way. If you bomb us, we can carry a bomb onto a bus and blow ourselves up. We can make you sleepless, we can make your nation live day and night in fear." So they try to retaliate, to prove that they are something, that they are not nothing. Both sides are trying to punish the other and prove that they are superior. And that is happening with many groups, whether Palestinian or Israeli, Hindu or Muslim, American or Arab. All that kind of striving is based on the illusion of self. If you suffer, we suffer also. If you are in safety, we will be in safety also. Safety and peace are not individual matters. If the other person is not safe, you cannot be safe. If the other person is not happy, there is no way that you can be happy.

In any family: if the father is unhappy, the son has no chance to be happy; if the mother is not happy, it's very difficult for the family to be happy. Happiness is not an individual matter. You have to see the nature of interbeing. When you make the other person happy, you have a chance to be happy also.

The complex of superiority brings a lot of suffering to you and to others. But when someone suffers from an inferiority complex, they also struggle and they make you suffer. Low self-esteem, inferiority, is another sickness. You cannot use a poison to heal a poison; the inferiority complex is also born from the illusion of a separate self. Three olive trees that sprout from the same root don't have a separate existence; two brothers also, two sisters also, two partners also. Considering yourself exactly equal to someone else is also a sickness because when you think there is a self then you compare and compete. You may think "Well, I am as good as you are, I will prove it." This will also cause a lot of suffering. So, psychotherapy in Buddhism is a little bit different. It is based on the wisdom of no-self. That is why when you remove the notion of self you are free from the three kinds of complexes, and there will be peace, reconciliation, brotherhood, and sisterhood.

With that wisdom, we can liberate ourselves and help liberate the world by means of our practice. We can live without any complex, whether of superiority, inferiority, or equality, because there is no self. To be a lotus flower is wonderful. To be a magnolia flower is equally wonderful. In the lotus there is a magnolia. In the magnolia there is a lotus.

The Buddha told us that human beings are made of non-human elements, such as animals, plants, and minerals. If a human being is aware of the fact that he or she is made of non-human elements, he or she will know how to protect the life of animals, plants, and minerals, and will not exploit, pollute, and destroy them. Because protecting the realms of animals, plants, and minerals is to protect the realm of humans. The teaching is clear and simple enough for all of us to understand, to touch, and to practice.

If you have only one way of thinking, one way of behaving, then you are confined to the limits of your culture. And with your habitual way of thinking, you imprison yourself in a framework of culture and behavior, and you cannot understand the suffering, the difficulties, and the dreams of people of other races and people who live in other areas. You have a view about freedom, about happiness, about the future, and you want to force that view upon other cultures and other nations, and you create suffering for them. You think that everybody has to follow a certain economic model, a certain way of thinking, and only then are they civilized people.

If that is how you think, then you have used a rope to tie yourself up, and you bind others with that rope and you cause danger and suffering for yourself and others. We need to have the opportunity to let go and learn other ways of thinking and behaving that are not ours. We have to practice opening our hearts, to learn about other cultures and other ways of thinking and behaving, so we can establish communication with other nations and cultures.

If you are born and raised in the United States, you should not let the American culture imprison you. You need to open your heart to learn other ways of thinking and behaving, including those of the country where your parents and grandparents were born. If you cannot understand the culture, the way of thinking and behaving in the place your parents and ancestors originated, then you cannot have communication and a good relationship with your parents, with your ancestors, and you may be completely cut off from the cultural stream that is one of your deepest roots. If you are a young Asian American raised with American culture you also need to let go, open your heart and learn about your original roots and the country of your parents and grandparents. Growing up in the United States you have received a culture, an education, a way of carrying on your activities, but do not think that it is superior. We have to open our hearts to learn about cultures and ways of behaving of people in other parts of the world.

When we have a stubborn attitude, caught in the values, culture, and way of thinking of our own civilization, we are backward and completely isolated. The United States right now is isolated. It is isolated not only in the areas of politics and the military, but in the way Americans think and respond to violence and terrorism. It is not the same as the way the Europeans or Africans or Asians think and respond. We need to listen to other nations so we can learn and not be caught in the view that our way of reacting and behaving is the best. When we are able to practice the teaching of the Buddha and come back to the present moment to be in contact with our true home, then we are not backward anymore, we are not discriminating anymore, our hearts are open to embrace all races, all cultures.

If you like to eat oranges, go ahead and eat oranges, but don't say that oranges are the best fruit. Besides oranges there are other fruits that are very good. You have the capacity to enjoy mangos, jackfruits, kiwis, and cherries. If in your whole life you only eat oranges, that would be a pity. If your whole life you can only be American, and wherever you go you have to have a Hilton Hotel, it's a pity. You have to be free from this prison so you can live with others and explore other ways, other arts, cultures, and traditions. That is civilization. Civilization is an open mind. Civilization is a view that is open, an attitude that is free. Civilization is opening your two arms to embrace all races, all people, and all species.

We can talk with President Bush, we can be friends with him, we can love him. We can also come to Osama bin Laden, speak to him and find out all the sufferings and difficulties of his people, all their wrong perceptions, and ask and find out why he has come to feel as he does. He can see that President Bush is also a brother, he is not the enemy, and he can see that the Americans also have their difficulties and suffering. Why do we think about hatred and punishment when we can liberate and help Osama so he can be in contact with his Buddha nature?

Conflicts can take place within ourselves, and when there is a conflict within, we suffer. According to the Dharma, it is possible to solve the conflict with the practice, it is possible for us to reconcile with ourselves in a nonviolent, gentle way. The Dharma provides us with practices that can help us reconcile with ourselves. Very often we cannot accept ourselves. There is a struggle within. Conflicts may also take place between two persons, and with the practice of good communication, deep listening, and loving speech, we can help each other remove wrong perceptions. The teaching of the Buddha is very effective in solving conflicts between two persons, whether they are father and son, husband and wife, brother and sister, and so on. Conflicts between two groups of people or two nations, can also be solved in that way.

Sometimes we are motivated by fear, as in the war with Iraq. We are afraid of each other. We want to be safe. And we think that in order to be safe we have to control, to occupy. And for the sake of safety, because of our fear, we commit atrocities in war. Sometimes it is both fear and craving. We crave power and to show that we are the strongest, and that is why we are able to kill and to destroy. We always find an excuse to kill and destroy. In order to be able to shoot them, bomb them, destroy them, we have to convince ourselves that they are evil and against God. We have to demonize them. That kind of thinking allows you to go to war and conduct a war. Wrong thinking is at the foundation of war. Wrong thinking has ignorance, discrimination, craving, and fear in it. If they are able to kill half a million people, one million people, it is because of their wrong thinking. You cannot look into your gun and shoot someone unless you believe that he is evil, has created suffering, is dangerous to you and to other people. In order to kill, you have to make people believe that the one you are trying to kill should be killed. This is what is going on. The mass media and public discourse may support this kind of effort, which is very dangerous. When we are so busy, then we don't have the time to intervene and we allow people to talk in that way, to write articles in that way, to make films in that way so that the majority believe in it and the war effort will be supported. The cause of this kind of tragedy is not just cruelty or violence, but it is our fear, our craving born from wrong thinking. And wrong thinking always creates suffering.

The terrorists who attacked the Twin Towers must have been motivated by a strong desire to punish. They must have had a lot of anger and a lot of hate. They were ready to die in order to punish. They may have believed that what they were doing they did in the name of justice, in the name of God. The person who blows himself up in the bus to punish others is ready to die. He may think that he is doing it for the sake of justice or as a holy kind of action. We have to find out what is the motivation, the foundation, of this kind of action. We cannot just call these people evil.

We know that some kind of thinking is at the foundation of their action. They believe they are on the right side, the side of goodness, of God, and they may be acting in the name of justice, of righteousness. If you think they are wrong in their way of thinking, you should help them remove their wrong perceptions. They may have wrong perceptions about themselves, they may have wrong perceptions about us, and these wrong perceptions are the foundation of hate and anger.

So far our political leaders have not tried to do enough in this direction. Motivated also by anger and fear, we believe only in our military power, to strike, to punish, and to destroy. But we see that in the last year we have created more hate, more violence, and we have created more terrorists.

If you listen to people around the world, you will see we have not succeeded in reducing the amount of hate and anger in the world. It is not so difficult to see that the roots of terrorism and violence lie in the way people think, and that in order to really remove terrorism we have to remove that way of thinking and help people remove their wrong perceptions about themselves and others, including us. We have not done that. It cannot be done with guns and bombs. That is why the practices of deep compassionate listening and gentle speech offered by the Buddha are very important. We need to say to other people in other countries: "Dear people, we know that you must have hated us a lot, must be very angry with us in order to have done such a thing to us. We want to understand why. Have we done anything that makes you suffer so much. Have we tried to destroy you as a religion, as a culture, as a people, as a nation? Please tell us. We may have said or done a number of things that have given you the impression that we discriminate against you, that we want to destroy you. But really we don't have the intention of destroying you and discriminating against you. So please tell us so that we know what wrong we have done to you. And please tell us what we can do in order to help you live in peace and safety."

Our political leaders have considered this kind of talking as too weak. But it takes a lot of courage to speak in this way and to offer deep listening. If we are sincere, and we really want to listen, they will tell us everything that they have in their hearts; that is the practice of deep listening. Even if they say it with anger, condemnation, a lot of accusation, we are still able to listen in order to understand why they have done such a thing. If we detect elements of wrong perception in them, then we know that later on we can release the information they need to correct their wrong perceptions.

And while listening, we may recognize not only do they have wrong perceptions of them and us, but we also have wrong perceptions about them and about ourselves. Because we are not saints, we are human beings, we have our shortcomings and we have done and said unskillful things that that have given them wrong impressions of us and our intentions. So, this is the kind of basic work for peace: creating mutual understanding. In this way, we move from understanding the causes of suffering to creating the compassion necessary for its cessation.

NOTES

1 Deer Park Monastery is in southern California and is part of the Unified Buddhist Church.

A Teaching On
The Second Noble Truth

RALPH M. STEELE

THERE ARE TWO KINDS of suffering—the kind that comes from within and the kind that comes from without—but often it's hard to sort out which is which, especially when you've internalized a culture designed to make you suffer.

For more than twenty years I practiced various meditation methods. I was the only person of color at retreats around the country 99 percent of the time. Although I was a Vietnam Veteran and a victim of the race riots of the 1960s in Kansas City, born into a culture built on slavery, for a long time I remained in a state of dissociation, ignorant of how I had internalized the colonization, oppression, slavery, racism, and genocide on which the United States of America is based. How could I have been so blind? I was born on Pawleys Island, South Carolina one of the Sea Islands, where many of the ships landed that brought the slaves that made this nation wealthy. Yet I was unaware that I was putting away certain aspects of myself to survive.

My wakeup call came when I was an ordained monk in Burma and Thailand in 1999 and 2000. I realized that by being away from the stressful life in the United States, I was taking a long-needed break. I was glad not to see any European Americans in Burma. Had I become hateful? If so, how did I get that way? After six months of intensive practice in Burma, I went to a monastery in Thailand where 80 percent of the monks were European American, and English was the spoken language. That's when things really hit home. Observing my mind states, I noticed busloads of unskillful mental qualities arising to fuel my rage and suffering. Despite my previous intensive practice, I felt that my work had just begun. I thought I had already experienced hell during intensive practice, resulting in a ruptured L-5 spinal disc, but I accepted the fact that this was another level of hell I had to overcome.

I had to get even more serious with *bhavana,* mind/heart training that included chanting; meditation practices in the four basic postures of the body;

right speech; hearing and teaching the Dharma; listening to the evening's talks and having conversations with other monks; and straightening out my view. Could I get all of this accomplished during this time? I had less than six months of my year-long sabbatical remaining before I would return to the country I now choose as my home. I wanted to master these skills, but for me that was like going to graduate school without completing undergraduate.

Going to Asia and working with the practice in cultures that have held this Buddhist practice for over a thousand years was a revelation. I suddenly understood that the American and European teachers of Buddhist practice had brought their own cultural baggage to the practice as it was taught in the U.S. This baggage included unconscious racism. Now I understood my unexplained rage at these teachers' meetings and at retreats. In taking on the practice, I had also taken on the spirituality of the European American style.

Because I gained so much from the practice, I had tried to ignore the European American way it was taught. I had left the "ethnic" part of my self at the door so that the white participants would not be uncomfortable. I did not want to draw attention to myself. I just wanted to learn. I had no clue that I was taking my sense of self and putting it away in order to be some one I was not. My sense of self should be awarded an Oscar for playing this role of ignorance.

Before becoming a lay teacher, I recall practicing at a meditation retreat. Out of 200 participants there were two persons of color. This is still the norm at the majority of retreats in the American Buddhist traditions. I went to one of the teachers and said that I have been practicing for 15 years, how come no one has made arrangements for people of color to be part of this practice? Why haven't we invited anyone from the Asian Buddhist communities? The response was, "That's a good observation, Ralph." We agreed that something had to be done. But I was on retreat so I went back to practicing. I went to war with my mental states about this situation. After a while, I found tranquility when my eyes were closed, and hell when they were open. This was when metta, or loving kindness, was being established as a practice here in America. At that first metta retreat in California in the latter part of the 1980s, I decided to become a teacher for the purpose of opening the door for people of color so they could come to retreats and feel comfortable. It takes a good ten years of practice and training to become a teacher, so my goal of bringing ethnic diversity to American Buddhism had to be put on hold because none of the other approximately 200 Theravada and Vipassana teachers were ready to do anything about this situation. Every four to six years we would get together at a Western Lineage Teachers Conference, and every two to four years at a Vipassana and Theravada Teachers Conference. I was the only one talking about people of color and cultural diversity.

Not all the problems were coming from outside. I needed to work on maturity around my own issues of belonging and power before I could come forward to address the unintentional racism and continued oppression within the Western Buddhist system. When I returned to the States after my sabbatical in Asia, I was brought face-to-face with unexamined parts of myself, the realm of my shadow, that had led me to behave in ways that caused suffering for myself and others. In learning to understand my shadow, I found that bhavana was not enough. I had to understand the history of oppression in our society to see how I had hidden from myself the ways I had oppressed others.

This work is something we all have to do. We all have to examine the shadow we all carry as part of this society before we can heal our unintended racism. Each of us has to skillfully do our individual work in this area so that we can work on the collective. Otherwise we'll just keep on causing suffering for ourselves and others, even when we think we're practicing and teaching the Dharma.

We can't focus just on the internal or the external. We have to focus on both. But because we don't know when our individual death will come, the Four Noble Truths have us start by focusing on the unnecessary suffering that comes from inside. That's the big issue. The Buddha wants to empower us. If we can learn not to pile suffering on ourselves, we can have more strength to deal with the suffering and stress that come from without. That's why he taught the Second Noble Truth: the cause of suffering and stress.

What's the cause of our suffering? What's the cause of our stress? There are two key words. The first is craving—not desire, but craving. Craving is our habitual thirst, our addictions, our obsessive-compulsiveness in looking for happiness and fulfillment in the wrong ways, as if equanimity could be found from using objects, substances, and people. When I was a 19-year-old soldier in Vietnam, I tried smoking five packs of cigarettes per-day, riding the white horse of heroin, and engaging in sexual misconduct, all these unskillful behaviors. And all I got was a tormented mind and body. I realized that that was not the way out of suffering.

The other key word is ignorance. Ignorance means not understanding. Not understanding what? Not understanding what we're doing! We can see our ignorance only if we practice skillfully, doing whatever is needed to get a better understanding of ourselves so that we can work with the collective problem. This can start by understanding our shadow: the way we hide our own motives from ourselves in ways that we've devised for ourselves and that we've picked up from the collective shadow of our society. We can do this by educating ourselves about the history, social injustice, and oppression of people of color and all people; interacting with other people from other ethnic origins; becoming culturally and ethnically diversified to broaden our view; reading literature we are not familiar with; undergoing therapy; and professionally working on our issues and ourselves to support our being an excellent person of integrity, for the collective well-being

And also by meditating. Our sitting meditation is training the mind. This is where the hard insights come. The first few minutes or so, images (mental qualities, images, or both) begin to move through the mind. Not just a little bit. A lot. We respond: "Oh, I want to stop this; oh I don't like this." Just interacting with that, trying to drive those images away, makes us even more restless. And that restlessness creates tension in the body. Fifteen or twenty minutes into the sit, we're dancing with this restlessness. We're blaming the thoughts, but the problem is that we don't see what we're doing. Like a monkey whose tail's on fire, we're just running down a street, setting more fires as we run down the street. The city we live in is in flames, hurting those close to us. And we have no idea that we are the cause of this fire! We have no idea.

So what are we going to do? It's like having dirty laundry. If we don't wash it, it won't get clean. If you wash the laundry a little, it'll get a little clean. If we give the kid within ourselves something to wash, we know how it's going to come out. So which part of us is going to wash our laundry? The kid, or the adult? Also, what kind of a laundry job are we going to do? Lukewarm or industrial strength?

When we begin training the mind, we need to bring some understanding of what we are doing to the task. Look and see, "OK, what am I doing to cause stress right now?" And after a while we might find out, "Oh, I'm not paying attention, that's all. I need to pay more attention to what I'm doing, right now. Oh, my arm is tense, oh, my chest is tense, oh, my belly is tense." Right there we begin to cultivate right view. We're beginning to have a better understanding. We're noticing, "Wow, as I begin to release this tension here, I'm beginning to calm down, my focus is strengthening, I'm not thinking about right arm or left arm here, it's just this object here." Right view…or ignorance: Which one are we going to choose? How many times have we sent a kid out to do an adult job? We know the kid always craves the chocolate, the candy, the sweets. We're sure to get distracted if we let the kid inside of us do our practice, because the kid is going to go for that craving, the habits, the instant gratification, every time.

We've got a choice. The adult is awareness itself. I'm saying awareness itself, not just awareness, because awareness can be scattered, but awareness itself can see what we're doing and the effects of what we're doing right as it's happening. If we see these things after they happen, it's too late. But as soon as we bring awareness itself to catch ourselves right when we're causing stress, yahman, then we can let go. There's some peace. That's wisdom—our sense of discernment. But it takes precision and relentless dedication.

It's all about training the mind. A Western Thai Forest Meditation Teacher, Ajahn Pasanno, said, when you're tired, practice; when you're happy, practice; when you're sad, practice; and when you're joyful, practice. It's like martial arts.

I initially came into the practice of meditation through Zen and martial arts during my high school years in Japan, and there the lesson was the same. My teacher told me not to complain, but to keep practicing and learning to overcome mental and physical difficulties or obstacles.

The cause of our suffering is not allowing the impermanence of life and death, the good and the bad, to flow. When we freeze up at the bad, we'll never overcome the fear of looking at our shadow. The cause of suffering is not being aware of the interconnectedness of the internal and external, not accepting, not being ready for the transitions of life, not being relentlessly mindful. Not understanding the uncertainty of life and death fuels our ignorance, supports unskillful behaviors, and causes suffering. It's like swimming in the Arctic Ocean for a few hours. If we're not prepared, we will die. But because of our commitment to the practice and working on ourselves, we are able to allow life and death to flow through our hearts, which results in nourishment, food for love and the collective.

This spiritual practice is universal. With discernment and insight we can learn to look at our cultural conditioning, language, ethnicity, temperament, and do whatever is therapeutically needed to integrate our shadow and to cultivate healing, because the time of death is uncertain. Practice is the arms of grace or the hands of the Dharma washing the inside of our body constantly, and once the mind/heart is trained to pay attention, then it's not difficult anymore. What's difficult will be to not pay attention! That's the beauty in the practice: gaining understanding that this heart of ours can be trained. Because of that, we can liberate ourselves from suffering in this very lifetime. We always have a choice, to keep things hidden in the shadow or to pay attention.

The Second Noble Truth is key, the biggest. If we don't understand that, our foot will never come out of the hole. And we will constantly complain, "Why is my foot in this hole? Who put my foot in this hole?" All the stories. Most people don't look at this particular truth here, this Second Noble Truth. But it's like when we get sick. If we don't understand how we got sick, we won't know how to cure our sickness. But once we understand the cause of our suffering, boom, it stops. It doesn't stop completely at first. It's only going to stop enough so we can say, "Ahhh, yes, I relax here." Then we have to bring in more discernment.

This is where maturity comes from. Maturity arises from practice. So in that moment of craving, who's going to jump in? The adult or the child? It depends on how strong the craving is and our level of maturity—can you see that? If you can, then you can see your addiction. And when we can see the stress it causes if we follow it—and when we realize that we don't have to follow it— we are able to drop it. That's when we'll understand how powerful it is to practice, and practice will become the thing you crave instead. That way our craving becomes our friend. Ajahn Jumnien, one of the Thai Forest Meditation Masters that I studied with, said, "Use everything as a tool for practice, and see through everything." We begin to find the joy in practicing, the sweetness. It just comes, a joy bigger than any other joy we have experienced. So this is practice, practice, practice, practice, practice, practice. And then all of a sudden, our life is our practice, and there's no moment when we are not practicing, turning the light on our collective and individual shadow, and letting go of the Second Noble Truth.

To Love Unconditionally is Freedom

MICHELE BENZAMIN-MIKI

THERE HAVE BEEN two practices that have guided me since taking on the path of the Dharma: gratitude for this human life and *ahimsa*, non-harming. Often I find some suffering inside me—some craving for something I do not yet have or some clinging to something I'm afraid will leave me. My response to whatever I find inside is gratitude for this human life.

My practice of gratitude involves remembering my ancestors. We all have a family history that makes up a great part of who we are, whether we agree with what our ancestors did or not. We suffer when we cannot see a part of ourselves or when we disown a part of our history. Whether that history was born out of oppression or privilege, violence or compassion, courage or defeat, grief or joy, remembering it uncovers suffering and moves us to grace and a possible future.

I am an artist and painter, and this history is only a small part of my story, but an important part. I walk upon the rich soil of many traditions, cultural and religious. My mother was Japanese and her root religion was Shinto and Buddhist, later to be Catholic. Her family was made up of farmers on her mother's side and Samurai on her father's side. My father was born and raised in America of mixed parentage, Czechoslovakian and German Catholics on his mother's side, and on his father's side Moroccan Sephardic Jew and Egyptian, and English Jewish. He is Catholic.

My parents met in Japan during the Korean War and were married in a Catholic church in Kobe. My mother and father traveled back and forth several times between the U.S. and Japan trying to decide where to put down roots for a family. I was born on one trip to America, my sister was born a year later on the trip back to Japan, and there we stayed until I was almost four.

A biracial marriage is complex and brave. Racism was my playground battlefield as a child. The racism was most directly experienced from my father's family because of his marriage to a Japanese woman, and was present in subtler ways from my mother's family because of my father being Caucasian.

My father's family was in the military and had their prejudices, and my mother's family wanted my mother to marry a Japanese man, preferably a doctor. The only people to attend their marriage ceremony were my Grandmother Noe Miki and my mother's friend.

Many circumstances led to their final decision to raise us in America. They felt it was best for us children to speak only English. We lived a poor to working class life in East L.A. and the San Fernando Valley. Later, when we could afford it, my mother visited her family in Japan. At the age of twenty-one, making good money on my own, I went back for the first time since I was four. It was strangely familiar, walking inside those enormous hollow bodies of bronze Buddhas in Kamakura, Nara, and Kyoto. I was amazed to see my mother resurrected there in her homeland, after having suffered many hardships while adjusting to life in America. I watched her reconnect to her heritage and root religion, and regain personal sovereignty. Despite language barriers, I formed bonds to my Japanese family that would later change my entire view of life and spirituality.

I returned to Japan every two years until my mother died in 1987 at age 59, when my sister and I returned to Japan with my mother's ashes and buried her in the family grave. My mother never became an American citizen.

In the practice of the Dharma, all the opposites of my life merged. I signed a peace treaty with all the warring factions inside myself, and became aware of the path set before me. My mother and father's family, Pearl Harbor and Hiroshima, Jesus and Shakyamuni Buddha, Mary and Tara, angels and bodhisattvas, my martial arts study and nonviolence principles—all these parts of me come together to lead me towards freedom.

Part of remembering my ancestors each day includes remembering our land ancestors, indigenous peoples and animals, plants, and minerals. In the Sutta Nipata (verses 600-611), it says: "Know ye the grasses and trees.... Then know ye the worms and the moths, and the different sorts of ants.... Know ye also the four-footed animals small and great, the serpents, the fish which range in the water, the birds that are borne along on wings and move through the air... Know ye the marks that constitute species are theirs, and their species are manifold." Buddhism also has the practice of looking deeply into the nature of things. In the words of Lama Anagarika Govinda: "To the enlightened man ... whose consciousness embraces the universe, to him the universe becomes his Body."

For all this, for the people and the natural world that make me, I wake up each morning and am thankful.

The second principle that I try and return to each day is nonviolence, *ahisma*. As an Aikido and meditation teacher, I am often asked if I would kill in order to protect a loved one or myself. I used to answer that yes, I would kill; I would kill the action, though, and not the person. I don't know if this is enough of an answer. Sometimes I answer with the story of a friend of mine who was participating in a peace rally. A passerby angrily threw out a question to him: "What would you do if you met the person who killed your loved ones? Don't tell me you wouldn't be angry and want to take their life!" He replied, "Yes, but then I would count on you, brother, to restrain me." We are not alone in our struggle; it is necessary to know to ask for help.

As I walk the path of the warrior, love and tolerance are my great teachers. I call myself a warrior because I am a woman who comes from a long line of female warriors and I am discovering my strengths on a path traditionally walked by men. I feel my role as a woman in Buddhism is to pay homage to, honor, and love deeply my own mother, grandmother, and the ancestral mothers and sisters within the Buddhist tradition. This earth is fertile ground for a woman warrior to walk upon.

To be able to love unconditionally is freedom. By loving myself and others, beginning each day with gratitude, and committing not to harm myself or others, I can let go of the clinging and craving that is at the root of my suffering. Each day, I can face the future without fear.

Mind Like a Mirror

GEORGE T. MUMFORD

I WAS WORKING with a group of inner city male adolescents several years ago. We did a role play where Asian American young men played the role of young African American men going into a store. Once in the store they were immediately approached and asked "Can I help you?" in a very disrespectful manner. They answered they did not need any help and were followed and watched as if they were expected to try to steal something.

It became obvious how awful it felt to be treated like a potential thief because of the color of your skin. But it would be too easy to say that the store clerks that treat potential customers as thieves were the bad guys and the young men being mistreated were the good guys who were the only ones suffering.

From my experience as a person of color, I have encountered similar treatment from both people of color and non-people of color. I experienced suffering because I felt I was treated unfairly and it felt unpleasant. I would experience anger and would either act it out by yelling some obscenity or hold it in to be released at some inappropriate time in the future. I suspect that the person mistreating me was also experiencing suffering in the form of fear or some other aversive unpleasant emotion.

As I apply the teachings of the Buddha to my life, I am able to see my suffering, what causes it, and how to lessen or eliminate the suffering.

A brief example comes to mind. I was standing in line to go through security in an airport and when my turn came, I stepped forward to hand a female Caucasian national guardswoman my boarding pass and identification. She yelled at me to step back. I know that I didn't do anything differently than the people ahead of me in the line. There was no way I could hand her my information without stepping forward. She reacted to me like I was threatening her even though I was acting like everyone else. As the only African American in the group I was treated as if I had done or was about to do something wrong. I did not react by getting angry, I responded by staying calm and letting her do what she had to do. I let go of my need to be right or to express my outrage.

The suffering is my unpleasant feeling of anger. The cause is my wanting things to be different, my wanting the person to treat me with respect, my wanting not to be associated with the unpleasant. When I let go a little, I have a little less suffering, when I let go a lot, I have a lot less suffering, when I let go completely, I eliminate the suffering completely.

How do I do this? I do it by understanding how things are and how things work. If you squeeze a lemon you get lemon juice. The juice is inside the lemon just as the suffering and anger is inside me, and under the right conditions it erupts. When I understand that the external situation is triggering something inside of me, I can switch my focus inside and see what I am holding on to and let go of it. I do not need to focus on the story, all I need to do is see how the anger is causing me suffering.

The focus needs to be on me, on my internal conditioning. The Buddha's concise teaching is to do good, avoid evil, and develop the mind. The poisons of greed, hatred, and delusion are gotten rid of by developing generosity, loving-kindness, and understanding. To do good, I need to cultivate good intentions, intentions of non-harming, intentions of goodwill, intentions of generosity. To avoid evil I need to use restraint so that I do not react to situations out of anger, greed, or confusion. I need to use skillful means (creative methods to get the right results) to change the harmful emotions to positive emotions. I do not have to react to my anger when someone mistreats me. I can feel it and not do anything to harm anyone including myself. In addition, I can prevent negative emotions from arising by investigating my intentions and discover how these emotions come into being.

With the young men I worked with, and in my own life, empathy builds compassion and eases suffering. The young Asian American men I worked with were able to feel on some level what it feels like to be a young African American man in our society and the African American young men were able to see the other's perspective as well. The participants talked about feeling disrespected, mistreated, harassed, distrusted, and unwanted, and they shared the anger, resentment and hatred that arose. It was difficult, but these young men began the process of developing the clear mind of compassion.

Developing the mind is a full-time job. Every moment we live is an opportunity to be mindful of people, places, and things as they are right here right now. We can train our mind to reflect the objects before it like a mirror, without the extra descriptions flavored by our likes, dislikes, or disinterest. Seeing clearly helps us to choose our responses to a situation so that our good intentions remain grounded in wisdom.

The Stories I Live With

SALA STEINBACH

THESE ARE THE STORIES I live with. They change as I change. These stories shape me because, like all of us, what I see now is a mixture of what is before me and what I have seen before.

I was born in Chicago in a black hospital because, in the 1940s, a black hospital or the county hospital were the only two choices. My father was in the Navy and stationed at the Great Lakes Naval Station, so my family moved to the middle-class suburb of Lake Forest to be near his work. One of my earliest memories is of playing in the woods that were next to our house. The woods caught fire one day. When the fire engines came, all our neighbors came to watch the fire. All the neighbors were cheering. I remember standing there with my parents and realizing that the neighhbors were hoping the fire would burn down our house. I remember the suffering and fear that my family and I felt.

Something was happening out there, but as a child I didn't know what it was. I could feel my family's own suffering but I couldn't see the suffering of others. What I know now is that everything that happens is connected to everything else that happens and cannot exist without it. In Buddhism, this is called dependent co-arising. Suffering exists and cruelty exists but it doesn't have an independent existence.

When I was 5 years old, we moved to Hyde Park, an integrated neighborhood on the south side of Chicago. Hyde Park was an island of sanity in what seemed to me to be an insane world. I learned the boundaries of my island/village. My twin sister and I could ride our bikes up and down streets and to and from school and feel safe. But we didn't realize we were only as safe as our neighborhood. One day, my sister rode her bike to the next neighborhood, with some friends who happened to be white, to go to the beach near their homes. A riot happened at the beach because this little black girl wasn't welcome there. They couldn't see that she was a little girl who wanted to swim with her friends, not a projection of what they thought she was.

Opening our hearts to that loss of feeling safe was also an opening for my sister and I to become activists in the civil rights and anti-war movements of the sixties and seventies. Although I had only a vague sense of it at the time, I knew that the people rioting on that beach in Chicago or beating up young people at lunch counter sit-ins in the South were more than just "racists." I was so much more than what they thought I was, so probably they were more than I thought they were, too.

I was at an Eastern women's college, the only black person in my class, when the church in Birmingham was bombed and four little girls were killed. I felt hurt and lost. Other students would come up to me and tell me how sorry they were for me and something about their sympathy made me feel worse. I tried talking to my father and figuring out what about my classmates sentiments made me feel so bad. I realized part of my suffering was that I had no ally close at hand to work out my feelings with. Now I see that the bombing was a loss for my classmates as well. These other students were also closing themselves off. All of humanity had been hurt by the loss of these four beautiful young girls, not just black people.

I tell these stories because these experiences make up part of the lens through which I see the world. When I came to Green Gulch Farm Zen Center on Sundays for a year and no one spoke to me, I wondered if maybe I wasn't wanted. Sitting in meditation helped me acknowledge that painful thought. It also helped me see that that wasn't all I was. I didn't have to hold on so tightly to the feeling of being unwanted. If that wasn't all I was, and I knew it wasn't, then maybe that wasn't all there was to the people around me either. In sitting, I can bow to the whole human being in myself and in all of us.

KANNON ON THE CARP

The Truth of the Cessation
of Suffering

Liberation from Suffering: Cessation and the Practice of Freedom

GAYLON FERGUSON

RECENTLY, A FRIEND of mine was daydreaming out loud about a future in which there would be meditation centers in every neighborhood—as common as convenience stores are now. "Instead of Stop and Shop," she suggested, "they could be called Stop and Stop!" The Buddha's Third Noble Truth—that suffering can end—can be summed up in that one word: "stopping." As it says in Chögyam Trungpa Rinpoche's *Cutting through Spiritual Materialism*, a classic guide to the path of Buddhist meditation: "There is no need to struggle to be free; absence of struggle is itself freedom." Stopping the inner battle is the basis for peace and non-aggression in our world. Only when we stop the battle within ourselves can we lay the groundwork for the truly compassionate activity of helping others to overcome suffering.

This is the heart of cessation: stopping the fight with ourselves. Traditionally, the opposite of making war on ourselves, endlessly judging and harshly criticizing ourselves, is spoken of as "making friends with ourselves"—the practice of loving kindness or *maitri* or *metta*. "Maitri"—a Sanskrit word that sounds like "my tree"—means friendliness, loving kindness or, simply, love. Just as compassion begins at home, a loving relationship with others radiates out from an inner affection, a friendly and fundamentally kind relationship to ourselves. This is a deep friendship with ourselves—not at all the same as those superficial relationships with what we call "fair-weather friends." We can all appreciate ourselves and our companions in moments of victory and shining success—but what of the times of loss and defeat, of discouragement and uncertainty?

What does it really mean to be kind to ourselves in this deeper sense? How is it different from indulging our every whim and desire for entertainment and escape? When does making friends with ourselves become mere indulgence?

The essence of meditation is non-struggle—not fighting with ourselves inwardly, developing a welcoming attitude toward our thoughts, our feelings, our bodies and minds altogether.

The founding Zen master of San Francisco Zen Center—Shunryu Suzuki Roshi—calls this welcoming approach a "spacious meadow." It involves welcoming our thoughts, our emotions, the sensations of the body, and the sights, smells, colors, and tastes of our world with an open-armed embrace. It means letting ourselves fall in love with the colors and sounds of ocean and sky, of freeways and streetlights. This can be as simple as really noticing the taste of orange juice in the morning—or as surprising as getting up to close the window against the noise outside and noticing that actually we enjoy the music floating in.

The disciplined freedom of cessation is much like the experience of leaving a stuffy, crowded room and stepping through an open doorway into fresh air. We give up editing ourselves—our minds and our emotions particularly— and simply let ourselves be as we are. We are neither exaggerating our potential—with wishful thinking of how great we are or will soon become—nor are we minimizing our faults out of fear that if we look too closely we won't like what we see. We are not dramatizing our emotions through elaborate fantasies of acting them out—how delicious continuing this love affair will be or how sweet the revenge on that person who hurt my feelings will feel. Nor are we repressing our emotions—our passion, our anger, our jealousy, feelings of puffed-up pride, lonely fear, and sadness. We simply let all this be and this letting be *is* cessation—the struggle to tightly control our experience stops, if only for a moment.

The heart of the problem is the constant attempt of all people to "fix" ourselves. In everyday life, we take things to be fixed because they are in need of repair—something is wrong with our car, for example—it needs more of this and less of that. Often, we regard ourselves in the same way—something about us is wrong or inadequate, in need of a little more this and a little less that. There is almost always room to indulge this view since, after all, who is perfect? But the view of the Buddha is that we are, all of us, fundamentally whole and complete as we are. In some traditions this is called our basic goodness or "Buddha nature." As Suzuki Roshi says, Buddha nature is just our human nature. We all possess an inherent, natural wakefulness. Our deepest longing is to reclaim this fundamental heritage of human goodness, basic compassion. Cessation is celebrating this fundamental goodness, uncovering an inner

strength and confidence that cannot be weakened or corrupted by the sometimes disorienting ups and downs of outer successes and failures.

Now the widespread human tendency to regard ourselves as in need of a
good "inner fix-it" repair job is particularly important for us as people of color.
People of color in the West grow up in societies saturated with ideas and values that invalidate their very existence. As Cornel West has written, affirming
exclusively Eurocentric standards of beauty often goes hand in hand with the
denigration of the moral and intellectual capabilities of Europe's "Others."
This is but one thread in a cultural fabric of white supremacy interwoven with
the strands of gender domination, homophobia, and pervasive economic
exploitation. Everyone reading this will have their own scars and stories to tell
from bruising encounters with that demonic trio of societal "isms"—sexism,
racism, classism. We are all survivors of many battles and many wars. We all
have our own sense of the meaning of Jimmy Cliff's "many rivers to cross." As
Charles Johnson phrases it: "the black experience in America, like the teachings
of Shakyamuni Buddha, begins with suffering."

The focus of the Buddhist practice of meditation is the internalized night-
mare of these outer battles. bell hooks has written movingly of the challenging issues of self-esteem facing many of us. In *Rock My Soul,* she points out:
"Most discussions of black people and self-esteem start by identifying racism
as the sole culprit. Certainly the politics of race and racism impinge on our
capacity as black folk to create self-love rooted in healthy self-esteem, sometimes in an absolute and brutal manner. Yet many of us create healthy self-
esteem in a world where white supremacy and racism remain the norm." What
makes such recovery of basic healthiness possible in the midst of the speed
and aggression and everyday assaults on human dignity of twenty-first century
social life? I want to acknowledge from the outset that the path to liberation is
not easy and will not be a smooth journey from confusion to clarity. But is it
possible that the ancient teachings of the Buddha—including instructions on
working with gentleness and insight into our own hearts and minds—can be
part of a path of liberation, which begins, as he taught, with self-liberation?

Yes. The teachings and practice of meditation allow us to activate the intimate yet public connection of the personal and the political. Outer change
proceeds alongside inner revolution. As hooks emphasizes, there has historically been some reluctance to include the psychological dimension in our
collective efforts to establish a more just and sane society: "Throughout our
history in this nation, black people and society as a whole have wanted to

minimize the reality of trauma in black life. It has been easier for everyone to focus on issues of material deprivation as the reason for our continued collective subordinated status than to place the issue of trauma and recovery on our agendas." Yes, there are real and pressing material priorities, but unless these go hand in hand with what Dr. Martin Luther King, Jr. called "the inner treasures" of the spirit, we will wake up to find that, again in King's prophetic words, "we have foolishly minimized the internal of our lives and maximized the external."

Of course, the church has traditionally been a place for healing the wounds of daily life, a safehouse for solace and recovery. It has also been in the arts—particularly the music of the blues and realistic fiction—that we find the exploration of the jagged edge of this connection between the intensity of private experience and the vast forces of historical change sweeping us from the Middle Passage through the horrors of enslaved life, the joy of emancipation, Reconstruction, Jim Crow and racial apartheid, the Civil Rights era and on into this, the new millennium. In Toni Morrison's masterpiece, *Beloved*, the elderly Baby Suggs, surrounded by her congregation, preaches a sermon of profound self-acceptance in a clearing in the woods: "Here—in this here place, we flesh; flesh that weeps, laughs; flesh that dances on bare feet in grass. Love it. Love it hard. Yonder, they do not love your flesh. They despise it. *You* got to love it, *you*." We have all, all of us, heard this message before. hooks says of her own mother's wisdom and skillful means, her "motherwit": "Having lived in the midst of white supremacy all her life, Mama recognized that it would be dangerous for us to live our lives trying to please racist white people, letting them set the standards for our identity and well-being."

The truth is that freedom is possible through our own self-determination. The opportunity for making friends with ourselves is an invitation delivered to our doorstep every day. According to tradition, the Buddha's last words were: "work out your salvation with diligence." The Third Noble Truth of cessation—of stopping the inner battle that undermines our confidence and well-being—is followed then by the Fourth Truth of the path—the way of experiencing the natural freedom of our basic being itself—freed from external additives. Again, the key point here is that we are not victims of our states of mind, we are agents in our own making, in the emancipation of our minds and hearts from the internal prisons of fear, anger, jealousy, and endless craving.

This is precisely the issue of an inner "decolonizing" of the mind and spirit: *any* external or conceptual standards that we impose on ourselves will eventually have disastrous consequences for our own sense of self-worth. Just as the menu should never be confused with the meal we are actually eating, we cannot rely on any set of ideas—or feelings based on those ideas—to tell us who we really are. Stopping or cessation means letting go of the mistaken idea that judging ourselves and comparing ourselves to others is the way to increase our wisdom, insight, and compassion. In a powerful teaching from Chögyam Trungpa Rinpoche, we find this startling line that sums up the essence of the Third Noble Truth: "I awaken into the wisdom with which I was born, and compassionate energy arises without pretense." Stopping means declaring a cease-fire in the battle of ego, freeing ourselves from vicious cycles of judgment and painful negativity. It is discovering the liberating message that we are, just as we are, originally good, fundamentally wise, and basically sane and loving.

A Child of the South in Long Black Robes

REVEREND MERLE KODO BOYD

B EFORE PLUNGING into this practice of Zen Buddhism, I was convinced I could keep my suffering to a minimum through foresight and cleverness. As an African American woman, I knew that the racism of others was beyond my control, but I worked to minimize the suffering it caused me through my choice of friends, neighborhood, and activities. When all else failed, I simply drew closer the armor I'd fashioned years ago in childhood.

I grew up in Texas during the forties and fifties, the years before the Civil Rights Act ended legal segregation. My childhood was generally happy but, at the same time, suffering and the longing to end it were as pervasive as the air. My parents experienced daily humiliations I felt rather than saw. Sometimes, returning home from shopping outside of our community, my mother would declare in a tight voice, "I'll never shop there again." Once, after deciding to take me to a white doctor for medical treatment, my father sat next to me in the dark closet assigned as a waiting room for black patients. He was silent, rigid, looked straight ahead, and avoided my questioning eyes. Even my uncle's estrangement from the family was attributed not to family tensions but to a flight from the South and some unspeakable incident he had witnessed. Only when I was an adult did my mother tell me that she suspected he had witnessed a lynching that occurred in their hometown.

At times like these, I sensed rage in my mother and shame in my father. I sensed vulnerability and powerlessness in parents I normally experienced as strong and powerful. At times like these, I knew that I would hurt them deeply if I asked questions or probed for more details. Dark memories were passed on, it seemed, without ever being spoken out loud. At home we were relatively safe, but travel out of town was full of quiet terror. On long trips to visit relatives, the reality of our vulnerability could not be avoided. Any incident drawing the hostile attention of a white person could result in violence from which no one would protect us. We were raised with not just a longing to end our suffering, but with a sense of obligation to do so, if not for ourselves, for the next generation.

In my family and in my childhood community, ending personal suffering meant getting an education, a decent job, and choosing the right man or woman to marry. Ending our suffering as African Americans meant taking action—boycotting, sitting-in, challenging laws in court, integrating schools, daring to vote, and generally risking the wrath and retaliation of white people. To encounter Zen practice was to encounter a new way of defining suffering, and therefore, a new way of ending it. The word "liberation" took on new meaning.

I was drawn to the meditation cushion by the vast spaciousness of a twelfth-century Chinese painting inspired by Zen Buddhism. The painting, *Solitary Angler,* was a picture of a lone man fishing quietly on a vast sea. The wide space of the sea was equal in importance to the small man in the boat. I was drawn at once to both the sea and the man. When I saw this painting in a book, my sense of self-recognition was so strong it startled me. The painting called to me in my own voice. I immediately sought out more books and found instructions for sitting *zazen.* Using a bed pillow and blankets, I began the practice alone in a corner of my bedroom.

It was natural that a book introduced me to Zen and became my first teacher. In the South of my childhood, Jim Crow laws defined my world. There were many places we were forbidden to go, but once I could read, I discovered that any place I found in a book was open to me. For a couple of years, I sat alone in my bedroom guided by books on Zen. I felt naked in this practice of zazen, and I was reluctant to expose myself to the racial realities I anticipated facing in a formal Zen center. I knew of no black people practicing Zen. The thought of entering a zendo knowing nothing of the etiquette and ritual was frightening enough. Being the only black person there would, I felt, draw more attention than I could stand. But the pull of practice was strong and, finally, I ventured out.

I had been sitting zazen for awhile by the time I heard the teachings of the Four Noble Truths and the Buddha's promise of the cessation of suffering. In the years that I have practiced there have been times when I wondered what this black child of the South is doing in black robes and *kesa,* the outer robe of a Buddhist priest. As part of my study for *jukai,* the taking of the Bodhisattva Vows, I began the practice of bowing to the ancestors in our lineage. Though I understood that all bows were to a shared self, a non-individual self, I sometimes felt uneasy and even disloyal as I bowed to Indian, Chinese, and Japanese men. As I chanted, I felt both included and excluded. Though I knew the bow honored the Buddha in all of us, I also felt keenly aware of all those not included in this specific list of names, ending with my own.

And still I bowed and sat zazen. From the beginning I was sitting in response to a call that spoke to me at the most intimate level. In this world of differences and conflict over differences, the recognition of myself in a practice with a Japanese form was a direct experience of a universal self.

Dogen Zenji's *Fukanzazengi* is one of the teachings at the core of my practice. It is also called *The Universal Promotion of the Principles of Zazen*. The key word is "universal." When delusion raises confusion in my mind, pitting my African American identity against my universal identity, creating the illusion that they are different, it is the practice of zazen that brings me back to reality. Its stillness can appear passive. It can appear to be the opposite of the action I was raised to see as the solution to injustice and suffering, but gradually I have come to see zazen as one of the most radical actions I can take.

Dogen refers to it as "the backward step." It necessitates a confrontation of a different kind than marches and sit-ins demanded. Sitting still, it is impossible to escape the busyness, the amorality of one's own mind. What gradually becomes clear is the way the mind works, bouncing from one thought to another, evoking first one emotion and then another. Still and silent, accepting all thoughts, emotions, and sensations no matter how painful or disturbing, zazen is the experience of taking a long unblinking look at oneself. Giving clear, nonjudgmental attention to everything, true equality becomes evident.

"Sitting fixedly," Dogen says, "think of not thinking. How do you think of not thinking? Nonthinking. This is the essential art of zazen...the Dharma gate of repose and bliss...." Over time there comes to be a space between thoughts, a space at the bottom of the breath, a space where one disappears. At first there seemed to be a huge gap between the calm and quiet experience of this space and the tight, seething experience of the incidents of casual racism that arise in my daily life. It has taken awhile for practice to teach me that zazen is not a posture. It is an embrace of each moment of my life, even those that evoke rage and the desire to pull close the protective shell formed so long ago. There are moments when it is clear to me that there is no difference between the universal self that recognized its call in an old Chinese painting and the African American woman who fled the South only to find a more subtle and grinding racism in the North.

The seething rage and the protective shell still appear, but the experience of practice has led me to be more willing to let them drop when I notice their appearance. Over and over again, zazen teaches me that there is a difference between pain and suffering. It is a powerful practice that has allowed me moments of softening even when face to face with someone who would diminish me.

For many years I have worked as a psychotherapist. It is my job to listen closely to the stories of people's suffering. One of the places I do this listening is in a small, mostly black, seaside town that is struggling to come back from the devastation of riots during the 1960s. I am told that the African American families in this town came north to work in the hotels that flourished when the town was a famous resort area. These families are now in their third or fourth generation. They now share neighborhoods with families who have moved here from Haiti, fleeing the poverty and political instability of that country.

It is a town to which people have come in the hopes of easing their suffering. I hear stories of generations of abuse, abandonment, and poverty. The young people, mostly young mothers, who tell these stories speak in flat tones that reflect the absence of any real hope that their lives will improve. However, they tell their story once again, just in case, and I listen. Together we move step by step through the problems and pains of their lives. Although I hope this helps, I know that problem-solving does not end suffering. Even when all immediate problems are solved, we worry and wait for the next one to arise. This is not the kind of cessation that the Buddha promised.

Zazen, in stillness and in action, is the embodiment of the Eightfold Path, the path the Buddha promised would put an end to suffering. This is how awakened oneness lives, embracing each moment no matter what it brings. Though I spend a great deal of time and energy resisting discomfort, I let out a deep sigh of relief when finally I give in and simply allow it to be what it is. Then I have energy to take care of it. It is a lesson I learn over and over again.

Each year when we celebrate the birthday of Martin Luther King, Jr., I feel that I am eleven years old again. That is the age I was when I heard about the Montgomery bus boycott. I felt liberated by the news. I had no expectations of change. I did not even think about an outcome. I was simply relieved to be shown a way to bear with dignity the humiliations we experienced. I was freed by their action and their courage to be who I was without shame or apology. The action of the Montgomery boycott arose out of taking an unblinking look at our situation and wholeheartedly embracing it. The action led to a change in the laws about seating on public buses, but that is not the memory that stays with me. What I remember is that this man and these people I did not know managed to change the way I saw and felt about myself as a black child.

This is a kind of liberation not dependent on changing, defeating, or appeasing others. It is not dependent on circumstances though the circumstances may be horrifying. In fact, it is not dependent on anything. It is simply our birthright, immediately accessible right where we are. Nothing stands between us and our circumstances. We can always take the backward step and claim ownership of our lives. In doing so we take ownership of the universe. To me this is true empowerment. The people in Montgomery walking miles back and forth to work were probably in pain, but they were not necessarily suffering. I am deeply grateful for their enlightened action.

Birthing and Blooming: Reflections on the Third Noble Truth

MUSHIM IKEDA-NASH

ONE AFTERNOON, during a seven-day freezing-cold Zen retreat, I figured out something about the Third Noble Truth. We spent much of the retreat sitting, meditating on the koans—the traditional riddle-like questions —the teacher gave us. When it was time for sanzen (a face-to-face meeting with the Zen master), I'd leave the chilly zendo, get in the bitter-cold waiting line, and then, when my turn arrived, run into the sanzen room, prostrate, sit down, state the koan and stammer out an inadequate answer. Then Roshi would say: "More zazen" and ring his hand-bell briskly to summon the next student. Usually I found the procedure terrifying and embarrassing, and I wasn't even sure what I was supposed to be doing. You're not supposed to sit in Zen meditation and think about things in a deliberate way. But if I didn't think about it, how would I find an answer?

Going to sanzen was also called "seeing the old man." Sasaki Roshi had done thousands of teacher-student interviews over the years. The intensity of the traditional face-to-face encounter between Zen teacher and Zen student is almost impossible to describe. To make it worse, I was always aware that the intensity was something I was generating, uncontrollably and neurotically. Roshi wasn't tense in the least, although sometimes he sounded slightly amused. He had even commented, publicly, that his students had such constipated expressions as we tried to answer our koans that we were even more amusing than cartoons.

This time was different, though. I'd finally reached a maximum point of frustration, boredom, and anger at the absurdity of the process, and had caved in under my own internal pressure. Hours passed. The koan Roshi had given me was, "How do I manifest my true nature as a flower?" I sat on my cushion, breathing "How? How?" in and out. I forgot to be anxious about whether I could answer the koan, whether I would look like a fool to Roshi, and whether I would ever make any "progress" as a koan student.

The koan had absorbed me. I entered the sanzen room, made my prostrations, and sat down on the cushion. I stated the koan. I breathed "How? How?" or it breathed me, silently, through my belly and blood. The universe bloomed.

Roshi said gently: *"It's very peaceful, isn't it?"* Then he rang the hand-bell and I left the room.

Since that moment, a kind of enduring happiness has entered my heart and rooted itself there, deeply and invisibly. The only time I have experienced anything similar was when my son was born, and he and I looked into each other's eyes for the first time, the breath still new in his body. Those moments are two experiences in my life as a Buddhist practitioner which convinced me that the Third Noble Truth, the end of suffering and dissatisfaction, is a reality.

*   *   *

Mahayana Buddhists are always taking impossible vows. We take the Bodhisattva Vow to save all beings, and we vow to end our delusions even though they are endless, and so on. Over the long run, what one teacher called "vow power" becomes a steady force in our everyday lives, reinforcing our spiritual motivation and providing a humbling and even humorous perspective. I get up every morning and renew my Buddhist vows, and then I laugh to myself. Once I saw an ant trying to drag a fallen chocolate chip cookie to its home. I am that ant.

When I first began to sit in meditation, in 1981, I thought I could get to a place that would always be quiet and calm if I tried hard enough and was lucky. So it was a big shock to me two years later when I moved into a Zen temple and discovered that I spent a lot of time feeling exhausted, on edge, and judgmental while following a steady schedule of meditation and manual work. In part, this was because we had just purchased an old, cockroach-infested house and had little money and a long list of renovations to perform. I was appointed treasurer, and found myself in the position of having to pay the mortgage and other bills when there was really no way to cover all our costs. Our situation was stressful. In addition, the teacher, a Korean Zen monk, occasionally resorted to what he termed "irritation Zen," and he would say insulting things to his students. On one particularly equanimous evening, he even wore himself out and complained, "I'm trying to make you people mad, but no one will get angry, so I have to go to bed."

I recently got a Christmas card from a devout Christian friend, who said she found Buddhism very attractive, particularly its "cool luminosity." Maybe other

Buddhists had gotten to cool luminosity, but not me. Of course, I've had many experiences during Zen practice of feeling very calm and settled, but they've always passed. As a parent in lay life, I've discovered that I can go in a matter of seconds from being a kind, tolerant mother to screaming at my son for a bad grade on a report card. Amidst the heat and tumult of family life, I've had to radically redefine what "peace" and "inner peace" mean. In fact, it was my son, when he was around twelve, who helped me figure it out. "Don't confuse inner peace with enlightenment," he said. "Inner peace is a feeling, but enlightenment is clarity and understanding. It can include inner peace but it is much more."

* * *

For me, Buddhist teachings and practice have provided a context of understanding in which to let go of some of my convoluted, judgmental thoughts. In the summer of 1999, my father-in-law died after a long illness. Seventeen days later, Mark, a teenage friend of the family, was in a car accident. The driver was instantly killed. Mark was in a coma, in the Intensive Care Unit of a local hospital, when my family and I went to visit him a few days later. A respirator and feeding tube were helping to keep him alive.

The accident and its consequences have permeated our lives with the realization that things we might take for granted can change overnight. About a month after the accident occurred, I found myself sitting in a stupor on our back deck one afternoon, unable to understand how this could have happened to Mark. The question grew larger and louder, filling my heart with pain. I wasn't sitting and meditating, but I was sitting and allowing that thought to absorb me. I didn't try to manufacture an answer; I just naturally entered the question in the way my Zen training had taught me, with a steady forward movement, like rowing a boat on a lake.

After around a half hour had passed, I gradually became aware of the potted bamboo and herbs around me, the warmth of the sun on my arms, and the white noise of cars passing on the nearby expressway. A bird rustled in the upper branches of an overgrown elm. The blue sky overhead was cloudless and vast.

It was as though someone had handed me a pair of prescription eyeglasses that made everything appear sharp and clear. My normal sense of the boundaries of my body dropped away, and I became my surroundings: the deck, which is really the tar-papered roof of the back extension of the apartment below us, the back yard, the plants, the trees, the bird, the neighborhood, the sun and the sky. My little section of the city of Oakland teemed with life: worms and bacteria in the soil, opossums and raccoons in the storm drains, birds, people, cats, dogs, and aphids, ants, flies, mosquitoes. Plants and tree leaves breathed in carbon dioxide, breathed out oxygen. Bacteria in my body digested what I'd eaten for lunch. And within this pulsing, intensely alive world, I was suddenly aware that at that very moment, some living being somewhere had been in an accident and had become injured. Some living being had just died. Something was being born and something was dying, near me or even in me or on me at the microbial level.

It wasn't that I suddenly felt calm or indifferent. But my question was answered in that the question below the question had been revealed. Unconsciously, I had believed until that moment that, somehow, because I knew and loved a young friend, he would be magically protected from harm or death. Could the same thing that had happened to Mark happen to my own son when he learned how to drive? Yes, it is possible. We do our best to keep those we love safe from harm; we have no guarantees.

My heart opened to let in this bigger picture of the continual unfolding of birthing and blooming and withering and dying. How amazing, that so much is going on in this very moment, around the world, throughout the universe. How big life is, and it embraces so much!

Finding True Freedom

VIVEKA CHEN

REFLECT for a moment on what led you to pick up this book. It may be that a sort of quiet curiosity brought you to these pages. Or you may have traveled a more painful route. The glassy smoothness of the day-to-day might have been rent by a death, a break-up, a layoff, the reality of war, or a run-in with racism. Something as acute as despair might have driven you here. What led you to these pages? What do you seek?

The Third Noble Truth is a response to our spiritual questioning. Over 2,000 years ago, Siddhartha Gautama Buddha realized and taught that, with dedicated training, it is possible to calm and even completely liberate self-created suffering. This liberation is the very enlightenment experience of the Buddha and it is available to all of us. We all have the potential to make this radical shift.

The revolutionary spirit of the Third Noble Truth is akin to the messages of civil rights leaders like Dr. Martin Luther King, Jr. who urge us to wake up and rise up from life-robbing oppression. The Buddha was a freedom fighter who launched a spiritual movement empowering people to end mental, physical, and spiritual enslavement.

From the time of the Buddha to today, Buddhism has repudiated the caste system in India that names some people "untouchable" and only fit for certain menial jobs. Today, many practitioners identify as "engaged Buddhists" who continue the struggle against injustice whether in our local communities or further afield. The Four Noble Truths teach that we are ultimately bound by our own spiritual ignorance. No matter how good our social and economic conditions, if we are deluded there can be no true fulfillment or peace for us. And even in oppressive conditions, freedom can be had by freeing the mind.

The greatest fulfillment of a human life is to mature, grow, and discover the spirit, bringing together heart and mind. Our longings and frustrations are linked to the ability to touch into and manifest what is deepest within. The Buddha said that we can "light up the world like the moon when freed from clouds" and he urged us to find "the heart's release."

In my own life, the Buddhist ethical teachings on nonviolence and interconnectedness provided a refuge I didn't even realize I was seeking. Up until learning about Buddhism, I had reacted with increasing cynicism and isolated outrage to the vast human-wrought suffering in the world—apartheid, homelessness, racism, and classism in Philadelphia and in my own university, and Reaganomics. The teaching pointed out the possibility of responding to the truth of suffering by becoming increasingly awake and skillfully active. It was tremendously empowering.

THE CESSATION OF SUFFERING

There are many kinds of suffering. The kind that we can liberate ourselves from is self-created suffering. Self-created suffering is caused, at the roots, by the contraction and isolation of our hearts. Moment by moment we form and feed different habitual patterns that either make us feel more alone or more connected with the world and all life. This is the process of karma (intentional action) which shapes the course of our lives. Buddhism is concerned with helping us recognize and reinforce the tendency towards openness and interconnection. This is how the heart is liberated. This is how we awaken.

The fact is that most of us are conflicted much of the time. One moment we are engaged in the world and the next we fall into diversion, any diversion. I know an amazing number of highly intelligent people who find celebrity gossip magazines and reality TV a placating lifeline. Better to think about someone else's life for a while. We can simply notice where our energies go. Are they are aimed at awakening? Invested in the lifestyles of the rich and famous? The key is just to persistently recognize it all with kindness and clarity.

The kind of mind states that result in self-created suffering are called the *kleshas*, poisons or afflictions. We all know these states well. Kleshas—such as delusion, craving, aversion, jealousy, fixed views, and pride—tend to create suffering. This is easily observable in our direct experience. My work as spiritual director at a Buddhist center involves a great deal of communication. If someone tells me about something they don't like that I have done, I can react with defensiveness and begin fueling thoughts about their lack of appreciation or their consumer attitude. I know that path. It leads to me feeling right (even if my thoughts aren't true) but to everyone feeling more isolated in the end.

From these contracted states we build a wall around the self to define and protect "me" and "mine" as a misguided means of seeking security. Whenever we create a "self" to cling to we also create "others" to protect ourselves from or as objects from whom to get our needs met. This is inevitably stressful, both for us and for those we start seeing as "other," be they enemies or even at times those we hold dearest.

On the other hand, when we act from unafflicted states of mind we create a momentum towards freedom from suffering and start to dissolve the protective, isolating walls we've built up from past habit. A freedom arises in each moment that we let go of the preoccupation of circling the wagons around "me" and "mine."

Going back to my personal example, when someone is sharing a concern or complaint, I can train to be aware of any defensive reactions simply as habits. There is recognition that I don't have to act on those knee-jerk impulses. In that moment of awareness, the healing state of mindfulness is introduced, allowing me to refocus my energies on listening more deeply to and understanding what is being shared. This builds a sense of connection and mutual concern rather than reinforcing the suffering of blaming.

The fact that we are the cause of much of our suffering, when honestly confronted, may bring up grief or shame but it is also a joyful recognition. Since we create suffering we can also stop creating it. This is the key to the cessation of suffering. By learning to work with our minds we can affect our karma. Of course, everything that happens to us is not a direct result of our karma. An earthquake can simply be the plates of the earth moving regardless of anyone's state of mind. The suffering of racism, sexism, homophobia, and other oppressions arises out of complex historical and socioeconomic conditions. There is most definitely suffering that is not self-created. But we benefit in any moment we refrain from taking a path that creates more suffering. Sometimes that benefit doesn't register right away but it is there, like a chokehold releasing its grasp, choice by choice, action by action. In these moments there is a shift in the balance of ease to tension, of contraction to openness, of intolerance to compassion. This balance is a moving, living equation that is always unfolding in ourselves and in the world that we collectively create. Moment by moment a person and our world can move closer to a tipping point where understanding and compassion outweigh confusion and oppression.

As we free ourselves from absorption in the suffering we have fabricated, we increasingly wake up to the existence and plight of other living beings. It begins to dawn on us that *everyone* (even those we consider enemies) deep down, ourselves included, basically wants to be well and free from suffering. It might seem ironic to free ourselves up from suffering only to voluntarily step right back into suffering, but this is where the Third Noble Truth takes us. Raised consciousness is inseparable from compassionate activity.

At any time and any place there is the possibility of collectively building a momentum where mutual concern and compassion proliferate as a real alternative. This momentum can begin in a communication, a household, a workplace, a campaign, a community, a meditation retreat. Action by informed action we can move towards the tipping point and create a sustainably compassionate world together.

The Discovery of Deep Deep Well-Being

My partner and I go to salsa shows in San Francisco. He has taken me to see some of the great salsa artists—Mongo Santamaria, Tito Puente, Eddie Palmieri. It's always a privilege to participate in the music. Gradually, the sound and mood come to envelop and connect everyone present, from the jamming musicians to the enraptured audience to the fast-moving dancers. It's easy to lose myself in that communal, joyful exuberance and I leave encouraged about the human race. These salsa shows are a Dharma teaching to me. The Four Noble Truths wake us up by confronting us with our suffering but they are equally about confronting beauty within us and all around.

The Yogacara tradition of Buddhism developed the word "Thusness" to try to describe the viewpoint of Enlightened experience. "Thus" is the way things are. "Thusness" is the "utmost wondrousness" of everything seen as it actually is. Thusness is the beauty that characterizes you and all beings. It is our deepest nature. We don't need to, and we can't, create this quality. It is already there.

When Thusness is recognized, we become complete. The missing piece of the puzzle of human existence snaps into place. When forgotten or as yet undiscovered, Thusness is still there, just obscured. Enlightenment is the state of thoroughly realizing, down to our bones, that this utmost wondrousness is who we truly are and always have been.

Words cannot adequately describe Enlightenment. There was an exhibit of Mongolian Buddhist art that came through San Francisco in which a large statue of Tara, a symbolic embodiment of compassion, suddenly confronted visitors around a blind corner. I found myself startled into tears upon meeting this image of tremendous compassionate beauty.

Thusness is in that moment of recognition. It is in salsa music. It is in glimpsed acts of kindness. It is in a youth. It is there when we sit with death, or mindfulness of breath. This beauty is always there, although we may not perceive or remember it. Learning to relax our fearful ego fabrication, Thusness is revealed like a clear blue sky appearing through the clouds.

May you and all beings find benefit in the teaching.

Coming Home

SISTER CHAN CHAU NGHIEM

RECONCILIATION

IDON'T REMEMBER hearing about my father's parents, or even seeing pictures of them, until I was eight and we went to visit them for the first time. It was the summer of 1982 and our parents had just divorced. Our mom is black, our dad is white. My dad had already seriously disappointed his white, upper-class, Texan parents when he joined the Civil Rights movement. They were completely alienated and enraged when he decided to marry a Black woman in Chicago in 1970. I think he saw them only once or twice after this until he and my mom divorced. My mom's family was much more accepting. My black grandma came to help my mom with me right after I was born and I grew up visiting my mom's side of the family regularly.

We drove from Chicago to Houston to meet my paternal grandparents. They were happy to meet their only grandchildren and kind to me and my brother. They let us go out shopping with their housekeeper and she got us whatever we wanted. My granddad gave my dad money to take us to Six Flags and Waterworld. We sat in the den with him and listened to him tell stories as he smoked cigars. His easy chair was full of holes from cigar ash that fell when he got too sleepy. He had a deep throaty chuckle and loved to tell jokes. I also enjoyed asking my grandma questions and listening to her share about her life. I wanted to love them, and it wasn't difficult. I saw their care for my dad and his love for them. I was shocked and hurt though, when my granddad told a story to my dad about a "nigger." My jaw dropped and I turned to my brother for help, whispering "Did you hear what he just said?" All three of us bristled, and I think he must have noticed because granddad kept to "nigra" or "colored" after that.

In 1998, my dad and I attended a twenty-one-day retreat with Thich Nhat Hanh and the Plum Village Sangha in Vermont. My granddad had died ten years earlier. One day I was doing sitting meditation in the gymnasium-turned-meditation hall. Thây (as Thich Nhat Hanh is known by his students) had been giving teachings on Touching the Earth, a practice in which we connect with our ancestors to heal the suffering in our relationships and to strengthen the goodness they have passed on to us. Often as an adult, I had reflected bitterly on my grandparents' racism and their refusal to accept their only grandchildren for so long. They rejected their own son and missed out on most of our childhood. I hated that my dad wouldn't have brought us to meet them if he were still married to my mom. In their eyes, the divorce was an admission of defeat, an acknowledgment that they had been right all along. Only under these conditions could we come into their lives.

During the retreat, I sat and breathed to connect with my granddad. "Breathing in, granddad, I am here for you. Breathing out, I will take good care of you in me." Soon I was in tears. Up came a very deep, old hurt of feeling rejected, discriminated against, unloved because of my skin color. It was very painful. But I had never embraced this pain with my mindfulness before. It had just been lying there, stuck in my consciousness. Now it could circulate freely, massaged by mindful breathing. I held my pain—this feeling that I had missed out on something important as a little girl—with tenderness and love and allowed the hot tears to flow down my cheeks.

As I held and began to release this block of pain and confusion, I meditated on my granddad, and began to look deeply into him. I felt his presence very strongly. Suddenly I knew he didn't *want* to be the way he was—in fact he made himself suffer tremendously because of his rigid beliefs about race. And I saw that it would have been very difficult for him to have thought or acted differently given the way he was raised and the consciousness of his generation. He could never fathom an interracial marriage and certainly not of his own son. I felt a deep sense of connectedness with him as I continued to breathe and I felt in the marrow of my bones that he loved me and my brother deeply, from the moment we were born, but was unable to express it until years later. And that he deeply regretted this. I knew that it caused him real pain to be caught in this way of thinking and not be able to get out.

I see now that our presence in his life was also an opening, an opportunity for him to be more inclusive and to let go of some of his long-held beliefs. If he hadn't been able to do this at least to some extent, he wouldn't have even let us in the door. He loved to watch my brother play around. My granddad had been a football player and a coach and he appreciated my brother's athletic strength and agility. I think he saw something of himself in his brown grandson.

As I practiced, I felt a deep communication between us. He let me know how proud he was of what I was doing, of all that I had done. He was happy that I had found a path of beauty and understanding that could transform the many generations of suffering in our family. I felt him very much alive in me. I knew I was his continuation and I vowed to live my life deeply to honor him and all the good qualities he had passed down to me—his perseverance, his calm, his thoughtfulness, his way of connecting to people, his general goodness. I cried for a long time—it was so beautiful to feel this love, this comforting and full warmth spreading through my chest, finally releasing this heavy burden of ignorance, separation, and pain. In its place I felt a lightness, a deeper confidence in myself, in the practice of mindfulness and in a very real connectedness with my ancestors. I let go of the judgment and resentment that I had always carried in my heart toward him. I loved him unreservedly, and for the first time I felt truly happy to be his granddaughter.

BLACK IS BEAUTIFUL

The first time I attended Thây, soon after I ordained as a nun, we were in his room in Lower Hamlet, Plum Village.[1] He was resting in the hammock and telling me about the different things in his room. He pointed to a picture on the wall of himself with a much fuller face, sitting on a large rock, surrounded by pine trees and a deep blue sky. Younger monks and nuns were standing nearby—it was Kim Son Monastery, California. In the photo he was wearing a brown leather jacket. His hands were resting gently on his knees. He said that photo was taken twenty years ago. He still had the jacket. He pointed to the short bamboo stick hanging horizontally from the ceiling next to his mattress on the floor. Coats and robes were hung on it. "Go look," he said. I looked at the very same jacket he wore in the picture; it had oval-shaped pockets with a diagonal zip down the middle. I commented that it was really original. Thây said, chuckling, "It's funky!"

I was taken aback, then laughed. I never could have imagined he knew that word! In an instant our generational, cultural, and teacher-student gap was no more. A big, lovely bridge stretched out over roaring, rushing waters of confusion, awkwardness, fear. I love him so much for learning and sharing that word with me. A seventy-five-year-old Vietnamese monk, he knew that word and exactly how to use it. What a beautiful teacher. He was right there with people of color in the sixties, giving and risking his life for peace and freedom—in Vietnam and in the U.S. He has consistently stayed in touch with young people and never let himself be caught in restrictive, outdated traditions no longer relevant to people's real, daily situations. I felt acknowledged, held, for who I was: a young American of white and black ancestry, just beginning to find my way in our largely Vietnamese community. It was a welcoming.

*   *   *

When I had been a nun about five months, I wrote Thây a letter about wanting to integrate my blackness more into my practice, to embrace it and make room for it. Most of the time in our community, I just feel like a Westerner, because most of the brothers and sisters are Vietnamese. But when black people come to visit us, I see myself and identify more strongly as black, not just Western. I want to connect with them as a fellow black practitioner. So at that time, there was a conflict in me—a feeling of love and attraction to black people, and at the same time, not knowing how to express it, how to relate to it. I felt unsure of myself and wondered if it was appropriate to approach someone just on the basis of race. And at the same time, it felt so important to meet each other on that level as well as all the other levels of our personality. I wrote to Thây that I felt I needed to affirm, understand, and nurture this part of me more.

Some weeks later, Thây visited us in the Lower Hamlet. He called all the sisters into his room and served us tea and sweets. He had asked us some time ago to paint the outside of the sisters' building, as it looked pretty old and grey. As we hadn't done anything about it yet, he decided to motivate us by asking us to go around and each say which color we'd like the building to be. The sisters answered quickly with blue or pink or a natural tone. When it got to my turn, I hesitated, not sure how to respond.

Suddenly, Thây broke the silence, "Black is Beautiful!" I couldn't believe he said that! The other sisters burst out laughing.

It was only later that I connected his response to the letter I had written him. It was unexpected in a very affirming and deep way. He didn't respond directly to what I wrote, but this answer gave me real nourishment and a great deal to think about. I felt really seen. I felt he was trying to tell me that I didn't need to work so hard to understand or figure things out. I just needed to practice, to enjoy myself, and then I would naturally touch the beauty in my heritage. Not through struggling, but by allowing my mind to settle down and be in the present moment. I felt he understood me so perfectly and helped me to get out of old, stuck ways of thinking with real lightness and grace. His declaration is a kind of koan for me, a teaching that I can always come back to, to find deeper and deeper layers of meaning. Who am I? What is it about me that is Black? How, why is it beautiful? How can I help that beauty manifest?

BUDDHAFULL

On a recent visit to my brother and his family in Washington, D.C., my sister-in-law and I were driving my nephew to school; it was his first month in pre-kindergarten. He pointed out the homeless people on the street and asked me if I give them money when I see them. I told him, "Sometimes." A few days later, when I was returning from an errand, a homeless man asked me to buy him some dinner. He was standing in front of a restaurant. I surprised myself by saying, "Sure!" and went in to get him a plate of fried catfish and vegetables. I told my four-year-old nephew about it that night as I was reading him a bed-time story. He asked me immediately, "Auntie, was he black or white?"

Why do four-year-old black children have to ask that? How is it that they already know that it matters, that it has consequences for them? I answered, unwillingly, "black." He was quiet. I don't think white children feel compelled to know things like this. Being black is already painful, right from the beginning.

Contemplating what it is about me that is black, I remember that I used to squeeze the bridge of my nose for hours as a young girl, hoping my nose would become skinny like a white person's. I remember that I was ashamed and scared when I learned the D.C. snipers were black. Their acts were one more reason for society to hate and fear black people. I was afraid in an almost unconscious way of some collective racial punishment. When they caught the snipers, some-how it was *me* that was caught; every black person was implicated. My black-ness is the part of me that feels self-conscious and a little nervous upon walking into a restaurant or a room full of unfamiliar white people, especially in the South. It is fear, insecurity on a cellular level, transmitted by my ancestors. It is wanting to fit in, to feel loved and safe, and not wanting to have to protect myself.

What is black about me is my way of understanding myself through my connection to family, friends, and community. It is the need to connect to the insight, humor, and suffering of my ancestors, to understand how it continues in me. It is my hunger to know other black people in order to know myself bet-ter and affirm who I am. It is an indescribable feeling of *home* sitting around the dining room table at my grandma's eating Sunday dinner and listening to my family talk, argue, laugh, and just be themselves. My blackness is also the way I can feel one with my body, the way *I am* the music when I dance. My mother, grandmother, great-grandmother, all the women on my mom's side, were natural dancers. They just had to see a move once and they could do it, effortlessly. That is deep wisdom. My blackness is the way I get chills when I listen to certain spirituals or gospel singing in a black church. It is also mysterious, containing many elements I have yet to understand and discover. And even as I want to embrace and know my blackness better, I do not want to be limited or suffocated by it. I see that blackness means different things to different black people. We share the same heritage of slavery and segregation, but the way we express and understand our blackness is unique to each one of us. My blackness is a deep desire for wholeness, for non-fear.

In 1999, I wrote the following in a letter to the Plum Village community requesting novice ordination: "I want to ordain because I want to affirm the reality of my own Buddha nature. For me, becoming a nun is a powerful and fierce 'yes' to my deepest aspirations to live mindfully and compassionately. I *can* live an awakened life and it is my birthright. This is very important because buried deep inside me is doubt and fear that realizing my true self is not possible." I have been ordained for four years now. I have struggled a great deal with self-doubt, and it has not been easy to maintain and cultivate faith in my practice. It is so hard to stop looking outside myself for beauty, for wisdom. Usually I am trying to be something, trying to achieve some goal in my practice: to meditate more, to concentrate better, to be more disciplined, to be more loving like my teacher. This often leads to disappointment and self-criticism, because I rarely live up to my expectations. But when I relax and stop trying so hard to be what I am not, Buddha nature, or mindfulness and clarity, arise of their own accord. When I can simply accept where I am at, make room for all my junk, and at the same time affirm the goodness already and always there, I touch peace and real freedom. When I let myself be, when I smile and am in touch with this deep desire to understand reality clearly and to love myself and others, that is already Buddha, and nothing less. It is my mind in an unclouded state, filled with generosity and compassion.

Cultivating Buddha nature is my foundation for understanding and realizing that "black is beautiful." When I am really alive and awake in the present moment, I can help the beauty of blackness manifest, by recognizing and strengthening the wholesome seeds my ancestors have passed on to me and transforming the unwholesome ones. I was thinking about the words "Black Power" and how for me they mean "Black Enlightenment," enlightenment of what it does and doesn't mean to be black. Enlightenment about how to be peace and happiness, right here and now. This is real power, the kind that has the capacity to transform, not only on the sociopolitical level, but on the level of the collective consciousness, and cause collective awakening. This kind of power or enlightenment is learning from the past without getting stuck in the past, embracing and healing my suffering so I am no longer a victim of it. It is knowing that I already am what I want to become (even if it takes awhile to figure this out), and that I can look inside myself for answers. It is an affirmation of my own and everyone else's capacity to wake up and live in mindfulness. So black is beautiful and black is also "Buddhafull."

If Buddhism is to really make a contribution to Western society, it must use the insights of the Dharma to heal the suffering of racism. Our teacher invites us to see Buddhism as a tree, always alive and growing. We have to contribute to it and renew it to ensure that it continues to grow strong and healthy. In applying the teachings to heal the pain of racism and prejudice, I am able to offer the beauty, wisdom, and experience of my ancestors to find new ways to express and live the insights of the Buddhadharma. One day, maybe soon, I want to sing in a Buddhist gospel choir. When I think of the power of engaged Dharma, I know that my nephew's generation has a chance at living in a very different America. It is up to us.

NOTES

1 In our tradition, every novice spends time attending his or her teacher as part of the monastic training. As attendant, you assist your teacher, clean his or her room, bring meals, serve tea, but most importantly your teacher has a chance to understand you better and you have the chance to observe and learn from being close to your teacher.

LET WISDOM ARISE WITHIN US

The Truth of the Path
to the End of Suffering

Reading the Eightfold Path

CHARLES JOHNSON

INTRODUCTION

IN THE SPECIAL SUMMER 2003 issue of *Turning Wheel: The Journal of Socially Engaged Buddhism* devoted to "Black Dharma," Choyin Rangdröl, a Vajrayana teacher, is asked why he decided to bring the Dharma to African Americans. He replied eloquently, "When I discovered that it was possible to avoid becoming ensnared in the mentality of an angry black man by applying Buddhism, I felt I had found a great treasure not just for me but also for my people. I could immediately see the potential for resonance in millions of black people's minds. I could see how this could reverberate down to the core of the hurt so many of us carry, and that one could emerge from Buddhist study and practice healed."

One perennial beauty of the 2,600-year-old Eightfold Path is that all the "great treasure" that Choyin Rangdröl discovered in the Buddhadharma can be found in its interwoven steps. Within its framework, the content of all the sutras and such critical Dharma leitmotifs as suffering, impermanence, dependent origination, the status of the self as an illusion, loving kindness toward all sentient beings, and the ultimate ontological truth of the emptiness of all things can be discussed and explored. For African Americans especially, this time-tested guide for spiritual and moral progress on the Path becomes the richest of refuges from a predominantly white, very Eurocentric and culturally provincial society almost completely blind to the dignity and deeds, well-being and needs, of people of color.

From almost any angle that we view black American life, historically or in the post-Civil Rights era, we find the First Noble Truth: the presence of suffering. In Washington State and throughout the country, more black men are in prison than attending college. Forty-seven percent of black students nationwide drop out of high school. The preponderance of single-parent households has further weakened our fragile communities and in the anti-intellectual and violent subculture of gangs, young black men celebrate "thug life."

These dysteleological dimensions of black life are not easily negotiated—or survived. To endure and prosper, one needs the understanding that we alone, and not an abstraction called "social forces," determine moment by moment our individual destinies and our happiness. My friend, mystery writer and Buddhist Candace Robb, addresses this nicely when she says, "Pain is something that comes in life, but suffering is *optional.*" Thus, the Eightfold Path is, and has been for two and a half millennia, such an exquisite manual for survival in this world where race is the grandest of all our lived illusions.

READING THE EIGHTFOLD PATH

The coming of Buddhism to the West may well prove to be the most important event of the Twentieth Century. —Arnold Toynbee

To study the way is to study the self. To study the self is to forget the self. To forget the self is to be enlightened by all things. To be enlightened by all things is to remove the barriers between oneself and others. —Dogen

All parts of the universe are interwoven with one another, and the bond is sacred. —Marcus Aurelius

According to poet-philosopher Ashvaghosha's *Buddha-charita,* a Sanskrit poem that presents the first legendary history of the Buddha (whose name means "Awakened One"), Prince Siddhartha's experience of enlightenment came during three "watches" or phases as he sat in meditation.[1] He saw most clearly during the first watch his thousands of births and former lives. During the second watch he "beheld the whole world as in a spotless mirror"[2] (here the frequently used metaphor of the "mirror," which occurs often in Buddhist literature,[3] suggests a consciousness free of all obscuring delusions), seeing the entire universe of births and deaths driven by higher and lower merit (karma). Finally, when he entered the third watch, the Buddha saw the twelve causal links in the chain of dependent origination[4] and the Four Noble Truths. It is the fourth of these truths that will be the focus of this examination. In Ashvaghosha's poem, written in approximately 100 C.E., the Buddha expresses the Four Noble Truths in a terse, fourfold description compressed into a single *sloka*:

> This is pain, this also is the origin of pain in the world of living beings; this also is the stopping of pain; this is that course which leads to the stopping.[5]

What is appealing about this simple, epigrammatic statement is that it is both eidetic and a description of the empirical evidence Shakyamuni encountered in the depths of meditation. *This is pain,* he says in the First Noble Truth, where "this" refers to the entire phenomenal field of perception, to all worldly experience, which is characterized by impermanence and some form of suffering or *duhkha* (*Duh* "bad"; *kha* "hole." Think of the hole amiddlemost a wheel, one that so poorly joins with a wagon's axle that we experience our ride through life as rough and bumpy). The second truth, *this also is the origin of pain in the world of living beings,* identifies thirst (*trishna*) or selfish desire arising from attachment as the root of *duhkha.* When he says, *This also is the stopping of pain* (the Third Noble Truth), the Tathagata is merely reporting that he has seen how some men and women escape *duhkha.* And the fourth truth, *This is that course that leads to the stopping,* points directly to the interconnected items of the spiritual and ethical program that brings deliverance, which we call the Eightfold Path, the *Astangika-Marga,* or the *Arya Astanga Marga.*

"Just as one would examine gold through burning, cutting, and rubbing, so should monks and scholars examine my words,"[6] the Buddha said. "Only thus should they be accepted; but not merely out of respect for me." He asked no one to believe or take his statements as articles of faith, or on authority. His was a philosophy that seldom, if ever, forced its adherents to proselytize. Rather, like a phenomenologist, the Buddha emphasized during his forty-five years as a teacher, "Do not go by oral tradition, by lineage of teaching, by hearsay, by a collection of scriptures, by logical reasoning, by inferential reasoning, by reflection on reasons, by the acceptance of a view after pondering it, by the seeming competence of a speaker, or because you think, 'The ascetic is our teacher.' But when you know for yourselves, 'These things are unwholesome, these things are blamable; these things are censured by the wise; these things, if undertaken and practiced, lead to harm and suffering, then you should abandon them."[7] A testament to how many people have agreed with his critique of the human condition can be found in the fact that at one time one third of the human race were the Buddha's students and followers[8]; and today Buddhism has 360 million adherents.

If one's own life confirms the first three Noble Truths, then the Eightfold Path ineluctably follows as the means for systematic spiritual practice. The term that precedes each step, सम्यक् (*samyak*), has often been translated by Westerners as the word "right." This is not inaccurate, but it can be misleading in respect to Buddhist ontology and the ethical position that account of reality produces. Among the several meanings of "samyak" we find "rightly," "correctly," "truly," and "properly." It also means "perfect," a translation Buddhist scholar Lama Govinda preferred (as does your servant) because "perfect" suggests wholeness and completeness, and sidesteps the dualism implied by terms such as "right" and "wrong." Each of the steps on the Path has a canonical interpretation; in fact, there are different readings spread across several schools, sects and traditions. Here I hold with the explanation of the eight steps presented in the *Mahasatipatthana Sutta* (The Greater Discourse on the Foundations of Mindfulness).[9] One learns after decades of meditation and mulling over these polysemous steps that each deepens and grows richer over one's lifetime, so that, any single interpretation of, say, "Conduct" (or Action) must be seen as reflecting only a fraction of its fullness. With this in mind, the steps on the Eightfold Path are:

Perfect View	*samyag-dristhi*	सम्यग् द्रष्टि
Perfect Thought	*samyak-sankalpa*	सम्यक् सङ्कल्प
Perfect Speech	*samyag-vach*	सम्यग् वाच्
Perfect Conduct	*samyak-karmanta*	सम्यक् कर्मन्त
Perfect Livelihood	*samyag-ajiva*	सम्यग् आजीव
Perfect Effort	*samyag-vyayama*	सम्यग् व्यायाम
Perfect Mindfulness	*samyak-smrti*	सम्यक् स्मृति
Perfect Concentration	*samyak-samadhi*	सम्यक् समाधि

Generally, in most Western translations the *Arya Astanga Marga* appears with its steps in this order. But this is not a linear movement. I will discuss them in terms of the progression above, seriatim, as most commentators do, with the caveat that the remarks about each stage will be filtered through and informed by the illuminating explanations of great teachers such as Thich Nhat Hanh. Strictly speaking, for a practitioner, the first realized steps on the Path are stages 3–5 (ethical living), followed by 6–8 (freedom from attachment), and ending with 1–2 (nonconceptual insight or wisdom)[10] Groupings and regroupings of the eight steps have consumed the energy of scholars for twenty-six hundred years. In his guide to Buddhism, John Snelling follows previous commentators when he suggests that "the path can be further subdivided into three main elements: wisdom (*panna*), morality (*sila*), and meditation (*samadhi*)."[11] (Incidentally, in different versions of the Path we find variations in the list, for example, the word "understanding" may appear instead of "view," and "resolve" often replaces the word "thought.") I believe *some* grouping of the eight steps can be useful. However, unlike Snelling, my preference is to group *Views* and *Thoughts* together as a "first philosophy" or the ontological side of the Path; *Speech, Action,* and *Livelihood* as a guide for civilized living in the shifting social world; and, lastly, *Effort, Concentration,* and *Mindfulness* as *praxis,* or the steps directed specifically at developing the skills and techniques, through Vipassana "insight" meditation, that shore up the other five. Naturally, all the steps presuppose, depend upon, complement, and complete each other; they are not taken one at a time, but worked on simultaneously, and as one matures with them understanding of the steps deepens. ("Morality practiced alone can lead to involvement with other beings, as one will not have a correct view of reality as 'voidness.' Wisdom practiced alone can lead to a kind of moral and spiritual alienation from persons and things.")[12] They are all aspects, as Heidegger might say, of a particular *Dasein* or "being-in-the-world" and, by virtue of that, the eight steps must be thought about holographically, or seen as prismatic sides of the same process of living. Taken as a whole, the steps of the Eightfold Path codify a profoundly human cultural vision that is in sync with the world as it is portrayed by quantum physics[13]: a vision American society at the dawn of the twenty-first century can benefit from immensely.[14]

PERFECT VIEW

In the *Mahasatipatthana Sutta,* the Buddha says,

"And what, monks, is Right View? It is, monks, the knowledge of suffering, the knowledge of the origin of suffering, the knowledge of the cessation of suffering, and the knowledge of the way of practice leading to the cessation of suffering. This is called Right View."[15]

There is no philosophical teaching more radical, emancipatory, non-essentialistic and empathetic than the Dharma. The Buddha's explanation of "Right View" states it demands a knowledge of the Four Noble Truths. He is concerned with but a single question, namely, why does suffering arise and how can we end it? Even more to the point is the question of *who* suffers? This is an ontological, epistemological, and moral question—the ancient problem of how one is to reconcile the One and the Many—which Buddhism addresses through the doctrine of "Dependent Origination." Thich Nhat Hanh, a master teacher of the Dharma, who was nominated by Dr. Martin Luther King, Jr., for the Nobel Peace Prize, calls this ontological stance "interbeing." His eloquent explanation of this neologism appears in *Living Buddha, Living Christ:*

"If we study the teachings of the Buddha and if we observe our own minds, we will find there is nothing permanent within the constituents of what we call our "self." The Buddha taught that a so-called person is really just five elements (*skandha*s) that come together for a limited period of time: our bodies, feelings, perceptions, mental states, and consciousness. These five elements are, in fact, changing all the time. Not a single element remains the same for two consecutive moments.

"Not only is our body impermanent, but our so-called soul is also impermanent. It, too, is comprised only of elements like feelings, perceptions, mental states, and consciousness.... According to the teachings of the Buddha, 'birth' does not exist either. Birth generally means from nothing you become something, and death generally means from something you become nothing. Before its so-called birth, this flower already existed in other forms—clouds, sunshine, seeds, soil, and many elements. Rather than birth and rebirth, it is more accurate to say "manifestation" (*vijñapti*) and "remanifestation".... When conditions are no longer sufficient and the flower ceases to manifest, we say the flower has died, but that is not correct either. Its constituents have merely transformed themselves into other elements, like compost and soil. We have to transcend notions like birth, death, being, and nonbeing. Reality is free from all notions."[16]

A lifetime of meditational practice has taught Thich Nhat Hanh that "in Buddhism there is no such thing as an individual."[17] Rather, all beings are relational and appear, as Dr. Martin Luther King, Jr. put it during the Birmingham campaign in 1963, "caught in an inescapable network of mutuality, tied in a single garment of destiny. Whatever affects one directly, affects all indirectly."[18] Knowing that "all life is interrelated," this civil rights leader, who was surely an American Gandhi, said, "We are everlasting debtors to known and unknown men and women.... When we arise in the morning, we go into the bathroom where we reach for a sponge provided for us by a Pacific Islander. We reach for soap that is created for us by a Frenchman. The towel is provided by a Turk. Then at the table we drink coffee which is provided for us by a South American, or tea by a Chinese, or cocoa by a West African. Before we leave for our jobs, we are beholden to more than half the world."[19]

Thich Nhat Hanh and Dr. King understand "Right View" as, first and foremost, a perception of reality as a *We*-relation. Even Buddhism, says Thich Nhat Hanh, "is made only of non-Buddhist elements, including Christian ones, and

Christianity is made of non-Christian elements, including Buddhist ones."[20] (Which is why many "Buddhists" refuse to call themselves that, preferring instead to simply and humbly say they are students of the Dharma.) This thing we call "self" is, depending on the spiritual angle from which it is viewed, everything. And nothing.[21] It is empty (*sunyata*), possessing no essence or intrinsic reality; it is, at best, a *process* dependent each and every moment on all other beings.[22] A verb, not a noun. Or we might discuss each individual as an ever-changing "event" or "occurrence" in terms of the metaphysical position Alfred North Whitehead presents in *Process and Reality*.[23] In *The Buddhist Vision,* Alex Kennedy (Dharmachari Subhuti), expands beautifully on this insight when he writes:

> …everything conditioned is part of a process whose essential nature is change. Nothing, however vast and long lasting, is exempt from this universal law…. A tree has no reality apart from the sum of the attributes which present themselves to our senses. It is like a pointillist painting, a cloud of dancing atoms, molecules, and perhaps more subtle forces in constant motion. Even these particles are, of course, not realities but are themselves compounded of smaller units which can be subdivided indefinitely. When we analyze any object, we can never come to a substance beyond which our analysis cannot penetrate. We can never find anything conditioned which has an underlying substantial reality…. All things, whether subject or object, are processes linked together in an intricate network of mutual conditions…. The ordinary man is distracted by the bright surface of the world and mistakes this for reality.[24] (Which, in Whiteheadean metaphysics, might be called the Fallacy of Misplaced Concreteness.)

"Perfect peace," said Shakyamuni, "can dwell only where all vanity has disappeared."[25] The word *nirvana* means "to blow out" (*nir* "out"; *vana* "blow"). In other words, when the mistaken *belief* in a separate "self" is extinguished like a candle's flame, the experiential realm of suffering and illusion, s*amsara,* which so often is created and conditioned by our notions and concepts about life,[26] is replaced—as a mirage might be or the shadows in Plato's cave— because underneath it all, *underneath it all,* is a perception of being that has always been present, like dark matter, though hitherto it was obscured by the illusion of the ego. *Samsara* and nirvana are but two sides—or phenomenological profiles—of the same world, and which one of these two incompossible visions we experience depends on our level of consciousness. In *On the Trans-*

mission of Mind, Huang Po insists, "Hills are hills. Water is water. Monks are monks. Laymen are laymen. But these mountains, these rivers, the whole world itself, together with sun, moon and stars—not one of them exists outside your minds! The vast chiliocosm exists only within you, so where else can the various categories of phenomena possibly be found? Outside Mind, there is nothing."[27] For this reason, after his awakening, the poet Bunan confesses,

> The moon's the same old moon,
> The flowers exactly as they were,
> Yet I've become the thingness
> Of all the things I see.[28]

"When you are able to get out of the shell of your small self," adds Thich Nhat Hanh, "you will see that you are interrelated to everyone and everything, that your every act is linked with the whole of humankind and the whole cosmos."[29] In other words, whatever it is, it is *you.*

And what would "wrong" view be? Again, Thich Nhat Hanh provides a powerful answer:

> Regarding something that is impermanent as permanent, holding to something that is without a self as having a self, we suffer. Impermanence is the same as nonself. Since phenomena are impermanent, they do not possess a permanent identity. Nonself is also emptiness. Emptiness of what? Empty of a permanent self. Nonself means also interbeing. Because everything is made of everything else, nothing can be by itself alone. Nonself is also interpenetration, because everything contains everything else.... Each thing depends on all other things to be.[30]

Suffering, then, arises from the belief in a separate, unchanging "identity" for things. That is the foundation for attachment and craving. Put another way, we cling to our static ideas about things, not the fluid things themselves, which are impermanent and cannot be held on to. (Nothing can endure change and remain unchanged.) In a universe of moment-by-moment transformations[31] all predications are risky; they *must* be highly provisional, tentative, and offered in a spirit of epistemological humility.[32] Words can be webs, making us think in terms of essences; language is all concept, but things in the world are devoid of essence, changing as we chase them. Life must always be greater than our ideas about life. For the Buddha, "Man's sensual desires are only attachments to concepts."[33] (It is not necessary, I hope, to explain how ugly and devastating are racial concepts when they are projected onto others.)

In 1997, I had the privilege and pleasure of interviewing Phra Tanat Wijitto, a young Thai abbot of skillful means in the town of Phrae near Chiang Mai. At the meditation center he was building, he explained to me that one must not be attached to even notions of Buddhism. ("I have taught you Dharma, like the parable of the raft, for getting across, for not retaining," said Shakyamuni. "You, monks…must not cling to right states of mind and, all the more, to wrong states of mind.")[34] Phra Tanat Wijitto was a true philosopher, which means that he had not surrendered his freedom. His focus during our two hour dialogue was on mindfulness at all times as the heart of Buddhism; on always knowing where the mind is, on its development and freedom from what William Blake once called "mind-forg'd manacles." He insisted that all the teachers and texts, rituals and traditions, and the Three Jewels (the Buddha, Dharma, and Sangha or community of the Tathagata's followers) were simply tools for our liberation and, once one reached later stages of development, they would be left behind. (That, he predicted for me.) The rituals performed by Thai monks he saw as unfortunate but necessary "bridges" to the Dharma because people could relate to them, as a child does to a simple lesson. At higher levels of attainment, he said, a practitioner no longer created "good" or "bad" karma—there simply was no karma (or "merit") at all.[35] Moreover, for this abbot, no two odysseys to awakening were exactly the same; one progressed alone, and what one experienced could no more be transmitted to another than one can explain to a blind man the beauty of an orchid. Put simply, to follow the Dharma is to live without a net. Or solid ground. Without a place to rest. Without mind-created or language-created constructs. (I was reminded by this of philosopher Ludwig Wittgenstein's advice, "Don't explain, *look!*") Furthermore, this gentle, percipient monk understood that Buddhism was synonymous with creativity. It, too, was subject to change, process, and transformation. He saw America as good for my practice of the Dharma because in this "developed" country, as he put it, we have more time for the practice of meditation and studying the sutras than do the far poorer people of Thailand. Some of the laity, he told me, will grasp the Buddhadharma in seven days, others in seven months, and still others will fail to understand it after seven years, if at all.

The Dharma is, if nothing else, a call for us to live in a state of radical freedom. It is not a Way for anyone who denies the fact that from the moment of our birth we have been dying, and that one day this universe itself will experience proton death—all that men and women have done will be as if it never was[36]—black holes will eventually evaporate into photons, leaving only a Void, from which (perhaps) another, different universe will arise.[37] In *The Diamond Sutra*, we are told that "those who find consolation in limited doctrines involving the conception of an ego entity, a personality, a being, or a separated individuality, are unable to accept, receive, study, recite, and openly explain this discourse."[38] That sutra ends with this verse:

> Thus shall ye think of all this fleeting world:
> A star at dawn, a bubble in a stream;
> A flash of lighting in a summer cloud,
> A flickering lamp, a phantom, and a dream.[39]

PERFECT THOUGHT

"And what," asked the Buddha, "is Right Thought? The thought of renunciation, the thought of non-ill-will, the thought of harmlessness. This, monks, is called Right Thought."[40]

In Sanskrit, the word *sankalpa* can mean both "thought" and "resolve." I imagine that those who prefer *resolve* do so to highlight the fact that harmlessness (*ahimsa*) toward all sentient beings necessarily follows from the understanding that we are never involved in "I/Thou" or "I/It" relationships, but instead only in "I am Thou" relationships. If all sentient beings are caught in a mutually interdependent process of manifestation and re-manifestation, then, according to the *Visuddhimagga*, "Bhikkhus, it is not easy to find a being who has not formerly been your mother...your father...your brother...your sister...your son...your daughter."[41] All clearly want the same two things that we do: to find happiness and avoid suffering. Toward all sentient beings there is but one proper response: compassion and loving-kindness (*metta*).

The Buddha was both an *arhat* who, in the Hinayana tradition, attained nirvana and will not return to the wheel of birth and death; and in the Mahayana tradition he was a bodhisattva who transcended samsara, but—due to his compassion—renounced full immersion in nirvana in order to work indefatigably for the salvation of all sentient beings. For the Dharma follower, even the "desire" for liberation from suffering can become a trap, a form of attachment, an instance of dualism ("I am not free; I wish to be free"), and so he must "let go" that craving as well. Better to simply attend mindfully to the "here" and "now," helping to reduce the *himsa* all around him when the occasion to do so arises, and to practice with no thought of personal "reward" or "gain." His resolve is expressed in the ancient Bodhisattva Vows found in most, if not all, Mahayana sects and schools:

> Sentient beings are numberless;
> I take a vow to save them.
> The deluding passions are inexhaustible;
> I take a vow to destroy them.
> The Gates of Dharma are manifold;
> I take a vow to enter them.
> The Buddha-way is supreme;
> I take a vow to complete it.[42]

as well as in Shantideva's *A Guide to the Bodhisattva's Way of Life:*

> First of all I should make an effort
> To meditate upon the equality between self and others:
> I should protect all beings as I do myself
> Because we are all equal in (wanting) pleasure and (not wanting) pain.
>
> Hence I should dispel the misery of others
> Because it is suffering, just like my own,
> And I should benefit others
> Because they are sentient beings, just like myself.
>
> When both myself and others
> Are similar in that we wish to be happy,
> What is so special about me?
> Why do I strive for my happiness alone?[43]

PERFECT SPEECH

> And what, monks, is Right Speech? Refraining from lying, refraining from slander, refraining from harsh speech, refraining from frivolous speech. This is called Right Speech.[44]

There are several observations to make about *samyag-vach,* the first being that in the *Sutra of Forty-two Sections,* the Buddha sharpened this injunction, saying, "Lie not, but be truthful, and speak truth with discretion, not so as to do harm, but in a loving heart and wisely. Invent not evil reports, neither do ye repent them. Carp not, but look for the good sides of your fellow beings, so that you may with sincerity defend them against their enemies.... Waste not the time with empty words, but speak to the purpose or keep silence. Covet not, nor envy, but rejoice at the fortunes of other people.... Cherish no hatred, not even against your slanderer, nor against those who do you harm, but embrace all living beings with kindness and benevolence.... He must not flatter his vanity by seeking the company of the great. Nor must he keep company with persons who are frivolous and immoral.... He must not take delight in quarrelous disputations or engage in controversies so as to show the superiority of his talents, but be calm and composed."[45]

Consider Shakyamuni's admonition *Waste not the time with empty words* in light of how in the U.S., and elsewhere in the world, we daily abuse the power of language, diminish and trivialize it when we use talk as merely another form of entertainment, or a way to amuse ourselves and others; to pass the time, or simply fill the silence that envelops us and is the ground and precondition for speech. Lying, slander, and harsh speech are obvious ways that we hurt others, wounding them with words. But as Martin Heidegger points out in *Being and Time*, "idle talk" is equally a violation of the being of language, which at its best is the means for dislodging consciousness from calcified, prefabricated thinking and disclosing truth.

"Discourse," says Heidegger, "has the possibility of becoming idle talk. And when it does, it serves not so much to keep Being-in-the-world open for us in an articulated understanding, as rather to close it off, and cover up the entities within-the-world. To do so, one need not aim to deceive.... The fact that something has been said groundlessly, and then gets passed along in further retelling, amounts to perverting the act of disclosing.... Thus, by its very nature, idle talk is a closing-off, since to go back to the ground of what is talked about is something which it *leaves undone*."[46]

Not only do we live in a culture where "idle talk" covers up and conceals interbeing, but also one in which different forms of violence have become entertainment and recreation. Violence is not only physical. It is also psychological and verbal. It begins in the mind. All my life I've wondered what would it be like to live in a society where, instead of men and women insulting and tearing each other down, people in their social relations, and even in the smallest ways, held the highest intellectual, moral, creative, and spiritual expectations for one another. One step toward achieving that is contained in an old Buddhist idea that urges us to momentarily detain all thought at three "gates"—or questions—before it crystallizes into speech. The three gates are, "Is what we are about to say *true*? Will it cause no *harm*? And is it *necessary*?" If all three answers are in the affirmative, then (and only then) have we realized *samyag-vach*.

Do some languages facilitate better than others the intuition of interbeing? Kobo Daishi (774–835 C.E.), founder of the Shingon school of Japanese Buddhism, privileged Sanskrit, believing that only this language could express the meaning of the mantras used in Shingon.[47] Clearly, there is a sharpening of one's intellectual understanding of the Buddhadharma if one reads Sanskrit, which means "refined" or "language brought to formal perfection."[48] But Sanskrit offers more than linguistic accuracy. It is the language of mantra (*man* "mind"; *tra* "refuge" or "protection") and of the Dharma. In its almost Mandarin, calculus-like exactitude, Sanskrit's rule for *sandhi* (the harmonizing of sounds) allows each syllable spoken to blend almost seamlessly into the next. When translating Sanskrit, you think and sing the world differently. Henry David Thoreau, the first translator of the *Lotus Sutra* into English,[49] praised its oldest texts: "What extracts from the Vedas I have read fall on me like the light of a higher and purer luminary which describes a loftier course through a purer stratum.... The Vedas contain a sensible account of God."[50] Joseph Campbell called it "...the great spiritual language of the world."[51] One of America's highly respected Sanskrit teachers, Vyaas Houston, says, "Even the earliest stages of learning Sanskrit require the one-pointedness of Yoga. Sanskrit tests and strengthens the skill of Yoga, and gradually it provides Yoga with its language, manuals, and maps for mastery."[52]

What is remarkable is that sometimes a Sanskritist can literally see interbeing in the slokas that comprise texts such as the many-splendored *Bhagavad Gita* or the sobering, veil-lifting *Astavakra Samhita*, a work in the Advaita Vedanta tradition. I said earlier that language is being; life is becoming. Yes. But now and then, with Sanskrit, language mirrors becoming and process. In the *Astavakra Samhita*, in Chapter XV ("The Knowledge of the Self")[53], the fourteenth verse declares that, "You alone appear as whatever you perceive. Do bracelets, armlets, and anklets appear different from gold?" In Devanagari script, that final line is written as:

कटकांगदनूपुरम्

When "bracelet" (कटकः), "armlet" (अंगदं), and anklet (नूपुरः) combine through sandhi, they are no longer three separate "events" but rather the manifestation of an entirely new form (*rupam*)[54], which is experienced, phenomenologically, as such. Here, grammar perfectly mirrors the cosmology of Hinduism, and additional examples for the startling, shape-shifting play of words in Sanskrit, interwoven entities combining and recombining endlessly, can easily be found in the *Bhagavad Gita.*[55]

In Sanskrit, the spoken word is holy, far removed from the "idle talk" of Heidegger's complaint. Each is energy unleashed. Each is a bridge between subjectivities. Each can potentially create a public, shared space in which we can raise the American *Sangha*—as "wrong" speech can destroy that possibility. Preserving this creative, primordial power is, I believe, what the Buddha intended, at least in part, when he described this third step on the Path.

PERFECT CONDUCT

And what, monks, is Right Action? Refraining from taking life, refraining from taking what is not given, refraining from sexual misconduct. This is called Right Action.[56]

The Eightfold Path is more process than end-product. It is like climbing a mountain in a circular, upwardly spiraling fashion, finding oneself forever returned to the same spot but at a different level. Thus, both the bodhisattva and the novice practitioner move through this splintered, relative-phenomenal world, where things arise and are unraveled in a fortnight. But it is *how* they move and act in the world that is important. "Doing" for the Dharma follower is an example of disinterested, deontological ethics which, like that found in Kantian philosophy, is "interested in the act, never the fruit."[57] In the *Astasahasrikaprajñaparamita*[58] ("The Perfection of Wisdom"), we learn that:

...a bodhisattva...should behave equally to all sentient beings. He should produce throughts that are fair to all sentient beings. He should handle others with thoughts that are impartial, that are friendly, that are favorable, that are helpful. He should handle others with thoughts that are non-confrontational, that avoid harm, that avoid hurt, that avoid distress. He should handle others, all sentient beings, using the understanding of a mother, using the understanding of a father, the understanding of a son and the understanding of a daughter...He should be trained to be the refuge of all sentient beings. In his own behavior he should renounce all evil. He should give gifts, he should guard morality, he should exercise patience, he should exert vigor, he should enter into contemplation, and he should master his wisdom! He should consider dependent origination backwards and forwards, and he should instigate, encourage and empower that in others.[59]

The strict, daily regimen of monks is far from easy, but how much more demanding is the life of the householder with half a hundred duties barnacled to his (or her) life, the *upasaka* and *upasika* (male and female Buddhist lay adherents) who strive to follow the Buddhadharma, not in a secluded monastery where the residents are free from worldly temptations, but in the roiling chaos of quotidian affairs—raising children; honoring parents, spouse, and ancestors; supporting colleagues and coworkers (and students) around the world in an ever-widening circle of giving. In other words, by transforming *samsaric* means for *nirvanic* ends. Living and working in *kamadhatu* (the world of desire) *and* being "capable of perceiving both unity and multiplicity without the least contradiction between them."[60] This is, I think, the greatest of spiritual (and moral) challenges. For the "bodhisattva...is not one to give weight to gain, honour and fame. He is not to give weight to fancy robes...a nice dwelling place.... He is not full of envy and meanness.... His understanding is deep. He eagerly hears teaching from others, and he incorporates all that teaching into the perfection of wisdom. He incorporates all the worldly arts and professions through their inherent nature, thanks to the perfection of wisdom."[61] (Can anyone doubt that Buddhists make the best employees and bosses?)

One of the perennially enchanting documents of Ch'an (Zen) Buddhism is the "Ten Oxherding Pictures," which inspired my second novel, *Oxherding Tale* (1982). These drawings depict the spiritual stages of Zen development that lead to enlightenment by portraying the search of a young herdsman for his lost ox (self). Each illustration is followed by commentary in prose and verse. The ten stages shown are (1) Seeking the Ox; (2) Finding the Tracks; (3) First Glimpse of the Ox; (4) Catching the Ox; (5) Taming the Ox; (6) Riding the Ox Home; (7) Ox Forgotten, Self Alone; (8) Both Ox and Self Forgotten; (9) Returning to the Source; (10) and Entering the Marketplace with Helping Hands.[62] It is this final panel that speaks significantly to the question of Perfect Conduct.

The version of the Oxherding Pictures important for this discussion was created in 1150 C.E. by Zen Master K'uo-an Shih-yuan (Kakuan Shien in Japanese). Some earlier versions of the Oxherding Pictures offered only five or eight drawings usually ending with an empty circle (Both Ox and Self Forgotten)[63], which fit nicely the *Arhat* ideal of Theravada Buddhism. "This implied," says Philip Kapleau, "that the realization of Oneness (i.e., the effacement of every conception of self and other) was the ultimate goal of Zen. But Kakuan, feeling this to be incomplete, added two more pictures beyond the circle to make it clear that the Zen man of the highest spiritual development lives in the mundane world of form and diversity and mingles with the utmost freedom among ordinary men, whom he inspires with his compassion and radiance to walk in the Way of the Buddha."[64] Shih-yuan's final, tenth picture is accompanied by this commentary:

ENTERING THE MARKETPLACE WITH HELPING HANDS

The gate of his cottage is closed and even the wisest cannot find him. His mental panorama has finally disappeared. He goes his own way, making no attempt to follow the steps of earlier sages. Carrying a gourd, he strolls into the market; leaning on his staff, he returns home. He leads innkeepers and fishmongers in the Way of the Buddha.[65]

Kapleau's gloss on the commentary of this tenth image deserves examination:

In ancient China gourds were commonly used as wine bottles. What is implied here therefore is that the man of the deepest spirituality is not averse to drinking with those fond of liquor in order to help them overcome their delusion.... In Mahayana Buddhism...the man of deep enlightenment (who may be and often is the layman) gives off no 'smell' of enlightenment, no aura of 'saintliness'; if he did, his spiritual attainments would be regarded as still deficient. Nor does he hold himself aloof from the evils of the world. He immerses himself in them whenever necessary to emancipate men from their follies, but without being sullied by them himself. In this he is like the lotus, the symbol in Buddhism of purity and perfection, which grows in mud yet is undefiled by it.[66]

Often we hear that the attainment of Oneness, or being awakened, is "nothing much" (for the belief in separateness was a chimera in the first place).[67] Like Bunan, the Oxherder discovers that "The moon's the same old moon/The flowers exactly as they were." He will take a drink. And perhaps eat meat, as does the Dalai Lama. But to none of this is he attached. Nor does he crave them. Like the abbot I met in Thailand, he does not fret about "good" or "bad" karma, because in his conduct all he is capable of are acts in accordance with *ahimsa,* which he does not name or judge as "good," no more than the lotus bothers to name the natural act of its efflorescence. And the Oxherder has a sense of humor and irony. How could he not? He knows that, despite all he has attained through a lifetime of practice, he is still an embodied being and, as such, will experience until the day of his death a residual stain of dualism, a tincture of samsara, and traces of suffering which he recognizes when they arise in his consciousness. All that he "lets go," and when he dies, falling like a raindrop back into the sea,[68] it is unlikely he will return (or return too often) on the Wheel of remanifesta-tion. He is, in a sense, a refugee[69]—homeless and groundless. He watches the ceaseless play of his thoughts, but is not naive enough to believe there is a thinker. (For a Buddhist, Descartes asserted but he did not prove his claim, "I think, therefore I am," because all that one can empirically verify is that "There is thinking going on.") He is alone-*with*-others[70] who are also refugees or tourists with no solid basis for security, and nothing permanent in this world. He pilgrimages through the Marketplace (the realm that turns on four, dualis-tic pairs of opposites: "getting and losing, disrepute and fame, blame and praise, happiness and suffering")[71] with fearlessness, probity, desirelessness (*nishpriha*), transcendent joy, and he delights in the *suchness* of everyday things:

> How wonderful, how marvelous!!
> I fetch wood, I carry water![72]

To the innkeepers and fishmongers, the Oxherder appears, in one sense, as nothing special, with no sanctimonious stink of self-righteousness on him since all sentient beings have Buddha nature and dwell in "an inescapable net-work of mutuality." But through his example—his compassion toward all beings, his gentle speech, and his unshakeable peace and happiness—he points them toward their own possibilities.

PERFECT LIVELIHOOD

> And what, monks, is Right Livelihood? Here, monks, the...disciple,
> having given up wrong livelihood, keeps himself by right livelihood.[73]

The Buddha counsels his followers to avoid occupations that produce harm.

He is referring to obvious evils such as dealing in slaves, producing weapons or intoxicating drinks, all activities that are as much a part of our world as they were of his. Few, I think, would deny that in the modern world humankind has inventively expanded upon the wealth of deeds that damage or destroy sentient beings, ranging from fast-vanishing animal species to the environment. Our Oxherder is free to find employment almost *any*where, provided the work he chooses doesn't violate what he has learned about Perfect Conduct and Perfect Speech, compassion and the Bodhisattva Vows.

Yet because so many people are involved in "wrong" livelihood, many Buddhists understand that, "...evil must be combatted by nonviolent means. We must battle against everything which drags men down, using criticism, exhortation, influence and whatever means are ethically sound and cause no harm to others."[74]

In other words, the flip side of avoiding a livelihood that harms is embracing a livelihood that heals. In his workshops, Thich Nhat Hanh distributes a page containing what he calls, "The Five Mindfulness Trainings." The first of these declares that, "Aware of the suffering caused by the destruction of life, I vow to cultivate compassion and learn to protect the lives of people, animals, plants, and minerals. I am determined not to kill, not to let others kill, and not to condone any act of killing in the world, in my thinking, and in my way of life." The second vow goes farther: "I will respect the property of others, but I will *prevent* others from profiting from human suffering or the suffering of other species on Earth." (Italics mine)

To put this another way, followers of the Buddhadharma, fully aware of impermanence, dualism, and relativity, yet also aware of the ubiquity of suffering, are obliged at some point to oppose the origins of duhkha in the social world. They will, I believe, share the dreams stated by Dr. Martin Luther King in his Nobel Prize acceptance speech in 1964, where he said, "Civilization and violence are antithetical concepts.... Nonviolence is the answer to the crucial political and moral question of our time.... The foundation of such a method is love.... I have the audacity to believe that peoples everywhere can have three meals a day for their bodies, education and culture for their minds, and dignity, equality, and freedom for their spirits. I believe that what self-centered men have torn down men other-centered can build up."[75]

To work for *this*, to find an occupation that realizes *this*, is to fulfill the step called Perfect Livelihood.

Perfect Effort

And what, monks, is Right Effort? Here, monks, a monk rouses his will, makes an effort, stirs up energy, exerts his mind and strives to prevent the arising of unarisen evil unwholesome mental states. He rouses his will...and strives to overcome evil, unwholesome mental states that have arisen. He rouses his will... and strives to produce unarisen wholesome mental states. He rouses his will, makes an effort, stirs up energy, exerts his mind and strives to maintain wholesome mental states that have arisen, not to let them fade away, to bring them to greater growth, to the full perfection of development. This is called Right Effort.

The first sentence of the *Dhammapada* declares, "All that we are is the result of what we have thought: it is founded on our thoughts, it is made up of our thoughts. If a man speaks or acts with an evil thought, pain follows him, as the wheel follows the foot of the ox that draws the wagon."[76] Of all the world's religions and philosophies, Buddhism is the most optimistic. It places creative control over the direction of our lives in our hands. You are your own master. Moment by moment, whatever suffering, joy, or peace we experience is always the direct result of our past and present decisions. If we wish to be free, we must liberate ourselves. No one can do this for us. No one can lead us. Or place insurmountable obstacles in our way. According to the *Dhammapada,* "those who are thoughtless are as if dead already."[77] By contrast, "He who is earnest and meditative obtains ample joy" because he knows, "It is good to tame the mind, which is difficult to hold in and flighty, rushing wherever it listeth; a tamed mind brings happiness."[78]

It is good to tame the mind.

As any teacher can tell you, the minds of most students are—well, *untamed.* Their minds, and those of most people, behave like Vivekananda's famous "drunken monkey," intoxicated with desire, consumed by pride and jealousy, trigger-happy with snap judgments, burdened by miscellaneous "likes" and "dislikes," his turbulent "mental panorama" causing him to leap uncontrollably from one thought and feeling to the next, dizzied by the elixir of powerful emotions banging and knocking through him like something trying to break out from inside. For him, the ego favors a bump in a carpet—push it down in one place and it pops up in another. The monkey does not know *how* to behave otherwise and is to be pitied. One tragedy of American education, in my view, is that from elementary school through post-doctoral programs, we place a staggering amount of intellectual, noematic content before the minds of our students, content covering all aspects of the universe, but we never teach them how to control the experienced world at its source: the noetic instrument[79]—the mind—that both receives this vast gift of information *and* makes experience possible.[80]

Disciplining the mind first involves *effort* directed toward developing the power of sustained concentration (*dharana*), followed by meditation (*dhyana*). The Buddha makes clear that this practice involves stupendous will and work, for no worldly opponent is as formidable as one's own "monkey mind."

But where, in terms of practice, should we begin?

Perfect Mindfulness

> And what, monks, is Right Mindfulness? Here, monks, a monk abides contemplating body as body, ardent, clearly aware and mindful, having put aside hankering and fretting for the world; he abides contemplating feelings as feelings…; he abides contemplating mind as mind…; he abides contemplating mind-objects as mind-objects, ardent, clearly aware and mindful, having put aside hankering and fretting for the world. This is called Right Mindfulness.[81]

The problem of life is, to a great degree, the problem of attention. Of *listening*, which is one of the attributes of love. Therefore, all steps on the Eightfold Path refer and return to the practice of Mindfulness. It is the root and fruit of the Dharma, a method for meditation taught by Shakyamuni himself. "Whoever, monks, should practice (this method) for just one week may expect one of two results: either Arahantship in this life or, if there should be some substrate left, the state of a Non-Returner."[82] Known as Vipassana, or "insight" meditation, a practitioner applies the forceps of his attention to one of the activities closest to him—the in and out flow of his breath. (Once, when my daughter was five or so, she saw me sitting, and referred to my practice as "medicating," and in a sense she was right; each meditation is both medicinal and the opportunity to hold a funeral for the ego.) But this is no easy task. Try, if you can, to focus on your breath and nothing else for five minutes. I doubt that you can do this. After a few seconds the labile mind will wander from fol-

lowing the breath to memories, projections for future plans, thoughts, rever-
ies, and the entire "mental panorama" that leaves only thirty percent of our
lives lived in the present moment, the *here* and *now*. All too often, thirty percent of conscious life is wasted by our minds dwelling on events in the unre-
coverable past; another thirty percent is lost pre-living the future. Put simply,
we are seldom fully one hundred percent in the present. Giving the mind
something to hold on to in order to keep it fully in the *here* and *now* favors a
technique used by every *mahout* who must train his elephant not to swing its
trunk wildly in all directions, which is, of course, dangerous for anyone who
gets in the way. The *mahout* gives the elephant a stick to grasp, and that both
calms and centers its attention. In Vipassana, the "stick" we try to hold on to
is our breathing itself.

This one-pointed grasping is sometimes called *ekagrata* (*eka* "one"; *graha* "to
seize or grasp"), and sometimes *ananyacheta* (*ananya* "exclusively devoted to";
cheta "meditation" or "mind"). Whenever the mind veers away from the in-
and-out rhythm of breathing, the practitioner dispassionately observes its
wanderings, then gently brings it back. He does not scold himself for his lapses.
His effort is concentrated on radical attentiveness to detail, physical and psychological, a focus directed at achieving complete awareness—right down to
the most subtle nuances and modulations—of what appears before consciousness as he sits. (Was this breath long or short, hot or cold? Are my shoul-
ders straight or slumped?) In due course, he understands why the Buddha said,
"Whatever is subject to arising must also be subject to ceasing." Suffering is no
exception to this law.[83]

Now, watch:

The practitioner sees that, like the rising and falling movement of his breath,
each thought, emotion, feeling, and ache in his back is impermanent, changing like everything else in the world, and will pass away like clouds moving
across the sky if he attends to them long enough. It becomes increasingly easy,
he discovers, to "let go" what the Buddha calls "evil, unwholesome mental
states" and use his will to "maintain wholesome mental states that have arisen."
In Vipassana he does not interpret evanescent mental phenomena as they arise.
It is quite enough to simply recognize the brief, flicker-flash passing of a feeling *as* no more than a feeling, a transitory mind-created object *as* no more
than a mind-object. "With the eye of Wisdom," says Alex Kennedy, "he sees
that.... He himself is Empty, all other things are Empty. He sees that the basic

nature of all reality is that ungraspable oneness which is called Emptiness.... It is not a blank nothingness but such a plentitude that all our ordinary categories of thought diminish and belittle it."[84]

This impermanence recognized through Mindfulness is an antidote for intellectual arrogance, and it brings with it a bracing moral discovery. The challenge of always "being good" is, obviously, daunting. Who can *always* behave morally? Is it not, after all, as impossible to control the mind as it would be to harnass the wind? What the practitioner realizes is that he need not worry about "always," because the challenge of the spiritual and moral life is simply this: to be good, truly moral and master of ourselves *for this moment only.* What time is there outside this moment that we should worry about it? This moment *here* and *now* is all that we are given or responsible for.[85] "Unwholesome mental states" will appear, rise and pass away like "a star at dawn, a bubble in a stream, a flash of lightning in a summer cloud, a flickering lamp, a phantom and a dream," if we do not sustain them by clinging and just let them disappear.

The direct result of this practice, according to Kennedy, is that our Oxherder is

> in full possession of his own body: he knows what his posture is, what he is doing and the direction and purpose of his movements...He is aware of his emotions. He knows whether he feels greed, hatred or delusion, or metta, generosity and clarity. He knows what he thinks: what thoughts and images are passing through his mind. And he knows where those thoughts have come from. He is able to distinguish what in his mind is simply the product of his past conditioning and what is genuinely creative....He is able to rise to challenges and deal with them with imagination and resourcefulness....He sees things with the eye of aesthetic appreciation, not of egotistical appropriation. He is profoundly moved by beauty in nature and in art....[86]

Mindfulness is not only practiced when sitting. It can—and should—be brought to each and every one of our activities, regardless of how humble they might be. When walking, eating, taking out the garbage, or talking, the Dharma urges us to practice a complete and dispassionate awareness of where we are and what we are doing. Such practice is transformative, as proven by seventy-eight-year-old S.N. Goenka, one of the world's foremost Vipassana teachers, who has taught its techniques to hundreds of thousands of people, among them hardened criminals at Tihar Jail, "India's largest and most notorious prison."[87] Recidivism dropped among inmates guided through Vipassana by Goenka, at prisons both in India and in America.

"This," Goenka says, "is universal. You sit and observe your breath. You can't say this is Hindu breath or Christian breath or Muslim breath. Knowing how to live peacefully or harmoniously—you don't call this religion or spirituality. It is nonsectarian."

The Dharma and its practice need not be "called" anything. Wisdom practices are the property of no single religion or philosophy.

RIGHT CONCENTRATION

And what, monks, is Right Concentration? Here, a monk, detached from sense-desires, detached from unwholesome mental states, enters and remains in the first jhana, which is thinking and pondering, born of detachment, filled with delight and joy. And with the subsiding of thinking and pondering, by gaining inner tranquility and oneness of mind, he enters and remains in the second jhana, which is without thinking and pondering, born of concentration, filled with delight and joy. And with the fading away of delight, remaining imperturbable, mindful and clearly aware....he enters the third jhana. And having given up pleasure and pain, and with the disappearance of former gladness and sadness, he enters and remains in the fourth jhana, which is beyond pleasure and pain, and purified by equanimity and mindfulness. This is called Right Concentration. And that, monks, is called the way of practice leading to the cessation of suffering.[88]

In the dialectic of samsara and nirvana, the experiential realms of ignorance and wakefulness, the dream-world of *samsara* is logically prior to and necessary for the awakening to *nirvana*. Gunapala Dharmasiri argues that this is the stance of Tantric Buddhism:

If samsara is only a mental construct, a maya, the Tantrics ask, why should we be scared of our own creations or dreams?....What is necessary is to master and get out of the dream. Once we get out of the dream, we will wake up to the nirvana which is this world itself....

We make a samsara out of nirvana through our conceptual projections. Tantrics maintain that the world is there for two purposes. One is to help us to attain enlightenment. As the world is, in fact, nirvana, the means of the world can be utilized to realize nirvana, when used in the correct way.[89]

For the approximately two million Buddhists in the U.S., the Eightfold Path is a map for the Way. But, like any map, it merely sketches the terrain bodhisattvas have traversed for two and a half millennia, leaving open for each follower of the Dharma an adventure of discovery and service: a genuinely creative journey through the mystery of being, which with each step leads to ineffable joy.

NOTES

1 *Buddhist Mahayana Texts,* trans. by E.B. Cowell, F. Max Müller and J. Takakusu, (Delhi, India: Motilal Banarsidass, 2002).http://www.sacred-texts.com/bud/sbe49/index. htm

2 *Ibid.,* Book XIV, p.1.

3 Alan W. Watts, *The Way of Zen* (New York: Pantheon Books, 1957), pp. 91–92. Compare the classic exchange of Zen poems by Shen-hsiu and Hui-neng. Shen-hsiu's poem says:

The body is the Bodhi Tree;
The mind is like a bright mirror standing.
Take care to wipe it all the time.
And allow no dust to cling.

According to legend, Hui-neng's poem, which follows, trumped Shen-hsiu's in terms of understanding the Dharma and led to his becoming a Buddhist Patriarch:

There never was a Bodhi Tree,
Nor bright mirror standing.
Fundamentally, not one thing exists.
So where is the dust to cling?

4 The twelve links in the chain are: (1) *Ignorance,* which gives rise to: (2) *Volitional action,* which gives rise to: (3) *Conditioned consciousness,* which produces: (4) *Name and form,* which leads to: (5) *The six bases* (the five senses and mind), which produce: (6) *Sense impressions,* which gives rise to: (7) *Feelings,* which then generate: (8) *Desire or craving,* which creates: (9) *Attachment,* which leads to: (10) *Becoming,* which gives rise to: (11) *Birth,* which leads to: (12) *Old age and death.* From John Snelling's *The Buddhist Handbook: A Complete Guide to Buddhist Schools, Teachings, Practice, and History* (New York: Barnes and Noble Books, 1991), p. 61.

5 Cowell, Müller and Takakusu, *ibid.,* Book XIV, p. 1.

6 Stephen Batchelor, *Alone With Others: An Existential Approach to Buddhism* (New York: Grove Weidenfeld, 1983), p. 39.

7 *Numerical Discourses of the Buddha: An Anthology of Suttas from the Anguttara Nikaya*, trans. and ed. by Nyanaponika Thera and Bhikkhu Bodhi (Walnut Creek, CA: AltaMira Press, 1999), p. 65.

8 *The World Book Encyclopedia* (Chicago: Field Enterprises, 1956), Vol. 2, p. 1,041.

9 Maurice Walshe, *The Long Discourses of the Buddha* (Boston: Wisdom Publications, 1995), pp. 348-49.

10 *The Shambhala Dictionary of Buddhism and Zen*, trans. by Michael H. Kohn (Boston: Shambhala Publications, 1991), p.63.

11 John Snelling, *ibid.*, p. 46.

12 Gunapala Dharmasiri, *Fundamentals of Buddhist Ethics* (California: Golden Leaves Press, 1989), p. 109.

13 "Two foundations of twentieth-century physics—quantum theory and relativity theory—both force us to see the world very much in the way a Hindu, Buddhist, or Taoist sees it...." Fritjof Capra, *The Tao of Physics* (New York: Bantam Books, 1984), pp.4–5.

14 The following statement has been attributed to Albert Einstein: "The religion of the future will be a cosmic religion. It should transcend a personal God to avoid dogma and theology. Covering both the natural and the spiritual, it should be based on a religious sense arising from the experience of all things natural and spiritual as a meaningful unity. Buddhism answers this description.... If there is any religion that could cope with modern scientific needs it would be Buddhism."

15 Walshe, *ibid.*, p. 348.

16 Thich Nhat Hanh, *Living Buddha, Living Christ* (New York: Riverhead Books, 1995), pp. 133–135.

17 Thich Nhat Hanh, *Being Peace* (Berkeley, California: Parallax Press, 1987), p.45.

18 *The Martin Luther King Jr. Companion*, ed. by Coretta Scott King (New York: St. Martin's Press, 1993), p. 94.

19 *Ibid.*, p. 91.

20 Thich Nhat Hanh, *Living Buddha, Living Christ, ibid.*, p. 11.

21 Consider these words of the Buddha from the *Anguttara Nikaya:* "It is impossible, O monks, and it cannot be that a person possessed of right view should regard any formation as permanent.... It is impossible, O monks, and it cannot be that a person possessed of right view should regard any formation as a source of happiness.... It is impossible, O monks, and it cannot be that a person possessed of right view should regard anything as a self. But it is possible for an uninstructed worldling to regard something as a self." From *Numerical Discourses of the Buddha, ibid.*, pp. 37–38.

22 In his outstanding work *Nonduality* (New York: Humanity Books, 1998), David Loy provides a concise account of *sunyata*. "It comes from the root *su*, which means 'to swell' in two senses: hollow or empty, and also full, like the womb of a pregnant woman. Both are implied in the Mahayana usage: the first denies any fixed self-nature to anything, the second implies that this is also fullness and limitless possibility, for lack of any fixed characteristics allows the infinite diversity of impermanent phenomena," p. 50.

23 A comparison of Buddhism's doctrine of dependent origination and Whitehead's project of developing a metaphysics based on quantum theory would make for a very useful study, since for Whitehead, who abandons the subject-object mode of thinking, entities are epochal units of becoming interconnected in a universe that is itself a process of becoming, and every actual entity is present in every other actual entity.

24 Alex Kennedy, *The Buddhist Vision* (York Beach, Maine: Samuel Weiser, Inc., 1987), pp. 170-71.

25 Paul Carus, *Gospel of Buddha,* (Tucson, AZ: Omen Communications, 1972), p.34.

26 "Because we label objects in the world with nouns we come to think of them as unchanging entities—isolated, interacting only by a system of mechanical exchanges. We even think of ourselves in this same way...." Kennedy, *ibid.,* p. 82.

27 *The Zen Teachings of Huang Po: On the Transmission of Mind,* trans. by John Blofeld (New York: Grove Press, 1958), pp. 81–82.

28 *World of the Buddha,* ed. by Lucien Stryk (New York: Doubleday, 1968), p. 343.

29 Thich Nhat Hanh, *Living Buddha, Living Christ, ibid.,* p.106.

30 Thich Nhat Hanh, *Living Buddha, Living Christ, ibid.,* p.183.

31 "I am composed of form and matter, neither of them will perish into nothingness, as neither of them came into being out of nothingness. Every part of me then will be reduced by change into some other part of the universe, that again will change into another part of the universe, and so on forever. And as a result of such a change, I too now exist, and those who begot me existed, and so forever in the other direction." Marcus Aurelius, *Meditations,* trans. by George Long (Roslyn: Walter J. Black, Inc., 1945), p. 50.

32 "Take away your opinion, and there is taken away the complaint, 'I have been hurt.' Take away the complaint, 'I have been hurt,' and the hurt is gone." Marcus Aurelius, *ibid.,* p. 35.

33 Dharmasiri, *ibid.,* p. 135.

34 *Teachings of the Buddha,* ed. by Jack Kornfield (Boston: Shambhala Books, 1993), p. 101.

35 Consider his words in light of Matthew 19:17, "Why callest thou me good? There is none good but one, that is God." And John 14:10, "Believest thou not that I am in the Father and the Father in me? The words that I speak unto you I speak not of myself, but the Father that dwelleth in me, he doeth the works."

36 "Consider that before long you will be nobody and nowhere, nor will any of the things exist which you now see, nor any of those who are now living. For all things are formed by nature to change and be turned and to perish in order that other things in continuous succession may exist." Marcus Aurelius, *ibid.,* p.129.

37 "Suffering alone exists, none who suffer;

> The deed there is, but no doer thereof;
> Nirvana is, but no one seeking it;
> The Path there is, but none who travel it.

From Alan Watts, *The Way of Zen* (New York: Vintage Books, 1957), p. 56. Consider also the Zen poem:

"To write something and leave it behind us,
It is but a dream.
When we awake we know
There is not even anyone to read it."

38 *The Diamond Sutra & The Sutra of Hui-Neng,* trans. by A.F. Price and Wong Mou-lam (Boston: Shambhala Books, 1990), p.35.

39 *Ibid.,* p. 53. Compare this to Aurelius's counsel, "Return to your sober senses and recall yourself. When you have roused yourself from sleep and perceived that they were only dreams which troubled you, then in your waking hours look at the things about you as you looked at the dreams...." Marcus Aurelius, *ibid.,* p. 62.

40 Walshe, *ibid.,* p. 348.

41 Dharmasiri, *ibid.,* p. 45.

42 Isshu Miura and Ruth Fuller Sasaki, *The Zen Koan: Its History and Use in Rinzai Zen* (New York: Harvest Books, 1965), p. 36.

43 Shantideva, *A Guide to the Bodhisattva's Way of Life,* trans. by Stephen Batchelor (Dharamsala: Library of Tibetan Works & Archives, 1979), pp. 114-15.

44 Walshe, *ibid.,* p.348.

45 Carus, *ibid.,* p.106-08.

46 Martin Heigegger, *Being and Time,* trans. by John Macquarrie and Edward Robinson (New York: Harper and Row, 1962), p. 213.

47 *The Shambhala Dictionary of Buddhism, ibid.,* p. 121.

48 All information on Sanskrit here is drawn from "Sanskrit and the Technological Age: Mathematics, Music, and Sanskrit," and "The Yoga of Learning Sanskrit," by Vyaas Houston, *Devavani: The Language of the Gods* (New York: The American Sanskrit Institute, no pub. date provided), pp. 1–8, and 17–27. http://www.americansanskrit.com

49 David P. Barash, "Buddhism and the 'subversive' science," *The Chronicle of Higher Education,* Feb. 23, 2001, pp. 13–14.

50 Houston, *ibid.,* p. 38.

51 *Ibid.*

52 Houston, *ibid.,* p. 20.

53 *Astavakra Samhita,* by Swami Nityaswarupananda (Calcutta: Advaita Ashrama, 1969), p. 100.

54 It is also interesting to note that the Sanskrit word for "form," *rupam* also means "beauty."

55 For example, see the final line in Book VI, verse 11 of *The Bhagavad Gita,* trans. by Winthrop Sargeant (Albany: State University of New York Press), p. 282.

56 Walshe, *ibid.,* p. 348.

57 Dharmasiri, *ibid.,* pp. 27–28.

58 Literally, "Eight thousand line wisdom perfection" sutra.

59 *The Perfection of Wisdom*, selections and trans. by R.C. Jamieson (New York: Viking Studio, 2000), pp. 65–67.

60 *The Zen Teachings of Huang Po, ibid.*, p.20.

61 Jamieson, *ibid.*, p. 71.

62 *The Three Pillars of Zen*, ed. by Philip Kapleau (Boston: Beacon Press, 1967), pp. 301–313.

63 *Shambhala Dictionary of Buddhism and Zen*, pp. 106–107.

64 Kapleau, *ibid.*, p. 301.

65 *Ibid.*, p. 311.

66 *Ibid.*, p. 313.

67 Consider this in light of Matthew, Chapter 6:27, "Which of you by taking thought can add one cubit unto his stature?"

68 "You have lived as a part. You shall disappear in that which produced you; rather, you shall be received back into the creative principle by a transformation." Marcus Aurelius, *ibid.*, p. 36.

69 Chögyam Trungpa Rinpoche, "The Decision to Become a Buddhist," *Shambhala Sun*, May 2001, pp. 28–33. The Dalai Lama, I should note, prefers that we see ourselves as "tourists" in this world, a point he explains in *Ethics for the New Millennium* (New York: Riverhead Books, 1999).

70 Stephen Batchelor, *ibid.*

71 H. Saddhatissa (New York: George Braziller, 1970), p. 140.

72 Poem by P'ang-yun, cited in Watts, *ibid.*, p. 133, and Snelling, *ibid.*, p. 139.

73 Walshe, *ibid.*

74 Kennedy, *ibid.*, p. 123.

75 *A Testament of Hope: The Essential Writings and Speeches of Martin Luther King, Jr.*, ed. by James M. Washington (New York: HarperCollins, 1991), pp. 224–226.
    It is instructive to compare the Eightfold Path to a document used during the Birmingham campaign, entitled, "Commandments for Volunteers," which civil rights activists signed. This Decalogue said: "I hereby pledge myself—my person and body—to the nonviolent movement. Therefore I will keep the following commandments: (1) Meditate daily on the teachings and life of Jesus; (2) Remember always that the nonviolent movement seeks justice and reconciliation—not victory; (3) Walk and talk in the manner of love, for God is love; (4) Pray daily to be used by God in order that all men might be free; (5) Sacrifice personal wishes in order that all men might be free; (6) Observe with both friend and foe the ordinary rules of courtesy; (7) Seek to perform regular service for others and for the world; (8) Refrain from the violence of fist, tongue, or heart; (9) Strive to be in good spiritual and bodily health; (10) Follow the directions of the movement and of the captain on a demonstration." These commandments can be found in my novel *Dreamer* (New York: Scribner, 1998), pp. 91–92.

76 *The Dhammapada*, trans. by Irving Babbitt (New York: New Directions, 1965), p. 3.

Compare Babbitt's rendering of these opening lines to those of Thanissaro Bhikkhu (Geoffrey DeGraff) in his translation of the *Dhammapada* (Barre: Dhamma Dana Publications, 1998), p. 1:

> Phenomena are preceded by the heart,
> ruled by the heart,
> made of the heart.
> If you speak or act
> with a corrupted heart,
> then suffering follows you—
> as the wheel of the cart,
> the track of the ox
> that pulls it.

77 *The Dhammapada, ibid.*, p. 6.

78 *Ibid.*, p. 8.

79 Obviously, I side with the Husserlian account of consciousness, expressed in his famous formula, "Consciousness is always consciousness *of* something," where the subject (*noesis*) and object *(noema)* are interdependent, both arising simultaneously to make experience itself possible. This rather Kantian interweaving of the Transcendental Ego and the phenomenal world provides a useful starting-point for discussing the Buddhist doctrine of no-self.

80 Think of this in light of Aurelius's advice: "Men seek retreats for themselves, houses in the country, seashores and mountains; and you too are wont to desire such things very much. But this is altogether a mark of the common sort of man, for it is in your power, whenever you shall choose, to retire into yourself. For nowhere with more quiet or more freedom from trouble does a man retire than into his own soul, particularly when he has within him such thoughts that by looking into them he is at once perfectly tranquil; and this tranquility, I am sure, is nothing but the good ordering of the mind. Constantly then grant yourself this retreat and refreshment." Marcus Aurelius, *ibid.*, p. 33.

81 Walshe, *ibid.*

82 *Ibid.*, p. 350.

83 H. Saddhatissa, *ibid.*, p. 74.

84 Kennedy, *ibid.*, p. 199.

85 "If you strive to live only what is really your life, that is, the present—then you will be able to pass that portion of life which remains for you up to the time of your death, free from perturbations, nobly, and obedient to your own deity within." Marcus Aurelius, *ibid.*, p. 126.

86 Kennedy, *ibid.*, p. 57.

87 Arun Venugopal, "Breathing-in-peace tour," *The Seattle Times*, May 4, 2002, p. A-11.

88 Walshe, *ibid.*

89 Dharmasiri, *ibid.*, p. 123.

Staying on Your Seat: The Practice of Right Concentration

LARRY YANG

THERE IS SOMETHING that resonates within us when we hear about the truth of suffering; something that calls to our hearts when we hear that an end to suffering is possible; and something that creates resolve and determination when we hear that there is a path to happiness and the freedom from suffering. Each of us, in our deepest internal wisdom, desires to experience the truth of our existence.

This innate wisdom indicates that within all of us is already a connection to the Buddha's Eightfold Path, his Fourth Noble Truth. We already have a taste of Right Understanding and Right Intention and, from this place of initial recognition, we can learn how to engage in the next three elements of the Eightfold Path—Right Speech, Right Action, and Right Livelihood—the practices of ethical behavior, called *sila*. Living in harmony with ourselves, other beings, and the larger world, allows a peacefulness to enter into our overall experience.

We can see this when we get caught in anger or rage. When this occurs, we are distressed not only in our emotions and our thoughts, but we can feel the turmoil in our bodies. Reflecting on times that anger has been strong, we can recognize the physical sensations of tension, elevated heart rate, and increased anxiety. In using our speech, our actions, and our livelihood with our highest sense of goodness, we calm our hearts and our bodies with the deep knowing that we are living our lives in the best way we can.

When we live and act from a place of non-harming and not causing suffering, we feel the goodness that we actually are, in that moment. When we cause harm or say hurtful things about ourselves and others, even though we may have methods of denial or escape, we feel the injury and negativity that arise from such actions. We begin to know on a deep experiential level, not just from our rational minds, that causing suffering will lead only to more of our own suffering. Living a peaceful life leads to more happiness. For *ourselves* as well as others.

If we cultivate peace with the external world through ethical behavior, this peacefulness also enters our personal experience, and it is in our internal life that the final three elements of the Eightfold Path emerge. Right Effort, Right Mindfulness, and Right Concentration are part of *samadhi*, the practices of concentration that deepen our exploration into what is actually happening in our moment-to-moment experience.

Just as any engine requires fuel, so our Dharma practice requires energy. This energy emerges from the practice of Right Effort. When we exercise our bodies, it is not just the physical exercise that builds strength, but also how we feed and care for our bodies in order to be strong. Similarly, in developing strength and concentration within our mind, we cultivate ways to increase its energy. We direct that energy towards our practice of Right Mindfulness—the activity of being aware moment-to-moment of what is happening to us. We may come to a deeper and deeper awareness of the sensations of our body—the tingling, the itches, the pains, the sounds. We may focus our mindfulness on the pleasantness, unpleasantness, or neutrality of our momentary experience. We may also direct our awareness towards the formations arising in our minds that include all our emotions and all our thoughts. Or, we can be mindful of how the Dharma manifests in each moment of our experience.

Each of these levels of mindfulness is cultivated and strengthened by giving our full attention to what is happening. This may sound simple, but it is not as easy as it seems. In this age of laptops, palm pilots, cellular picture phones, and multiple other technologies, we have taken multi-tasking to new heights, often measuring our success by how many things we can do in a moment, rather than experiencing the moment for what it is. All those things that we can "do" are not equivalent to who we really "are." It is as if we are distracted into the compulsion to fill our moments with as many activities as possible, not sensing that each moment might be completely full, just as it is, without any efforts on our part. To focus on who we really are and what our experience really is, takes a dedicated effort in concentration.

Concentration can be described as cultivating a non-distracted mind. It has been said that concentration is a process of unifying the mind. The power of the unified mind is far greater than the sum of the mind's fragmented experiences. It is like having one candle in each far corner of a room, creating a diffuse and dimly lit room; but bring all the candles together, and the light becomes bright and illuminating.

We start a practice of concentration by focusing on the sensations of the inhale and exhale of a breath—whether it is soft or hard, damp or dry, long or short. Whether the breath is harsh or smooth, cool or warm—we allow it to be just as it is. Inevitably, we get distracted. When we are aware, we have a choice to gently bring our attention back to the inhale and the exhale—not forcing ourselves and not judging ourselves for having our minds wander, just coming back to the breath with a deliberate, but tender effort. In the gentle return of our mindfulness to the breath is the beginning of the concentrated mind.

Imagine a young puppy. A puppy is born not knowing how to sit in one place. When we try to train the puppy, we know that it will take time and patience. We tell the puppy to "stay," and the puppy runs off…we tell the puppy to "stay" again, and the puppy runs off. It is no use to punish the puppy or treat it unkindly, rather it is just the gentle coaxing and constant redirection that will eventually train the puppy to sit. Thus, we train our minds to sit in one place, not needing to run off in different directions or with different activities. And it takes time and a great deal of care.

This training and practicing of our minds is not unlike the training or exercise of our bodies when we experience going to the gym. Strenuous exercise can often be hard to sustain. In doing the physical exercise we can be even harder on ourselves. We can be brutal on our body, expecting it to accomplish certain levels of activity, and risk injuring our body. Or, we can go slowly, noticing our progress and our limits, enjoying the sensations and results as they come. His Holiness the Dalai Lama has said that "concentration is merely another form of workout of another form of muscle."

We often are distracted from our spiritual practice. Particularly in difficult times of trauma, pain, or suffering, we may lose perspective. Our practice in concentration encourages and supports us to continually return to our deepest intention and motivation for practice, even if life becomes traumatic, difficult, or oppressive.

This is particularly relevant for people and communities of color because of our historic and continuing experience with oppression and social trauma. Sometimes the pain that emerges may be so great that it is difficult to examine the pain on the moment-to-moment basis that Dharma practice asks of us. At times this pain may arise without warning or expectation.

As a person of color entering a retreat or meditation hall with all white folks, there are times that I have experienced deep distress and anguish. Even if my intentions are to feel interconnected, the sense of isolation and the experience of not seeing others like myself can trigger past feelings of injury or exclusion.

I have felt unseen, excluded, and/or uninvited. There have been times that I have heard Dharma talks that have been insensitive, at best, and often harmful when the person speaking is unaware of different cultural experiences. And there can be a passive indifference to difficult and complex issues around diversity, discrimination, and oppression. This kind of ignoring only furthers the experience of being unseen, unvalued, and unacknowledged.

In my early practice, I sat a seven-day metta or loving kindness retreat in which I was the only person of color in a room of almost 100 practitioners. Even though I attempted to direct my attention towards metta, what arose more frequently were feelings of being "the only one" or "not belonging" or of anger at the inequality in the room. When I went to approach the teachers for assistance on being the only person of color in the space, the response was that a teacher would discuss it with me after the retreat was over because the focus was on the metta practice. I stayed as long as I could, but to my own chagrin I left on the sixth day, one day before the end of the retreat, and before I could have contact with a teacher on the issues that arose for me.

I have come to realize that my experience at that retreat was a door into my concentration practice. In spite of the difficult cultural circumstances of the retreat, there was something that was being practiced that resonated with my deepest experience. I knew deep inside that the cultivation of loving kindness could provide relief in my life. I felt on some nonverbal and intuitive level that developing the energy of the heart could only produce benefit for me and the people around me. When I was caught in the pain of the retreat's cultural conditions, and when my mind was lost in anger or sadness or frustration, I would return to this internal knowing of why I came to the retreat in the first place. Like returning to the breath each time I get distracted, I returned to being seated in my spiritual practice—I returned to my Dharma seat.

As events unfolded at that time, my effort and my concentration were not developed enough to allow me to feel comfortable enough to stay in the retreat until it ended. I left early. Of course, there were regrets of not being able to finish, judgments that I was not "good enough" in my practice, and frustrations that I did not connect with the guidance of a teacher. But similar to being mindful of the breath, I endeavored not to judge myself for being distracted, but rather, to learn how the distractions affected me and how I might respond in the future.

Most of all I realized that when I, as a person of color, experience the pain of difference, I often am diverted from my deepest intentions...intentions of staying in my Dharma seat and staying engaged with my meditation practice. I have used the experience of this metta retreat to expand my ability to see and experience the pain of the moment and yet, not prevent me from practicing. To move from my Dharma seat only compounds the suffering with an additional sense of loss. This invites an act of Right Concentration.

There is a life event of the Buddha that has provided guidance to me with these kinds of challenges. The story comes from the process of the Buddha's own enlightenment.

After years of searching for a spiritual path that would lead to total and permanent liberation from suffering, Prince Siddhartha Gautama, the Buddha-to-be, decided with all the resolve and commitment that he could muster to sit under a tree and not rise until he was fully awake—fully enlightened. As he sat in meditation, he penetrated and experienced the wisdom of the true nature of existence. However, before his attainment, Mara—his supreme foe, the god who tempts all beings into worldly experiences—was determined to prevent Siddhartha's liberation from occurring. Mara amassed all of his power and armies to force Siddhartha out of his state of meditative absorbtion. It is said that Mara caused unimaginable forces of destruction to arise and attack the future Buddha.

Mara created windstorms that could have uprooted mountains, but when they reached Siddhartha, the edge of his robes was not even ruffled. Mara called upon maelstroms of tornadoes and torrential downpours to wash away and drown the meditating prince, but the floods did not dampen him so much as a dewdrop. There were showers of rocks the size of mountain peaks, showers of hot coals, and showers of every conceivable weapon of destruction that assailed Siddhartha—yet they all were transformed into celestial flowers and fell at his feet. After nine of these unsuccessful attempts to unseat the future Buddha from his path towards liberation, an enraged Mara gathered the hundreds of thousands in his army. With the roar of their screams in the background, Mara declared to the Buddha-to-be:

"Get out of that seat! That seat belongs to me and to me alone! These are my witnesses to my owning that seat you are in!"

And there arose a deafening roar from his armies extending in all directions—north, south, east, west—"Yes, we are his witness! He belongs there!"

And Mara continued, "You, dear Prince, sit alone. Who is your witness?"

Then, the Prince, close to his liberation, undisturbed by any of the obstacles created by Mara, reached down with the simplest possible gesture, that was filled with ease, to touch the ground with the middle finger of his right hand. In doing so, the Buddha called upon the Earth Mother to witness his inalienable right to his Dharma seat. So brilliant was the power of the Mother Goddess when she appeared that Mara and all his armies were dispelled into all corners of the Universe.

Many times I have found this story of the Buddha's own struggles and difficulties helpful in strengthening my own practice. When I feel that my balance is being pulled from underneath me, or when I feel that I am going to lose my Dharma seat, I recall the resolve and concentration of the Buddha. I invoke the strength of the Buddha and the courage of all peoples who have lived through experiences of suffering and oppression. And as a physical reminder I can touch the ever-present Earth ™ as the Buddha-to-be did in his practice—I can ground myself in the deep knowledge that I have a choice to stay exactly where I am, and to experience whatever it is that is in front of me. In that choice to stay in my seat, is the act of concentration.

Part of my practice when I meditate is to take the Three Refuges and then say silently to myself "I surrender to the Dharma." When I need additional support during times of distress or anxiety of mind, I will add the words "I deserve the Dharma." We each deserve the Dharma. And if we choose to sit in it, just like Prince Siddhartha, we all have a Dharma seat that cannot be taken from us. It is a seat that is always there for us, regardless of the circumstances of the room, because everyone without exception deserves the benefits of the Buddha's teachings. When we take that Dharma seat, no one…no one can take it away from us or knock us off that seat. There may be distractions or painful experiences that try to knock us off, but no one can take our seat away. Regardless of how Mara tempts or tortures us, we do not have to relinquish our seat; we don't have to move from our seat of freedom. And even if we leave that seat, it will be there whenever we choose to return.

It is as James Baldwin wrote: "Freedom is not something that anybody can be given. Freedom is something people take, and people are as free as they want to be."

From the act of staying in our Dharma seat, from returning to our practice over and over again, from that experience of concentration—is how we reconnect back to the first elements of the Eightfold Path—the Wisdom of Right Understanding and Right Intention. It is from the stillness and tranquility of Right Concentration that the liberating understanding of the true nature of our experience can emerge. As we work through this cycle of the Eightfold

Path over and over again, we begin to turn the wheel of samsara, the wheel of suffering, in a different direction—a direction that is aimed towards our freedom, and the lasting happiness that the Buddha described to be within our reach.

Race, Racism, and the Dharma

BONNIE DURAN

THE DHARMA is the most important source of insight and inspiration to me as I heal from racism and discrimination and as I work towards social justice. The Dharma has taught me important truths about being a "minority" and the powerlessness, discrimination, and prejudice that often come with that status.

Growing up, I strongly identified by and with my racial identities and unconsciously believed the negative stereotypes. As a Native American (Opelousas/Coushatta) mixed race child growing up in a culturally diverse neighborhood in San Francisco, my white friends were often discouraged from playing or spending time with me. Although I scored well on standardized tests, the nuns who were my teachers tracked me into secretarial training and out of college preparatory courses. Girls from the Catholic school I attended would go to the predominantly white Catholic boys schools for monthly dances. I was rarely asked to dance. I unconsciously internalized these messges that I was worth less than others and was fearful, shamed, and obsequious towards authority. Although hurtful and limiting, experiences like these seem minor next to those of my parents, who passed down intergenerational fear, shame, and rage from much more serious, life threatening experiences

When I entered college and began to understand that I was the victim of racism, I was at first enraged by blatant prejudice and was hopeless about my life chances. I engaged in political work, and participated in the burgeoning Native cultural revitalization movement that was sweeping urban areas all over the U.S. and in other communities of color. As an undergraduate in the 1970s, I was very involved with the American Indian student rights, people of color movement at San Francisco State University. After years of political, cultural, and social work, I came to be disenchanted, particularly with the anger, separation, and other afflictive emotions that unmindful political community work and youthful party life can cultivate. As a mixed race person, I often felt that I had no solid cultural ground anywhere.

At 23, I moved to Europe to live the expatriate life and after a number of years, found my way on the well-traveled path to Nepal and India. I arrived at Kopan Monastery in Nepal to study Buddhism and then went on to Bodhgaya and Dharamsala for more retreats and Dharma teachings. Being a Native person in India and Nepal had excellent advantages. I looked much more like the people here than I did in Europe and I traveled around Nepal and India with Tibetans and was accepted by many people as an American sister.

Back in the U.S. a year later, I took advantage of the retreat opportunities provided by the growing Western Theravada community and also found my way back to Native spirituality through the Lakota Sun Dance, Sweat Lodge ceremonies, and the Native American Church. At that time, the Western Buddhist community, outside of the Asian immigrant churches, was predominantly white. Unlike my experience in India and Nepal, I often felt very out of place and invisible at Sangha meetings and could hardly afford the retreats. I loved the Dharma though, and did not leave the practice.

Through intense meditation practice and the wisdom of the Dharma, I came to uncover how I had internalized negative racist and sexist opinions and also came to see more clearly the truth of those experiences in my social and professional interactions. I am more attuned to the words in my head that hold me back and condition my unkindness towards others and myself and I work to lessen their impact. The racist opinions and beliefs that creep into the most innocent social or business interaction or decision are more clearly distinguished and can be resisted. There were other benefits as well. I began receiving straight As while completing a doctorate at UC Berkeley; before meditation I was barely a B student.

In 1999 I was introduced to Vallecitos Mountain Refuge, and the wonderful work Linda Velarde and Grove Barnett were doing to bring the Dharma to social activists, with special emphasis on people of color. I attended my first people of color retreat with Joseph Goldstein and George Mumford in 1999 and have sat annually with these teachers since then. With the help of Ralph Steele, a group of New Mexicans from that retreat started a people of color Sangha in 2002. We have now extended our group to included white people who want to sit with us and support us as people of color. In the Native American talking circles that take place after our weekly sit, we often discuss the ways the Dharma helps us to overcome our internalized oppression and ways to more skillfully deal with the hurt we all encounter. Although healing is a lifelong process for us all, my life is much more peaceful and clear.

Undoing Racism through the Dharma

I believe we all have a duty to uncover, resist, and transform racial oppression and injustice. The following are a few ways the Dharma helps us in that wholesome project.

Integrity: Finding Right Speech

Right Speech, Right Action, and Right Livelihood are the elements of the Eightfold Path that deal with virtue or integrity. Right Speech has three elements: truthfulness, timeliness, and usefulness. Applied to anti-racist work, naming the truth of racist words or deeds is a tricky business. Skillfulness is a function not only of recognizing when racism is at play, but also knowing the most useful time to bring it to awareness and the most lucid language to invoke understanding. In regard to admonishing another or ourself, the Buddha advised that we should investigate five conditions:

1. Do I speak at the right time, or not?
2. Do I speak of facts, or not?
3. Do I speak gently or harshly?
4. Do I speak useful words or not?
5. Do I speak with a kindly heart, or am I inwardly malicious?

Wisdom: "Be Less Not More"

Right View tells us that race exists on the level of "relative" reality. Race is based upon dualist thinking: black/white, male/female, self/other, good/bad, praise/blame, etc. On an ultimate level, race/ethnicity is a fiction, and identification with it is unskillful. Nondualism is beyond binary oppositions that inevitably create separation, hierarchies, and oppressions.

Concentration: Finding the Widsom to Let Go

Right Effort, Right Mindfulness, and Right Concentration fall under the heading of concentration. Racism and other forms of discrimination are so fundamental to how the modern world organizes itself, that without some form of continued spiritual practice (Right Effort) promoting clarity and love, it will be very difficult to make a meaningful and lasting difference. Social justice efforts that do not include the cultivation of clarity and love are doomed to failure. Meditation is key to uncovering the many stories we play in our own minds that are centered in fear. As we meditate, we can see our own propensities towards self-hate, racism, sexism, homophobia float away and we also see more clearly how these work in others. When we cultivate the *Brahmaviharas* (loving-kindness, compassion, sympathetic joy, equanimity) we are substituting afflictive emotions with skillful means.

As we develop skills to name, accept, decondition, and depersonalize these unskillful habits, we learn skillful ways to work more efficiently in our relationships, jobs, communities, and political life. As we cultivate wisdom and compassion, it infuses all aspects of our life.

MEDICINE: MINDFULNESS AS HEALER

The clarity provided by my sitting practice allows insight into the projected privilege of whites, men, heterosexuals, tall people, thin people, rich people, and others who are afforded higher status. For example, retreats are particularly useful for uncovering unrecognized but predominant mind states. In the first days of retreat, I am often surprised at the pervasive arrogant, privileged and competitive mind states that are the result of my identification as a college professor. Mindfulness allows me to see more clearly and with compassion the institutional and individual racism and privilege around me and allows more space and grace when confronting the illusions and delusions of race. The intention and skill we bring to social justice work will determine if our efforts are meritorious, wholesome, and productive of happiness, or the cause of more delusion, ill-will and other forms of suffering.

Native traditional practices like the Sun Dance, Sweat Lodge ceremonies and the Native American Church also reduce suffering and are based on the same universal truths as the Dharma. In many ways, to be a "pipe carrier" is to follow the Buddhist precepts to be truthful, kind, and not to harm. The principle of *Mitakuye Oyasin*, All My Relations, is to know our fundamental connectedness and equality with everything—it is to know selflessness, *anatta*.

Much gratitude to my teachers.

Right Action, Buddhism, and Our Participation in the World

REVEREND KENNETH KENSHIN TANAKA

INTRODUCTION

MY EARLIEST BUDDHIST EDUCATION started in my 8th grade at a Jodo-Shinshu Buddhist temple ("church" back then) in Mountain View, California. My Dharma School ("Sunday School" then) introduced me to the life of Shakyamuni, the Four Noble Truths, the life of Shinran (1173–1262, the founder of Jodo-Shinshu), and his teachings. These had a much greater appeal to me than what I was getting at a Seventh Day Adventist Church, which I had attended the previous two years. Though the minister and members were devoted and caring, I could not appreciate their strict code of conduct, their "fairytale-like" teachings, and could not find an adequate answer to the gnawing question, "Why could an all-loving God create a world filled with such suffering and problems?" This dilemma (which I would learn years later is one of "theodicy"), as well as other problems, were pleasantly absent in Buddhism, which began with the very premise that "suffering is intrinsic to life." I felt much more at home in the Buddhist teaching.

I felt at home for another reason. I was supported ethnically and culturally, since virtually all the members were of Japanese descent, and there were plenty of cultural expressions that I was familiar with. I must have felt this sense of familiarity even more keenly than my American-born third-generation friends at the temple, for my family had arrived from Japan just four years earlier (though my family's connection to the United States goes back to the 1890s with my great-grandfather). The temple and Buddhism provided for me much-needed confidence, as it had taken a toll on me to be person of color living in a society that was far less diverse than it is today. The conservative Christian church that I had attended reinforced my sense of marginalization. To the contrary, at the Buddhist temple I was able to deepen my religious understanding, develop my leadership skills, and, as a result, thrive academically.

However, ethnic and cultural factors alone are not enough to sustain one's religious pursuit, particularly to make it one's career. By the end of my junior year at Stanford while majoring in Cultural Anthropology, I had decided to make Buddhism my career, either as a priest or an academic. The decision was motivated in great measure by my wish to make some meaningful contribution to an American society wracked by the social upheavals of the '60s and the early '70s. Like many of my peers, I felt a sense of excitement to participate in the collective effort to do "right" and to "change society." We were constantly critical of the evils of the "establishment," but I felt I had to find the "right" conduct for myself in a way that included a strong dosage of practice. Shinran, who served as my model, had spent twenty years as a monk engaged in rigorous practice before finding spiritual reconciliation through the Pure Land teaching of his teacher Honen at the age of twenty-nine.

However, the Jodo-Shinshu tradition I encountered in the 1960s was weak in its articulation of right conduct and practice. I went to Thailand for answers. Encouraged by my Anthropology professor, Robert Textor, I arrived at Wat Borwarneewais in Bangkok in the fall of 1970. I was placed under the tutelage of Venerable Khantipalo (a noted British-born Theravada monk), who was gracious enough to take me under his wing. Through that experience of living the life of a novice monk, I saw with my own eyes the utmost dedication with which many (though not all!) monks engaged in their practices.

Despite my respect for the monks, I quickly came to realize that I could not remain a monk for life. In all honesty, I yearned for a life as part of a family with children in a committed relationship with a woman, as well as for a more active involvement in a community and in the larger society. The monastic life of solitude (where one hardly spoke to anyone all day) was simply not what I could live with. Such an experience made me realize how precious human interactions are and how much I needed them for my survival. I thus disrobed after three months in the monastery and returned by way of going around the world, taking great care to visit the holy Buddhist sites of India, Sri Lanka, and Nepal.

Once back in the United States, I felt a greater confidence in being a Jodo-Shinshu Buddhist, for, once again, I had a model in Shinran. He had left the monkhood to marry and have children, to lead a life as "neither monk nor lay" (in his words *hiso-hizoku*). However, as noted earlier, my tradition lacked a clear and concrete articulation of its views on how to think about right conduct, practice, and participation in the world for laypersons, especially with families, seeking to live spiritual lives. What I have articulated in this essay constitutes a segment of my attempt to meet the needs of Jodo-Shinshu Buddhists living in the present-day U.S. and to share with others who are curious about the tradition. In so doing, I obviously had to push the boundaries of what is normally considered Jodo-Shinshu—for example, adopting the Six Perfections as the centerpiece of right conduct and practice to the degree that I do.

While the numbers of non-Japanese priests and lay members continue to increase in Jodo-Shinshu temples, the majority remain Japanese Americans, especially in California. As people of color, many Japanese Americans may find the guidelines empowering, for they emerge out of their cultural and ethnic heritage and not from the dominant Christian culture. I would be pleased for them if they find it so. For those unfamiliar with Jodo-Shinshu Buddhism, I hope the questions and answers below give you some understanding.

In my personal case, Buddhism served as "training wheels" when I once lacked confidence as a person of color, but today I resist any attempt to identify Buddhism with any particular ethnic or cultural group. Buddhist teaching is universal and belongs to all people regardless of ethnicity or culture. Such is the real appeal that Buddhism has for the U.S. and other countries.

What is the aim of Buddhism?

The purpose of practicing Buddhism is certainly not simply to be a "good" person. The goal of Buddhism is to become "real" by becoming more aware of the true nature of oneself and of one's relationship to the world. If our motivation is only to be good people, we can easily become self-righteous and bitter when things do not go our way. When we are motivated, however, by a desire for awareness, we often become "good" as a natural outcome of that process.

Shakyamuni Buddha began his search to understand himself, not to change the world. "The aim of Buddhadharma is to know oneself," goes the first line of a famous saying by Master Dogen, the founder of Soto Zen. In the Jodo-Shinshu tradition I am part of, we turn to the well-known saying by Master Shan-tao, one of the seven masters of Jodo-Shinshu: "To realize Shinjin awareness for oneself and then to share it with others" (*jishin kyoninshin*).

Efforts to contribute to the world in other than religious ways are important. But efforts to help and to make the world a better place to live must not be divorced from the quest for spiritual enlightenment for oneself and others.

But how can I encourage this spiritual enlightenment?

The primary way to increase this spiritual enlightenment is to listen to the Dharma, which enables us to realize its transformative effects in the context of our daily life experiences. It is in this context that chanting, meditation, and other "practices" are considered as aids to our listening. A Jodo-Shinshu Buddhist can engage in any of the well-known forms of Buddhist practice, even sitting meditation, so long as he or she does not see those efforts as the direct cause of enlightenment. The purpose of any of these efforts is to serve as a mirror to increase our awareness about our imperfections and increase our gratitude to our family and friends, the community, and the world.

I like to call these activities "self-effort," rather than "self-power," an ambiguous word in Jodo-Shinshu. Although Shinran (the founder of Jodo-Shinshu, 1173–1262) rejected the idea that we can actually liberate ourselves through our own power, he never rejected our efforts to understand the teachings. The two are quite different.

Efforts that we can make at home in our daily lives are extremely important. For this, we need to take advantage of the religious value of our home shrine. In Jodo-Shinshu Buddhism, the shrine can be the spiritual center of daily life. Sadly, however, the shrine is too often associated with death and the deceased loved ones. This was never more apparent than when high school students at a summer youth program exclaimed, "Creepy!" Perplexed, I responded, "What's creepy? How can you feel that way? You should feel safe and sound to be sleeping in the Buddha hall (*hondo*)!" But to no avail, the students wanted to sleep elsewhere and dragged their sleeping bags to the gymnasium.

This came as quite a shock to me. But as I thought about it, it is true that the home shrines are often cluttered with portraits of our deceased loved ones; in some cases, so much so that Amida's representation in the shrine can't even be seen. This practice helps keep the image of Buddhism as a religion for the dead and the afterlife. The correct custom dictates that the portraits of the deceased be placed away from the shrine and not within the shrine itself. Maintaining the shrine can be a wonderful household activity. Each member, including children, can help with the offering of the fresh flower and other offerings such as one's favorite snacks (e.g., Oreo cookies), and with keeping the shrine clean and neat.

What are other things we can do daily?

Eating time is a great time to remind ourselves of the teachings. Before and after meals, we do *gassho* as our humble expression of thanks for our food. We remind ourselves of the sacrifice made by the animals and plants. The taking of their lives for food is not our inherent right as humans, but a selfish act necessary for our survival. So eating is a privilege.

"Namu" in *Namu Amida Butsu* can be understood in this context to mean "I am deeply grateful for"; "Amida Butsu" represents all the plants, animals, fowl, and fish that have been sacrificed for our food. So, when we say the Nembutsu, we are more aware of "oneness" with the world. Without the world, there is no "I"!

I've found these ideas are well-known. But often they have not sunk in, and remain only as ideas in our head. Because of our human nature to forget, it's vital that these truths be internalized through daily reminders.

Through the sharing of these life experiences, Jodo-Shinshu teachings come alive. For example, when we are angry and sad, the cause is usually our ego, though it's often hard to admit or see it. Yes, the person who is "making" us angry may be a real jerk, but we must still remind ourselves that it's our desire to expect him to be at least "normal" that causes our anger. Such is our foolish nature! Having understood our assumptions and expectations from this spiritual perspective, we are better able to assess our circumstances by coming closer to the Buddhist ideal of "seeing things as they are" and thus more able to engage in Right Action.

What is meant by "right" here? Can you provide a more concrete set of guidelines as a framework for bringing the teachings to my daily life?

The Six Perfections (*paramitas*), a basic Mahayana Buddhist practice, can serve as point of reference. Please realize, once again, that in Jodo-Shinshu our primary motivation for following these guidelines is gratitude, and not a desire to be morally or spiritually good.

Because these Perfections were the practices primarily of monks and nuns, we as modern laypersons with school, work, and family obligations will not be able to fully (in reality, "slightly" is more accurate!) live up to the high ideals of the Perfections. Nevertheless, they point us in the right direction and clarify for us the Budddhist ideals and, more importantly, serve as mirrors to see ourselves more clearly. The Six Perfections are:

1. Sharing (*dana*): Being open to other opinions and to give of yourself in time and materials without expecting anything in return.

2. Conduct (*shila*) : Being responsible to oneself and to others in one's action. The key here is responsibility: we must be responsible for what we think, say, and do. However, the Ten Wholesome Actions (perhaps the most well-known precepts for laypersons in Mahayana schools) can assist those seeking a more concrete set of guidelines. The Ten Wholesome Actions are to refrain from the following ten activities:

   Taking life

   Taking what is not given

   Being involved in sexual misconduct

   Telling what is not true

   Slandering others

   Speaking ill of others

   Being involved in frivolous talk and gossip

   Being greedy

   Being hateful

   Being attached to unwholesome views.

3. Effort (*virya*): Making an earnest, sincere effort to cultivate ourselves and resolve conflicts and problems.

4. Patience (*kshanti*): Being patient, so as not to expect immediate solutions.

5. Meditation (*dhyana*): Being mindful or attentive to our motives and capabilities in our thoughts and actions. Trying to be honest with our own thoughts and feelings, to cultivate the mind of equanimity with regard to others, and not to always insist upon one's opinion as correct. The mindfulness can be strengthened by reciting "Namu Amida Butsu" (aloud or silently) whenever possible. For those desiring mental calm, you may avail yourself of the various forms of Buddhist meditation, or try *seiza*, Quiet Sitting (discussed later).

6. Wisdom (*prajña*): This in Jodo-Shinshu is none other than Shinjin awareness. This awareness encompasses our understanding of the truth of the Four Marks of Existence, which help us to see life much more clearly. The Four Marks function like the car windshield wiper on a rainy day that helps us to see more clearly what lies in front of us.

Of these Six Perfections, wisdom is the most important since it is the brain and heart. Wisdom serves as the source of our motivation, energy, and understanding for carrying out the other five Perfections. If the source is flawed, we cannot be effective.

How do you find calm and quiet in the craziness of the world?

I have found what I call Quiet Sitting (seiza) effective in meeting my need for calm and quiet especially during the course of a busy and hectic schedule. I simply sit in a chair with my back straight (leaning against the back of the chair is acceptable), arms resting on my lap, and my eyes closed. I inhale through my nose and then exhale through my mouth until my abdomen caves in as air escapes. I repeat this at a natural pace for my bodily rhythm.

Whenever I breathe out, I repeatedly recite "Namu Amida Butsu" quietly or silently in my mind.[1] After even five minutes of this, I am able to feel rested and a little more mindful. And when I breathe in, I think of the many people (such as my children) and current interests that fulfill and give meaning to my life. My very existence is the result of all that I receive from the outside. They are the "power through others," which is one way of appreciating the meaning of Other Power or Amida's Vow. And when I breathe out repeating the Nembutsu (Namu Amida Butsu), I am able to express my appreciation in the most profound way possible. This seiza can take place wherever you feel comfortable: outdoors, at the office, in your kitchen, in a bus, or before your home shrine.

I've heard that some people, including Buddhists, feel that Buddhists are not supposed to get involved in matters of the world, such as charities for the poor and also social and medical issues such as abortion, organ transplants, and the environment? Is that true?

The first category—social welfare (what you call "charities")—has been a large part of the Buddhist tradition from its earliest period. For example, selfless giving (dana) is a way of sharing with others who need help without expecting any return or recognition. Bodhisattvas are people of deep understanding and caring whose purpose in life is to help others. All Buddhists, by virtue of their spiritual growth, will automatically try to live the bodhisattva ideals.

The great Buddhist ruler of India, King Ashoka, third century BCE, is a prime example of one who lived according to Buddhist ideals. Throughout his vast empire he set up clinics and drug dispensaries for the sick. He also made the traveler's task safer and easier by building convenient hostels and tree-lined roads. Buddhists coming after King Ashoka have looked up to him as a model of social welfare and personal humility. Such people are careful not to let their deeds become a source of self-righteousness and false pride.

One such person in the Jodo-Shinshu tradition is Lady Takeko Kujo (1887–1928), a daughter of Monshu Myonyo Otani who was the twenty-first Abbot of the Nishi-Hongwanji Branch. During her short forty-two years of life, Takeko Kujo dedicated much of her adult life to giving greater voice to Buddhist women, for which she is regarded as the founder of the Buddhist Women's Association (*fujinkai*). When the 1923 Great Kanto Earthquake devastated the Tokyo area, she marshaled rescue efforts for the victims, which led to the building of Ashoka Hospital in line with the spirit of the Indian Buddhist king. It is said that Lady Kujo died from physical exhaustion stemming from her social welfare efforts.

The Buddhist emphasis on the mind and self-reflection puts more emphasis on personal growth before helping others. We cannot truly help others if we have not helped ourselves first. The good feeling we get when we give to a charity or a beggar is not necessarily bad, but from the Buddhist view can be a distraction. Motivation often determines the outcome of our action. If we hold some prejudicial attitudes toward someone or some groups of people, yet try to be charitable to them, our actions will not be as effective as if we were free from negative views. Again, the aim in Buddhism is to cultivate oneself in order to awaken to how things are and not just to be a good person. One becomes a good person as a natural outcome of awareness. But one should not make being morally good the primary goal, for that would be another form of ego. Basically, if we understand the teachings, we will automatically want to get involved. Look at King Ashoka and Shinran and their accomplishments. I believe this is also true for great people in other major religions: Gandhi, Dr. Martin Luther King, Jr., Mother Teresa, and Elie Wiesel, to name a few.

In Jodo-Shinshu, we must remember that our actions are to be rooted in our spiritual life of "expressing our deepest gratitude for the benevolence" (*ho'on gyo*). This benevolence is normally thought of as that of Amida Buddha, but I feel that the source of our gratitude must expand to include more, i.e., the other Buddhas, family members, teachers, friends, society, sentient beings, physical matter, and the universe.

How would you state the basic values for Jodo-Shinshu conduct in the world?

Professor Sen'e Inagi, a noted Jodo-Shinshu scholar and teacher in Japan, suggests the following five values based on Rennyo Shonin's teachings:

1. Listen to the teachings throughout one's life.
2. Refrain from quarreling with other schools and religions.
3. Fully actualize the mind of equality (*byodo-shin*) that sees and treats people and events in our lives with equanimity.
4. Respect and honor life.
5. Abandon superstitious and magical practices.

More concretely, this is how I find these values play out in my life:

I believe the world-universe in which we find ourselves, despite its downside and tragedies, is fundamentally compassionate. This vision finds expression in the *Larger Sutra*'s Bodhisattva Dharmakara, who through selfless sacrifice aspires to spiritually nourish and liberate all sentient beings.

The universe is an interconnected network in which I play a vital role. As a member of this community, I must do my share to contribute to its welfare. We cannot wistfully depend on transcendent beings to bail us out from the grave environmental, medical, and social crises that now threaten the survival of the world.

In making my contribution to the world, I should not be motivated by a desire to be a "good person" or feel righteous that I have done a "good deed." What I give back to the world pales in comparison to what I receive from the world. Plus, given my ego-centered ways, a "good" deed today will quickly be snuffed out tomorrow, or even the next moment, by acts driven by selfish motives.

I believe that most criminal offenses are a result of causes and conditions reflecting the socioeconomic environment of the offender. Though the offender must bear the responsibility for his or her actions, as a member of society I should help correct the underlying social problems as well as help rehabilitate the offender. Furthermore, I should not feel righteous in looking down upon these people, for I am reminded of Shinran's insight:

> It is not that you keep from killing because your heart is good. In the same way, a person may wish not to harm anyone and yet end up killing a hundred or a thousand people. (*Tannisho*, Chapter 13)

I believe there are no absolutes in matters of the conventional, everyday world. Crucial issues, in particular, involve complex sets of factors and yield no ready-made, black and white answers. Here are my guidelines, drawn from the teachings:

1. If at all possible, utmost effort must be made to preserve and foster life, and not to take life.

2. If I must terminate life, utmost care should be taken to be well informed about the subject. The decision-making must include a serious consideration for the welfare of all whose lives would be impacted; for a person is involved in a much wider interconnected set of relationships.

3. Whatever decision I make, I must be willing to bear my share of the responsibility for its consequences and not shift blame or responsibility onto others.

4. I do not make my ultimate aim in life to accumulate wealth, gain fame, or garner power.

5. I strive to live simply and to share my energy, time, and resources for the betterment of the world.

6. I strive to refrain from idle talk and to neither purposely create discord among people nor speak ill of others without any constructive intention.

7. I do not feel any need to consult or petition supernatural forces to satisfy worldly objectives or to allay my fears and anxieties. I, therefore, do not rely on horoscope reading, fortune-telling, or superstitious beliefs to serve as a guide in my life.

In sum, I cannot help but look to Shinran Shonin, whose life of ninety years was dedicated to reaching out to the world by sharing the teachings in person and through writings. This spirit is exemplified by a verse that concludes virtually all chanting during Jodo-Shinshu services:

> May this merit-virtue
> Be shared equally with all beings
> May we together awaken the Bodhi Mind,
> And be born in the realm of Serenity and Joy.

NOTES

1 *Namu Amida Butsu* is a chant of reverence to Buddha Amida. This chant is a key practice of Jodo-Shinshu Buddhism.

Don't Waste Time

REVEREND HILDA GUTIÉRREZ BALDOQUÍN

THERE IS A FAMOUS QUOTE by my Dharma great-grandfather, Shunryu Suzuki Roshi: "In the mind of a beginner there are many possibilities. In the mind of an expert, very few."

When I began to practice the teachings of the Buddha—and I purposely don't say, "when I began to practice Buddhism," because Gautama Buddha did not teach Buddhism, he taught the Dharma—I believed myself to be an expert on how to change the world, eliminate all the suffering that was assailing this planet, and consequently, be happy forever after. What fueled this conviction was in large part my sociopolitical and historical experience, at an early age, of revolution, immigration, family breakdown, and a deep sense of otherness, inferiority, aloneness, and loss. In other words, I *know* how bad things are, so I have the answer. And because I remember as a child experiencing deep fear and confusion and witnessing the pain, despair, fear, and anger of the adults around me, as an adult I had to figure a way out of it.

For me, the "way out" took the form of social activism, the practice of re-evaluation counseling, and a deep search for understanding the dynamics of oppression and human conflict. Yet after twenty years on that path, and regardless of achievements and successes, the feelings and emotions of little Hilda were still driving my life, along with the recurrent message that something was missing. That sense of otherness and feeling afraid, inadequate, and alone were never very far away. I knew there had to be an answer, yet my intellect could not come up with it.

Dogen Zenji, the founder of Soto Zen, says in the *Fukanzazengi*, his universal instruction in the practice of *zazen*, "Put aside the intellectual practice of investigating words and chasing phrases and learn to take the backward step that turns the light and shines it inward." The Dharma found me at a time when everything I had constructed to be real, permanent, and true came crashing down.

One of the constructions I had lived by was that one day racism would end—of course, due to my efforts. The deep realization that this was not going to happen in my lifetime, or in the lifetime of generations to come, began to set me free. I embraced the Dharma with the tent-revival passion of the newly converted. It has yet to fail me.

Now, in my experience, the Dharma comes in many shapes, forms, and colors. I have found Dharma not just in the classical teachings but also in the words of my grandmother, on roadside billboards, in fortune cookies, even on television. For example, at a time when I was in the grip of internalized oppression as a first-generation university student, and contemplating dropping out, I saw an ad for the United Negro College Fund, reminding me that "a mind is a terrible thing to waste."

My *abuela* often said to me, "La vida es corta, no pierdas tiempo"—life is short, don't waste time. Dogen Zenji tells us in the *Fukanzazengi*, "You have gained the pivotal opportunity of human form, do not pass your days and nights in vain." And inscribed on the *han*, the wooden instrument that calls Zen students to zazen, are the words: "Great is the matter of life and death. Awake, awake. Don't waste time."

I became very curious about all these messages to not waste time. So, being a good Capricorn, I got down to business. I continued to practice with deep faith—an unequivocal commitment to meditation as the tool, to the precepts as the container, and to the vow of saving all sentient beings as my heart's intention. The more I sat, the more I began to feel in my bones what it would mean to be free of all my suffering.

I found support and inspiration for this in the sutras. In the *Heart of Great Perfect Wisdom Sutra,* one of the most beloved texts in Mahayana Buddhism, we are privy to a conversation between Avalokiteshvara, the bodhisattava of compassion, and Shariputra, one of Buddha's disciples. The sutra opens with the following statement: "Avalokiteshvara Bodhisattva, when deeply practicing the *prajñaparamita* (wisdom), clearly saw that all five aggregates in their own being are empty, and thus was relieved of all suffering." The five aggregates are how Buddhism describes what makes up a human being: form or body, feelings, sensations, perceptions, and consciousness.

So I began to put some pieces together. Mindful attention helped me see that what I experienced as being solid, this very body, my feelings, my thoughts, my sensations—are impermanent. They come and go, and if I am able to just be present with them in the movement of coming and going without holding on to them or identifying with them, I don't suffer. What a discovery! It was at that moment that I ceased to be an expert.

Up to that point, I had very much embraced Buddha as the teacher and the Dharma as the teachings. However, I could not embrace the Sangha as my community, because when I looked around me to find support, connection, and companionship among my fellow practitioners, racism and heterosexism reared their heads, dressed in flashing liberal colors. I began to seek an answer for the dissonance I experienced, because I knew I could not do this practice alone. It is difficult, it is hard work, and there are no shortcuts, for in this practice we confront the most difficult individual in all of our lives—ourselves. So I knew I needed the Sangha, the community. Also, I had discovered that when I encountered difficulties, if instead of turning away from them I paid very close attention to what was happening, awareness would arise.

And this is what I discovered—the Dharma is like water. As it flows it takes the shape of whatever space it encounters. When I ran into difficulties they weren't due to the Dharma or the practice—the Buddha taught liberation. No, I was running up against the conditioned circumstances of our human experience. So I began to pay close attention once more. And this is what I saw: For the first time in the history of their westward journey, the teachings of Shakyamuni Buddha have taken root in culturally heterogeneous societies. Yet issues of race and racial oppression, as well as sexual orientation and other dimensions of power differences, are rarely explicitly addressed in Western Buddhist Sanghas. In light of this, beginning to explore issues of oppression, its impact on the human species, and the role of our conditioned "selves" in perpetuating it, is like undertaking the pilgrimage of a lifetime.

Describing this journey, Jan Chozen Bays, Zen teacher and co-abbot of Great Vow Monastery in Oregon, asks: "How do we encourage and delight each other in the only journey that really matters?" What is this journey? It is the journey to freedom. And what are some key tools needed in this journey? The tool of spiritual inquiry and the tool of deep practice. And what happens when we begin to apply these tools? We develop the discipline, walk steadfast on the Dharma path, and by doing so we can gather the fruits of our efforts in this very lifetime!

For me, an aspect of this discipline is to pay attention to what in my life I hold onto very tightly! The focus of the pilgrimage I have undertaken with my practice is twofold: seeing through the limitations of identity, and deeply studying the teaching that there is no solid, separate self. In my experience, systems of oppression necessitate notions of identity, and consequently, our habitual attachment to this notion perpetuates oppression. It is the nature of oppression to obscure the limitless essence, the vastness of who we are—that the nature of our mind is luminous, like a clear pool reflecting a cloudless sky. The teachings that are being passed down to me consistently ask of me, at times demand of me, to look deeply and challenge my habitual conditioned views. These views, which are part and parcel of this human existence, have the karmic capacity to overshadow true reality.

In the Second Noble Truth, the Buddha taught that the causes of suffering are greed (desire), aversion (hatred), and delusion (ignorance)—the Three Poisons. When we get stuck in any of these three, we confuse our inherent wholeness and the wholeness of others and spend our lives swimming—or, for those of us less skilled, drowning—in the river of suffering.

Into this river flow many streams. One is our habitual tendency to cling to what feels good and to reject what does not feel good. Another is our attachment to who we think we are. And a third stream of suffering that I have experienced is believing in a reality that has been conditioned by oppression. In this third stream, ignorance and fear are key ingredients. One reason oppression remains so firmly rooted is because our clouded minds project this distorted reality, and our conditioned selves—who we think we are—are kept very busy maintaining this reality.

Fear is at the core of oppression. I have observed in myself the manifestation of certain mind states that go along with this fear and how they play out at different levels. There is a grasping for security at the personal level that makes me believe that "I" exist. At the interpersonal level, there is an aversion to intimacy when I tell myself that I can't trust anyone and therefore I am not safe—which, at a deeper level, means I don't trust myself. I also see myself craving control by having to know it all and being able to provide all the answers. This, in turn, feeds into the delusion of separateness. I justify my craving for control by telling myself that I am alone.

These mind states can only continue to exist in the soil of ignorance. When we are immersed in them we create structures and systems that mirror our grasping, our aversion, our need for control, and our separateness. I call this dynamic the "systematization of mind states." In her book, *Emancipation and Consciousness*, my friend and colleague, the late Ricky Sherover-Marcuse, spoke of it as the "sedimented nature of mystified consciousness."

The sedimentation of mystified consciousness congeals into "character structures" and "personality types"—naturalized and normalized cages for the individuals who inhabit them. The habits engendered by domination become forms of living through which individuals reproduce the system of domination.

In endless turns of the wheel of samsara, these systems and structures, now institutionally embedded, separate us into "haves" and "have-nots," into painful and divided camps of targets and non-targets of oppression. The reflection of our confused minds is mirrored on a large scale in society and we continue to drown in the streams of suffering. Lost in the pain and confusion that is oppression, our lives become entangled, rigid, impenetrable—like a ball of rubber bands with us at the center.

When I allow these mind states to live on unabated, I hold tight to my views because they offer a sense of security. Yet this is false. The reality I construct is limited and what I think, believe, and hold fast to about the world completely obscures the true reality: the Buddha nature in us all.

Viveka, a Dharma teacher in the Western Buddhist Order tradition, states:

> The so-called original face of all beings is Buddha nature. It is unlimited, a completely open dimension of being, and ultimately ungraspable. Buddha nature is the potential for enlightenment that every human being possesses. Reflecting that we share this nature is recognition of our basic solidarity. It is to recognize the preciousness of human life across national boundaries, class distinctions, and color lines.

So what makes it possible for us to experience this "recognition of our basic solidarity?" By opening ourselves to the light of mindfulness and allowing this light to shine on our moment-to-moment experience, we begin to create the conditions for awareness to manifest. With awareness we can see that our mind's ignorance creates the conditions that perpetuate oppression. And from within this awareness we can then see and experience our ability to move from woundedness to wholeness with each breath. We can be free right now!

Awareness gives me the clarity that as soon as I am present in this moment, my suffering lessens. This clarity helps me to see I am responsible for my feelings, for my choices, and for my liberation. This, my friends, is true freedom. However, to get there is the work of a lifetime. It is hard work, at times painful and despairing, at times blissful and heartful. Only through my Dharma practice have I really experienced a radical shift in how I now pursue social activism. Now, instead of bringing politics into the Dharma I bring the Dharma into politics. A teaching that brings it all home can be found in the words of Ché Guevara: "At the risk of sounding like a fool, I believe that a true revolutionary is guided by feelings of love."

Once, during an intensive seven-day retreat, I was complaining to my teacher about the unbearable physical pain I was experiencing. I said, with desperation and clenched fists, "Why do I have to have this human body?" She took a deep breath, looked at me with deep kindness, and gently replied, "Think about it. If you did not have this body, you would not have the opportunity to become enlightened." A wave of gratitude began to sweep over me as my relationship to the pain shifted instantly.

Suddenly I understood the preciousness of the opportunity of having been born in a human body, and how our body allows us to experience those places where our work needs to happen. Now, in this very moment, is the only time we can undertake the work of liberation. Most important, we have the tool to do it.

His Holiness the Dalai Lama reminds us, "Our lives are like a flash of lightning." Let's not waste time, let's get on with the work that really matters. As we say in the Zen tradition, "practice as if your head was on fire." Can you think of a more noble endeavor?

Adapted from a talk given at Creating Community,
a retreat for Lesbian, Gay, Bisexual, Transgender and Queer people,
people of color, and the wider community.

DAIKOKU

The Truth Of Bringing the Teachings Home

This Was Not an Area of Large Plantations:

Suffering Too Insignificant for the Majority to See

ALICE WALKER

This was not an area of large plantations, since the land is hilly with some bottoms of rich soil. Whites usually had small or medium-sized farms with slaves....Percy Sanders, a descendant of an early black family in the area, recalled hearing as a child about George Slaughter, a white farmer's son by a black woman, who came to a horrible death because "he didn't keep his place." Ambushed by white men, including his own father, he was shot while riding his horse because the saddle horse was "too fine." The story goes that when he was found "the horse was drinking his blood."

—Constance Curry, (from the introduction to *Mississippi Harmony,*
Memoirs of a Freedom Fighter, by Winson Hudson and Constance Curry)

WHEN I WENT to live in Mississippi in the sixties and to work in the Civil Rights Movement, whose aim was to emancipate and empower African Americans who were still, thousands of them, treated as badly as and sometimes worse than slaves, I met Winson Hudson. She was trying to write the story of her life. I helped her, until I left Mississippi to live in New England. We sat under a tree and I wrote what she dictated. Today her story has become a book that will be available in a few months.

I begin my talk with this harrowing quote simply to ground us all in the reality of being African Americans, African Indians, African Amerindians. We are that mixture of peoples, brought together very often and for centuries in the most intense racial confusion, hatred, and violence. This horrible story, which has haunted me since I read it, is typical of the kind of psychic assault we endure, while it is exactly the kind of assault today's white majority takes no notice of, just as it took no notice two and three and one hundred years ago.

This story, so chilling —The horse was drinking his blood? His own father was one of the assassins? His crime was that his horse was too "fine"?—unfortunately is one in a storehouse of such stories those of us present might hear or expect to hear, on any given day of our lives. What do we do with the shock? What do we do with the anger? The rage? What do we do with the pain?

When I read this story last month I was sitting in a Federal Courthouse, preparing to do jury duty. I felt ill immediately. But not as ill as I would feel an hour later upon entering the courtroom, when I was confronted with the fact that three young men of color, one Asian, two Latino, were to be tried for the murder of a policemen, whom they allegedly killed when he interrupted their burglary of a steak house. One glance at the accused trio revealed the faces of malnourished children, barely out of their teens. The choice before the jury would be Life Imprisonment without Parole or the Death Penalty. The judge, white and middle class, well fed and well educated, seemed prepared to impose either choice.

Here were the contemporary brothers of George Slaughter.

My first version of this talk began with a poem by Basho:

> *Sitting quietly*
> *Doing nothing*
> *Spring comes*
> *And the grass*
> *Grows*
> *By itself.*

I was thinking of how I found my way from the backwoods of Georgia as a young woman into the company of the finest poets. It was a route of unbelievable, serious magic. As a child my family had no money to buy books, though all of us loved to read. Because I was injured as a child and blinded in one eye, the state gave me a stipend which meant I could buy all the books I wanted. When I went North to college, my first stop after settling in my room was the bookstore, where I entered a state of ecstasy seeing before me all the books of poetry I was literally dying to read. It was there in the Sarah Lawrence College bookstore that I encountered Basho and Buson and Issa, Japanese Buddhist haiku poets who had lived centuries before. And also a book called *Zen Telegrams* by Paul Reps. We connected on the profound level of Nature. That is to say, in these poets I discovered a kindred sensibility that respected Nature itself as profound, magical, creative and intelligent. There was no hint, as in other poetry, that simply because he was able to write about Nature, man was somehow, therefore, superior to it.

So this is the way I was going to start. But then I thought: It is more honest to start with the hard stuff. The stuff that makes addicts and slaves of Africans a hundred and fifty years after the Emancipation Proclamation. For I knew while sitting in that courtroom, having read the story of George Slaughter and acknowledging the young men before me as today's version of him, that the pain I was feeling is the same pain that sends our people reeling into streets and alleys looking for a "fix" to fix all that is wrong with this gruesome picture. It is the pain that undermines our every attempt to relieve ourselves of external and internalized white domination. The pain that murders our every wish to be free. It is a pain that seems unrelenting. A pain that seems to have no stopping and no end. A pain that is ultimately, insidiously, turning a generous, life-loving people into a people who no longer feel empathy for the world. We need only listen to African American comedians to see that our traditional compassion for Life has turned into the most egregious cynicism.

We are being consumed by our suffering.

We are a people who have always loved life and loved the earth. We have *noticed* Earth. How responsive and alive it is. *We have appreciated it.* We have been a nation of creators and farmers who adored the earth even when we were not permitted to own any part of it larger than our graves. And then only until a highway needed to be built or a condominium constructed on top of them.

I remember distinctly the joy I witnessed on the faces of my parents and grandparents as they savored the sweet odor of spring soil or the fresh liveliness of wind.

This compassionate, generous, life-affirming nature of ours, that can be heard in so much of our music, is our Buddha nature. It is how we innately are. It is too precious to lose, even to disappointment and grief.

Looking about at the wreck and ruin of America, which all our forced, unpaid labor over five centuries was unable to avert, we cannot help wanting our people who have suffered so grievously and held the faith so long, to at last experience lives of freedom, lives of joy. And so those of us chosen by Life to blaze different trails than the ones forced on our ancestors have explored the known universe in search of that which brings the most peace, self-acceptance and liberation. We have found much to inspire us in Nature. In the sheer persistence and wonder of Creation Itself. Much in Indigenous wisdom. Much in the popular struggles for liberation around the world, notably in Cuba, where the people demonstrate a generosity of spirit and an understanding and love of humankind that, given their isolation and oppression by our country, is almost incomprehensible. We have been strengthened by the inevitable rise of The Feminine, brought forward so brilliantly by women's insistence in our own time. And of course by our own African American struggle for dignity and freedom, which has inspired the world. In addition, many of us have discovered in the teachings of the Buddha wise, true, beautiful guidance on the treacherous path life and history set us upon.

Having said this, let me emphasize that I did not come to the study and practice of Buddhism to become a Buddhist. In fact, I am not a Buddhist. And Buddha would not have minded this in the least. He would have been happy to hear it. He was not, himself, a Buddhist. He was the thing Itself: an enlightened being. Just as Jesus Christ was not a Christian, but a Christ, an enlightened being. The challenge for me is not to be a follower of Something but to embody it; I am willing to try for that. And this is how I understand the meaning of both Jesus and Buddha. When the Buddha, dying, entreated his followers to "be a lamp unto yourself," I understood he was willing to free his followers even from his own teachings. He had done all he could do, taught them everything he had learned. Now, their own enlightenment was up to them. He was also warning them not to claim him as the sole route to their salvation, thereby robbing themselves of responsibility for their own choices, behavior, and lives.

I came to meditation after a particularly painful divorce. Painful because I never ceased to care for the man I divorced. I married him because he was one of the best people I'd ever encountered and he remained that way. However, life had other plans for us both. I left my home, as Buddha left his two thousand and five hundred years ago, to see if I could discover how I at least could be happy. If I could be happy in a land where torture of my kind was commonplace, then perhaps there was a general happiness to be found.

The person who taught me Transcendental Meditation was teaching out of the Hindu tradition and never mentioned the Buddha, the Four Noble Truths (about the fact of human suffering, its causes, the necessity to engage, endure and transform it) or the Eightfold Path, which provides a guide to moral, conscious living. What she did teach me was the deeper value of sitting quietly, doing nothing. *Breathing.* This took me back to childhood days when I did this without thinking. Days when I was aware I was not separate from the cosmos. Days when I was happy. This was actually a place where poets, time out of mind, have frequently lived. No wonder I felt at home there.

And so I laughed. The laughter bubbled up, irrepressible. I saw the path to happiness and to liberation at a glance. It was inside myself.

Now I understand that all great teachers love us. This is essentially what makes them great. I also understand that it is this love that never dies, and that, having once experienced it, we have the confidence always exhibited by well-loved humans, to continue extending this same love. Buddha, presumably raised as a Hindu, was no doubt disheartened by its racism, i.e., the caste system that today blights the lives of 160 million Indians. Indians who were once called "Untouchables" and now call themselves "Dalits" or "Those broken to pieces." They are not allowed to own land. They cannot enter the same doors, attend the schools, or drink from the same wells, as the so-called higher castes. Their shadow must never fall on those above them. They are brutalized and the women raped at will. *Niggers* of India, they are.

Traditionally it is taught that the Buddha discovered someone old, someone sick and someone dying, after having lived a very sheltered life, and that because of this suffering, inherent to all humankind, he struck out into the world to find a remedy. There's no mention, usually, of the horrible caste system, everywhere in place in his area, which I personally find impossible to imagine the Buddha ignoring.

I like to think of the young prince, Siddhartha, observing this hypocrisy of his native religion, perhaps touching or loving an "untouchable," and deciding there had to be a better way. A higher truth. I like to think of him leaving his cushy home and delightful family, his loving wife and adorable son, and striking out into the wilderness.

Which is to say, I felt Buddha's spirit long before I began to study his words. I felt him not as a god or as the son of a god but as a human being who looked around, as any of us might do, and said to himself: *Something here is very wrong. People are such beautiful and wondrous creations, why are they being tortured? What have they done that this should be so? How can there be an end to their suffering?*

The Buddha sat down.

Most of the representations of the Buddha show him sitting down. Sometimes he is lying down. Sometimes he is walking, though this is rare. Sometimes he is shown leaping to his feet and flinging up his arms in joy. Anyone who meditates recognizes these states. First, the sitting. The concentration on the breath. Sometimes the lying down, feeling our connection to The Mother, the great support of Earth. There is the walking, which integrates our bodies with our mind state. Then there is the feeling of exuberance when we realize we have freed ourselves. *Again.*

How does this happen?

I imagine there are people who turn to Buddha because they've lost a lot of money. My experience however is that almost everyone I've met that has turned to Buddha did so because they have suffered the end of a love affair. They have lost someone they loved. Perhaps they have lost a country, as well, or parents or siblings or some function of their bodies. But very often, people turn to the Buddha because they have been carried so deeply into their suffering by the loss of a loved one that without major help they fear they will never recover. (I actually love this about Buddhists; that though their reputation is all about suffering and meditating and being a bit low key sexually and spiritually languid, they are in fact a band of hopeful lovers who risk their hearts in places a Methodist would rarely dare to tread.)

This is what happened to me. I had lost my own beloved. The pain of this experience seemed bottomless and endless. Enter my teacher for that moment of my life, the Buddhist nun Pema Chödrön and her teachings on a set of tapes called *Awakening Compassion.* Under her guidance, far in the country away from everyone, on my own retreat of one, I learned an ancient Tibetan Buddhist meditation practice called Tonglen along with the teachings that accompanied it, called Lojong. This involved, during meditation, learning to breathe in the pain I was feeling, not to attempt to avoid or flee it. It involved making my heart bigger and bigger just to be able to hold it all. It involved breathing out relief and happiness for myself and for everyone on Earth who was feeling as miserable as I was. I stayed at this practice for a year.

It worked.

So that today I sometimes wonder what my suffering over the loss of a loved one was really about. And I have almost concluded that it was again the love of the Buddha reaching through two thousand and five hundred years wanting me to understand I had some control over how much suffering I endure. Wanting me to try a remedy he had found and to see for myself whether it works.

My novel *The Color Purple* was actually my Buddha novel without Buddhism. In the face of unbearable suffering following the assassinations and betrayals of the Civil Rights movement, I too sat down upon the Earth and asked its permission to posit a different way from that in which I was raised. Just as the Buddha did, when Mara, the king of delusion, asked what gave him the right to think he could direct humankind away from the suffering they had always endured. *When Mara queried him, the Buddha touched the Earth.* This is the single most important act, to my mind, of the Buddha. Because it acknowledges where he came from. It is a humble recognition of his true heritage, his true lineage. Though Buddhist monks would spend millennia pretending all wisdom evolves from the masculine and would consequently treat Buddhist nuns abominably, Buddha clearly placed himself in the lap of the Earth Mother, and affirmed Her wisdom and Her support.

It has been enormously helpful to me to learn that Buddha's wife and son eventually joined him in the wilderness and that she became both a follower and a teacher. There was love between them, for sure. How I wish we had a record of some of her thoughts. The male effort to separate Wisdom from the realm of the Feminine is not only brutal and unattractive but it will always fail, though this may take, as with Buddhism, thousands of years. This is simply because The Feminine is Wisdom, and it is also the Soul. Since each and every person is born with an internal as well as an eternal Feminine, just as everyone is born with an internal and eternal Masculine, this is not a problem except for those who insist on forcing humans into gender roles. Which makes it easier for them to be controlled.

Sometimes, as African Americans, African Indians, African Amerindians, People of Color, it appears we are being removed from the planet. Fascism and Nazism, visibly on the rise in the world, has always been our experience of white supremacy in America, and this has barely let up. Plagues such as AIDS seem incredibly convenient for the forces that have enslaved and abused us over the centuries and who today are as blatant in their attempts to seize our native homelands as Columbus was 500 years ago. Following the suffering and exhilaration of the sixties a pharmacopia of drugs suddenly appeared just as we were becoming used to enjoying our own minds. "Citizen Television," which keeps relentless watch over each and every home, claims the uniqueness and individuality of the majority of our children from birth. After the assassinations of Martin Luther King, Jr., Malcolm X, Ché Guevara, and so many other defenders of humanity, known and unknown, around the globe, we find ourselves in the year 2002 with an un-elected president who came to office by disenfranchising black voters, just as was done, routinely, before Martin Luther

King, Jr. and the rest of us were born. This is a major suffering for black people and must not be overlooked. I myself, on realizing what had happened,
felt a soul sickness I had not experienced in decades. Those who wanted power
beyond anything else—oil and the money to be made from oil (which is the
Earth Mother's blood) —were contemptuous of the sacrifices generations of
our ancestors made. The suffering of our people, especially of our children,
with their bright, hopeful eyes, is of no significance to them. George Slaughter —the surname would have been his master/father's, and deadly accurate—
was not killed, we intuit, because his "saddle horse was too fine," he was killed
because *he* was too fine.

This is the bind we are in.

*There is a private joke I have with myself: The question is: Why did Europeans
enslave us in Africa and take us to the United States?*

The answer: Because we would not go voluntarily.

The African Americans who are aiding and abetting the rape and pillage of
Earth, helping literally to direct the bombs that fall on the innocent and the
exquisite, are still another cause of our suffering. We look into their eyes and
experience a great fright. They appear so familiar, and yet, somehow, we feel
they are not. I do not call their names because essentially they are, as we are,
energies. And they are familiar because they have been around just as long as
we have. It is also necessary to acknowledge that some of those energies we
find so frightening exist within ourselves.

This poem, which I think of as one of my "bitter" poems, expresses something of their position, when they can bear to acknowledge it, throughout the
long centuries:

"They Helped Their Own"

> *They helped their own*
> *They did not*
> *Help us*
> *We helped*
> *Them*
> *Help*
> *Themselves*
> *Beggars*
> *That*
> *We are.*

Underneath what is sometimes glibly labeled racism or sexism or caste-ism, there lurks covetousness, envy, and greed. All human states that can, through practice, be worked with and transformed. This is the good news for our oppressors, as it is for humans generally, since we all have these qualities to a degree. The equally good news for us is that we can turn our attention away from our oppressors—unless they are directly endangering us to our face—and work on the issue of our suffering without attaching them to it. The teaching that supports that idea is this:

Suppose someone shot you with an arrow, right in the heart. Would you spend your time screaming at the archer, or even trying to locate him? Or would you try to pull the arrow out of your heart? White racism, that is to say, envy, covetousness, and greed, (incredible sloth and laziness in the case of enslaving others to work for you), is the arrow that has pierced our collective heart. For centuries we have tried to get the white archer even to notice where his arrow has landed; to connect himself, even for a moment, to what he has done. Maybe even to consider apologizing, which he hates to do. To make reparations, which he considers absurd.

This teaching says: Enough. Screaming at the archer is a sure way to remain attached to your suffering rather than easing or eliminating it. A better way is to learn, through meditation, through study and practice, a way to free yourself from the pain of being shot, no matter who the archer might be.

There is also the incredibly useful assurance that everything is change. Everything is impermanent. The country, the laws, the Fascists and Nazis, the archer and the arrow. Our lives and their lives. *Life.* Looking about at the wreckage, it is clear to all that in enslaving us, torturing us, trying to get "ahead" on the basis of our misery, our oppressors in the past had no idea at all what they were doing. They still don't. As we practice, let this thought deeply root. From this perspective, our compassion for their ignorance seems the only just tribute to our survival.

Who or *What* knows what is really going on around here anyway? Only the *Tao,* or *Life* or *Creation* or *That Which is Beyond Human Expression.*

> *Sitting quietly*
> *Doing nothing*
> *Spring comes*
> *And the grass*
> *Grows*
> *By itself.*

This place of peace, of serenity and gratitude does exist. It is available to all. In a way, this place of quiet and peacefulness could be said to be our shadow. Our deserved shadow. Our African Amerindian shadow. In European thought the shadow is rarely understood as positive, because it is dark, because it is frequently behind us, because we cannot see it; but for us, ultra-sensitive to the blinding glare of racism and suffering daily the searing effects of incomprehensible behavior, *our shadow of peace*, that we so rarely see, can be thought of as welcoming shade, the shade of an internal tree. A tree that grows beside our internal river and bathes us in peace. Meditation is the path that leads to this internal glade. To share that certainty is the greatest privilege and joy.

I am grateful for the opportunity to join you in this first ever African American Buddhist retreat in North America. Though not a Buddhist, I have found a support in the teachings of the Buddha that is beyond measure, as I have found comfort and support also in those teachings I have received from Ancient Africans and Indigenous people of my native continent and from the Earth Itself.

The teacher who has been most helpful to me, in addition to Pema Chödrön, is Jack Kornfield, an extraordinary guide and human being, whose books and tapes, among them *A Path With Heart, After the Ecstasy the Laundry*, and *The Roots of Buddhist Psychology*, I would recommend to anyone who seeks a better understanding of the Enspirited Life; Sharon Saltberg's book *LovingKindness: The Revolutionary Art of Happiness* has been an incomparable gift. Recently, in a book called *Knee Deep in Grace*, I discovered the teachings of the Indian female yogi, householder and mother, Dipa Ma. Her instructions and observations seem endlessly potent.

I am deeply grateful to all the teachers who came before these four that I have mentioned. Teachers from Vietnam (Thich Nhat Hanh has been a beloved teacher), Thailand, Burma, India, China, and especially Tibet. I thank the Dalai Lama for allowing himself to be a symbol of good in a world that seems, at times, hopelessly tilted toward evil. I thank Martin Luther King, Jr. for the warm, brotherly, touch of his hand when I was young and seeking a way to live, with dignity, in my native land in the South. And for the sound of his voice, which was so full of our experience. I thank him for loving us all so very much. If he had been able to live and teach, as the Buddha did, until the age of eighty, how different our world would be. It is such a gift to have his books and recordings of his words; and to be able to understand his death as a teaching on both the preciousness of human existence and impermanence.

And, as always, I thank the ancestors, those who have gone on and those who are always arriving. It is because our global spiritual ancestors have loved us very dearly that we today sit together practicing ways to embody peace and create a better world. I feel personally ever bathed in that love.

Let's sit for ten minutes.

Let us bring our attention to the life of our young brother, our murdered ancestor, George Slaughter. We know he was a beautiful young man, and that it was this beauty and his freedom expressing it that caused his father, *himself unfree*, to seek his death. *We can see George sitting on his stunning saddle horse.* We do not know if his half-sister, white, confused by her liking for her darker brother, gave it to him. We do not know if his mother, dark and irresistible, as so many black women are, gave it to him. We do not know if he bought it himself. All we know is that *he is sitting there, happy. And the horse, too, is happy.*

George Slaughter, an English name. We might think of Bob Marley, half English, with his English name: perhaps George had a similar spirit. A kindred look and attitude.

> *May you be free*
> *May you be happy*
> *May you be at peace*
> *May you be at rest*
> *May you know we remember you*

Let us bring our attention to George's mother. She who came, weeping, and picked up the shattered pieces of her child, as black mothers have done for so long.

> *May you be free*
> *May you be happy*
> *May you be at peace*
> *May you be at rest*
> *May you know we remember you*

Let us bring our attention to George's father. He who trails the murder of his lovely boy throughout what remains of Time.

> *May you be free*
> *May you be happy*
> *May you be at peace*

May you be at rest
May you know we remember you

Let us bring our attention to those who rode with the father, whose silence and whose violence caused so much suffering that continues in the world today.

May you be free
May you be happy
May you be at peace
May you be at rest
May you know we remember you

And now let us bring our attention to George's horse. With its big dark eyes. Who drank George's blood in grief after the horror of his companion's bitter death. We know by now that the other animals on the planet watch us and know us and sometimes love us. How they express that love is often mysterious.

May you be free
May you be happy
May you be at peace
May you be at rest
May you know we remember you

I cherish the study and practice of Buddhism because it is good medicine for healing us so that we may engage the work of healing our ancestors. Ancestors like George. Ancestors like George's father.

Both George and his father are our ancestors.

What heals ancestors is understanding them. And understanding as well that it is not in heaven or in hell that the ancestors are healed. *They can only be healed inside of us.* Buddhist practice, sent by ancestors we didn't even know we had, has arrived, as all things do, just in time.

> *Adapted from a talk given at the African American Dharma Retreat*
> *and Conference. Spirit Rock Meditation Center, August 2002.*

"How Can I Be a Buddhist If I don't Like to Sit?":

Learning to Listen with Love to Self and Others

ROSA ZUBIZARRETA

WHAT DOES IT MEAN to practice Buddhism? I remember vividly the day a friend confessed to me that she felt deeply drawn to Buddhist teachings, yet felt hesitant to consider herself a Buddhist since she was not at all drawn to sitting practice. Her confession felt like a revelation to me; until then I had felt alone and awkward in my own preferences.

My earliest exposure to Buddhism was probably around age nine. Seeking solace from the emotional trauma of my parents' divorce and from the loneliness of being an immigrant child and social outcast, I perused world religions in the Compton's encyclopedia my mother had bought from a door-to-door salesman. Years later, I found a small inscription I'd written from that time: "Dear God, please grant me nirvana."

My interest in Eastern religions continued during my teen years. During college, a feminist awakening led to a greater skepticism. After all, wasn't the focus on "mind" and "absolute reality" just a more subtle and sophisticated way to denigrate the world of body and matter, the realm so often associated with women? It wasn't until encountering Tsultrim Allione's *Women of Wisdom* that the conflict began to resolve and I felt a renewed call to Buddhism.[1]

The summer of 1987, as I was struggling to get over the end of a disastrous romantic relationship, a poster announcing a lecture about the Chod teachings from the Tibetan Buddhist tradition caught my eye. I knew these powerful teachings designed to overcome the fear of death had been created by a woman in the fourteenth century.

I still remember vividly listening to the words of H. E. Tai Situ at the event. He began by carefully explaining that to be a Buddhist meant taking refuge in the Buddha, the Dharma, and the Sangha. Taking refuge in the Buddha did not only mean taking refuge in the historical Buddha; it meant taking refuge in the

Buddha nature of all sentient beings. Taking refuge in the Dharma did not just refer to the historical teachings of the Buddha; it meant looking deeply at everything, as a manifestation of the natural laws of the universe. Taking refuge in the Sangha did not consist only of finding inspiration in the community of ordained monks and nuns; it also meant understanding the nature of inter-dependent origination, and being grateful for everyone and everything in our path as an opportunity for awakening.

I couldn't honestly say whether Tai Situ actually said the words, "If you believe this, you are already a Buddhist," or if I only heard them in my own mind. Nonetheless, the gist of his message was clear: all that was needed in order to "be a Buddhist" was to take refuge in Buddha, Dharma, and Sangha. Everything else, all of the teachings of the Buddha, I was free to test against my own experience. At last, I had found a home for my heart, one with a strong and solid foundation as well as doors and windows wide open for my questioning mind. I delighted in taking refuge over and over as a practice, being nourished by affirming my own deepest truth.

But what about sitting meditation? Tai Situ had spoken at length about Buddha nature, likening it to a sun that is ever-present, even when we are not able to perceive it directly due to the clouds of suffering caused by our own obscurations. So, how might we shift from our present state of suffering to a clear and stable experience of Buddha nature? With a shrug, he concluded firmly that in Buddhist tradition, meditation is the "best way we know" to do so....

Just as everything else had rung true for me, I now felt a "disconnect" inside. I resonated deeply with the need to shift from the experience of suffering to the experience of the cessation of suffering. At the same time, from a brief and distressing introduction to Vipassana, I already knew that "sitting practice" was not likely to be the most helpful path for me, and that I would need to find other ways. Given my early experiences of isolation, I did not have the inner strength to "bear witness" alone to the pain that surfaced when I sat in meditation. On a few occasions, my attempts at sitting practice had allowed me to connect with a deeper "inner stream" beneath my emotional turmoil. But the instructions were to simply "let go" of the experiences of inner joy and insight that would surface, and that only served to increase my alienation.

Thank goodness, Tai Situ had not said that I needed to sit in order to be a Buddhist! Instead, I began reading the detailed Tibetan overviews of all the various forms of practice and "stages of the path." Initially, I felt drawn to the Vajrayana, very advanced and powerful practices which involve visualizations of deities. In my eagerness, I wanted to take the express train to enlightenment! Yet these practices involved taking vows to see one's teacher as an enlightened being, and every action of theirs as an enlightened action. Given the kind of family dynamics I had experienced while growing up, I realized that this would not be the path for me. Instead, I found myself moving backwards, much like Alice in Wonderland, from an initial fascination with Tantric practices, to falling in love with the Mahayana Bodhisattva Vow to commit one's self to relieving the suffering of all sentient beings, to a deep appreciation for the practice of ethical conduct and generosity (the foundation of Theravada practice), to my initial practice of taking refuge, and even further back, to the "Four Preliminaries" that are considered a preparation for taking refuge vows. I felt I could spend a lifetime contemplating that we are of the nature to change, to grow old, to die, and to be separated from those we love, daring myself to gaze unblinkingly at these uncomfortable truths every day as a prelude to the fundamental question, "How, then, shall we live?"

Most of this time studying and exploring different types of Buddhism was time spent alone, except when I had the opportunity to listen to Dharma talks by visiting lamas. For three long years as a child, books had been my only friends, so in some ways this time I spent as a solitary student of Buddhism felt quite natural to me. Yet I began to feel a growing longing for a community with which to practice, a longing which led to the next stage in my Buddhist path.

I found myself being drawn to the writings of Thich Nhat Hanh, both to his radiant joy as well as to his willingness to engage with the suffering caused by social injustice. I was particularly drawn to his teachings about deep listening, since the self-help, peer-based practice of re-evaluation counseling had been one of the most powerful healing practices in my life to that point. As a result, I began to explore the local communities of practice which had begun to form in this tradition.

While Thich Nhat Hanh's gentle instructions helped me become somewhat more comfortable with sitting practice, I found that I much preferred the walking meditation. And after some friends and I started the Mindfulness, Diversity, and Social Change Sangha in Oakland, California, Council circle became my favorite practice. Offering deep listening to each person in turn, practicing patience as we listened without interruption, each week we wove a web of caring and presence. Within that web, each one of us was gently held as we connected with the truth of our own experience and limitations, as well as the truth of the aspirations that inspired our practice.

So I related deeply to my friend's "confession" about disliking sitting meditation. This was especially poignant to me because this woman had dedicated
her life to the bodhisattva path of compassionate communication and had a
way of listening deeply beneath any anger, hate, or violence, to the suffering
being who desired to be happy. Even though she felt a great connection to
Buddhist teachings, she did not feel comfortable seeing herself as a "Buddhist,"
simply because she did not like to sit. I can't help but see this as an enormous
loss to our growing Buddhist communities in the West. After all, in Asia,
laypeople who may never sit are considered an integral part of the larger religious community.

In the years following that conversation, I have continued to feel called to a
variety of listening practices. Whether one-on-one or in group settings, simple yet skillful listening allows us to honor our suffering, our conflicts, and
our differences—the truth of our relative experience—as well as our absolute
nature, the interdependent radiance within us all.

At the same time, I continue to explore various meditation approaches. Loving kindness meditation retreats with Sharon Salzberg, where we concentrate
on offering love and compassion to self and others, have been particularly
helpful. Still, listening compassionately—both to my own truth and to that of
others—is where I feel most alive.

Harold Thurman Whitman said, "Don't ask yourself what the world needs,
ask yourself what makes you come alive, and then go do it. Because what the
world needs is people who have come alive." I hope you will discover your own
forms of practice, in whatever way helps you connect with the Buddha nature
in all beings, in whatever way helps you understand the Dharma inherent in all
living things, and in whatever way helps us all to realize our profound interconnectedness.

Our lives depend on it.

NOTES

1 London: Routledge and Kegan Paul, 1984.

Internal Disarmament

LOURDES ARGÜELLES AND ANNE RIVERO

I T IS RAINING. We are sitting in our small retreat quarters at Deer Park Monastery in southern California. On our table is a copy of *Interbeing*, a precious little book by Thich Nhat Hanh. We have spent most of this week-long retreat in sitting and walking meditation, struggling to remain in the present moment, but today, a "lazy day" as it is called here, we rest in our small room, talking and reflecting on anger, action, and our last journey to India.

Several years ago, the two of us had worked with a few others to create a successful animal welfare program in a Tibetan Buddhist monastery and nearby Tibetan refugee community in South India. The program provides medical care, including rabies vaccinations, to a large number of stray dogs, household pets, and farm animals. Several monks, nuns, and laypeople have been trained to assist the program staff veterinarian in carrying out the hands-on veterinary work. Young Tibetans associated with the program will soon be sponsored to attend veterinary school and return to practice in this and similar settings.

By many accounts, the program appeared to be a success. The local office of the government of Tibet had called the program incredibly useful. The abbot of the monastery, residents of the refugee camps, and Indian subsistence farmers in the surrounding area all had shared their positive experiences with the program. His Holiness the Dalai Lama had recommended that other Tibetan monasteries and refugee communities consider developing similar initiatives. As we looked back years later, however, we did not feel completely at peace with our recollections of our animal project experience. We had tried to be skillful in our program design and to take into consideration the needs of the animals, the people, the community, and the environment. From the start we were eager to involve not only the Tibetan community, but also the Indian farmers who struggled for a subsistence livelihood in the lands surrounding the monastery grounds and the Tibetan refugee areas. Our hope was to assist them in taking care of their old or infirm domestic animals, animals that insured their livelihood. We had tried to address environmental concerns and had exchanged ideas with many Tibetan Dharma friends who were also saddened by the conditions of animals in and near the monastery grounds. In initiating the program we had followed monastery and Office of Tibet protocols and had secured the commitment of several patrons who promised to continue financing the project for several years until it could become self-sustaining. We felt the work was truly a step in mindfully practicing for the sake of all sentient beings, but something still did not feel right. Then during that quiet afternoon, sitting with the rain and Thây's little book, we realized how much we had been motivated in our work by not only a desire to help all beings, but also by a great deal of anger.

The program we had initiated was indeed successful by conventional indicators, but it had been inspired to a large extent by our anger and frustration at the suffering of animal beings and at folk-Buddhist concepts of why that suffering was inevitable. Because we were acting from this root anger, we brought considerable unnecessary pain to many involved, including ourselves. We recognized that with our tendency to be time-pressured and often exhausted, frustrated, and angry in our everyday lives, we had gradually become more isolated and had allowed our formal Dharma practice to be given less emphasis than our social activism priorities. The tendency to anger was the direct result of a weakening of our Dharma practice and the absence of a strong Sangha. The perceived urgency of the situation of the animals and our own individualistic tendencies toward using the energy of anger to drive the tasks of activism and change no doubt contributed to our loss of focus on the management of our own negative states of mind and the detrimental effects of that negativity. In reflecting upon our own anger, we came to renew our understanding about the connections between Buddhist practice and social activism.

It became more clear that in relying solely on hard and fast ethical principles, even Buddhist ones, without continued mindfulness and deep looking inward with the support of a strong spiritual community, we had been in danger of losing our way. The positive reception of the project had distracted us away from mindful reflection on the process and had played on our strong attachment to results. Only later, with time for quiet self-examination, did we recognize that we had not kept an optimal balance of inner and outer work. When we finally took the time to look below the surface of the positive outcomes of the project, we were able to see several not so positive effects. With our unbalanced emphasis on outer work, our own Buddhist practice had continued to deteriorate, as had our connections with friends and teachers who, in our self-righteousness, we had perceived as ill-willed or not sufficiently caring.

In reflecting upon the state of mind that would be most helpful in our social engagement we are reminded of what His Holiness the Dalai Lama calls "internal disarmament" which involves the ongoing work of taming our own ego-based delusions, self-righteousness, and negative emotions. Internal disarmament is a necessary complement to external disarmament, and non-violent activism, and seems a necessary requirement for the practice of the Noble Eightfold Path. Internal disarmament represents a deeper level of mindfulness and transformation than mere insight and intellectual awareness. Whatever one's spiritual tradition, highest priority must be given to finding time and space for individual and shared spiritual practice while remaining committed to social praxis.

As we have engaged in these reflections, we have begun, individually and jointly, to redefine our practice guidelines and priorities. For Lourdes, awareness that the seeds of her anger had been deeply watered in the past by the dramatic political events in her native Cuba, the painful experiences of exile from her country, and the subsequent resettlement in an alien and aggressive society has emphasized the need for maintaining a mindful practice of remaining in the present moment at all times, but especially when engaged in social activism. Thus, mindful breathing, walking meditation, and *gatha* recitation will be needed to complement her more formal ritualized practices from the Tibetan tradition.

For Anne, the mindfulness practices also seem to be more urgently needed at present in her efforts to counteract the seeds of frustration, impatience, anger, and anxiety that had been watered and fertilized by painful family experiences. She gives high priority to a regular sitting practice, which most often takes the form of a meditation on the breath, as taught by Thich Nhat Hanh, but which also may, at times, be devoted to a more complicated and structured practice involving elements such as visualizations and use of mantras in the Tibetan tradition. Anne also greatly benefits from mindfulness practices which contribute to present moment focus as an aid in neutralizing the sense of constant rushing through insufficient time.

Both of us will continue searching for ways to work with other activists from Buddhist and non-Buddhist traditions and from a variety of political perspectives. In this process the reflections on our experiences in India will be a constant reminder that the path of liberation for all sentient beings is to be walked in a state of both internal and external disarmament.

Carrying the Dharma en Español

JULIA SAGEBIEN

How I Became a Buddhist

I WAS BORN in Havana in 1954, in a sweltering August night. It was so hot that my mother tells me that she went to the ocean every day to float her belly to relieve the weight and that she could only stand to eat watermelon for the last three weeks of her pregnancy. Perhaps I had been a yogi who failed in *tummo* (the Tibetan practice of generating inner heat usually practiced in freezing caves) in my last life and my incessant complaints had all resulted in a tropical new life.

My French, Italian, and Spanish ancestors, on both sides of the family, had been in Cuba for three generations. This was certainly their home. My fate, like that of many in the exile generations, would be somewhat different. My first memory at three years of age would be on an airplane traveling to Lima from Havana—sleeping bunks for the first class passengers, people moving about through narrow corridors in dimmed light. Waking up to life in Peru, a country so different from Cuba, nourished an exhilarating and lifelong sense of wonder. In Peru, there were majestic mountain ranges, a cold ocean, Andean people and their ancient rich culture, and English and German primary schools. Though my father had taken a position in Lima as a temporary post, the Cuban Revolution made it impossible to go back home. The search for a home would eventually lead us to Mexico, Panama, Puerto Rico, the Dominican Republic, and the United States.

A peripatetic life could perhaps predispose one to see the world as impermanent, based on relative conditions, not very solid at all. But moving to Miami at fifteen years of age was perhaps the experience that most indelibly marked me as a good candidate for Buddhism. My first day of high school, I had to read "Jabberwocky," Lewis Carroll's onomatopoeic poem, as homework. Not one word in the entire poem was in the dictionary. My Cuban relatives had never seen them either. My parents could not help since they had not yet arrived in the U.S.A. I panicked.

Did I know any English at all? How would I survive? Deeply embarrassed, I confessed to my English teacher that I had failed to complete the assignment. Mrs. Braithwaite looked at me with great kindness and said, "Oh, my poor child." Maybe it was all incomprehensible, but at least I had found out that there would be kind people around to help me out along the way.

If Buddhism is a form of existentialism without complaint, I certainly entered the path as Camus's stranger. Everything seemed to further deepen my sense of alienation and the glimpses of what eventually I would know as emptiness. At pep rallies and football games, dozens of "Panthers"(mostly blond boys and girls) would scream "Kill!" to the marching tune of off-key brass bands. I can't remember the name of the team we were supposed to kill. I just remember that I did not understand why this was happening or how I was supposed to be an accomplice in this crime.

Outside of the small enclave of Little Havana around Miami's 8th Street, South Florida in the late '60s was the deep American South, a good world, but a world very different from mine. High school race riots fueled by rumors of nearby Ku Klux Klan rallies only made my participation in pot-laced rock and roll concerts, peace marches, and Vietnam Moratoriums more enthusiastic and simply necessary as a counterbalance.

Hormones only confused the family dynamics even more. In my teens, I did not discover boys. I discovered a confusing emotional void. My sexual orientation was, as I had feared since I was five years old, "different." My mother's hormones were raging too. She was going through menopause. She did not speak English, nor did she drive. Her husband was away on business most of the time. Her oldest daughter, today a Superior Court judge in Puerto Rico, was at Barnard College in New York City burning her bra as a feminist protest. In Miami, she was losing her youngest little genius child, her precious princess, to an incomprehensible world. Although she couldn't realize it at the time, it was all incomprehensible to me too. We became close in our shared bewilderment, in our sad empty hearts.

How I Found My Teacher

At seventeen I dropped out of high school with a straight A average, great standardized test scores and a deep depression. Fortunately, I was rescued by

Hampshire College a very progressive liberal arts school in western Massachusetts. Finally, I was back in a world of intellectual and spiritual curiosity. While at Hampshire I explored all the spiritual options that came my way. I took a transcendental meditation course. I attended a Gurdjieff group in New Hampshire. I took yoga. I met Trungpa Rinpoche at Harvard. He was giving a lecture entitled "Open Secret." He did not say much at all. Just that the Dharma was an open secret. There were near riots. Neither the academics, nor the spiritual shoppers were getting their money's worth. Rinpoche (as he was known by his students) really seemed to enjoy the fracas. I liked this guy.

I took a leave of absence from Hampshire in the summer of 1973. I worked at a fancy macrobiotic restaurant in Boston in order to save money for a trip to South America where I hoped to find my roots (or something that made sense). A good friend and Gurdjieff colleague invited me to accompany him to a seminar at Tail of the Tiger retreat center in Vermont. Chögyam Trungpa was going to teach a seminar on Carlos Castaneda's *The Teachings of Don Juan.* I remember very little about the seminar—250 hippies in a small Vermont farmhouse and the fact that Rinpoche liked the book but warned us that it did not offer a path we could easily follow. During one lecture, Rinpoche asked Baba Ram Dass to sit at his feet and talk about the bodhisattva ideal. Unbeknownst to Ram Dass, while he spoke eloquently and sweetly about how to be a bodhisattva, Rinpoche would be putting the ashes of the cigarette he was smoking on Ram Dass's head. I really liked this Rinpoche guy.

Through sheer coincidence, I met Rinpoche one-on-one. We quickly developed a warm, tender, and trusting bond. We talked and laughed about many things, like how we owed our friendship to the communists who drove us out of our respective homes. He asked me to join him at the first ever Vajradhatu Seminary. I was nineteen, but I had "a life." Why would I give it up? At the time, I was a vegetarian and I did not drink alcohol or take drugs, but the confusion about what to do was so overwhelming, that I decided to drink an entire bottle of wine and smoke a joint. Bingo! I realized in quintessential Vajradhatu/Shambhala style that Rinpoche and the Seminary were the "something" that I had been looking for my entire life. Later on that day the mail came with a letter and a poem from Rinpoche. That was it. I called my mother and told her I was going to Wyoming to study Buddhism. She said "Wyoming, where is that? Buddhism, what is that good for?" As I flew into Jackson Hole, I knew I was finally home. I was home amongst the homeless.

EVERYDAY DHARMA IN IBEROAMERICA

My path has been full of richness. I was close to my teacher. I have had health and time to practice and study. I have met and studied with the most accomplished meditation masters born in Tibet and with those born in exile. I now study primarily with the Venerable Thrangu Rinpoche and with Sakyong Mipham Rinpoche. My path has also been an embarrassing continuity of moments where I have missed the point. Moments when I have failed to see the nature of my mind, when I thought my projections were real, when I did not put others before me, when I indulged in distraction, laziness, and arrogance. I am still stubbornly attached to my habitual patterns and to the familiar "home" of my confused mind. I am also haunted by my karmic debt to the lineage.

In the mid-1990s, Chögyam Trungpa's son, Sakyong Mipham Rinpoche, asked me to help develop Spanish and Portuguese-speaking Shambhala Centers in Latin America and Spain. As Iberoamerican Liaison for Shambhala International, I was finally put on the spot. I could pay back the lineage a fraction of what I had received by bringing it all back home.

I took a sabbatical and a leave of absence from my university job. For the three years I held this post I spent most of the time in Chile and Spain and a little time in Brazil, Colombia, and Cuba (Iberoamerica includes the Iberian Peninsula as well as the Spanish and Portuguese-speaking Americas). It was challenging, but relatively easy. I seemed to be doing great things, but it was just that many of these great things were, fundamentally, already done. The practitioners in these centers had a sincere and deeply heartfelt connection with Dharma. An older student like me simply had to encourage them to trust their own intelligence and embody through practice and study the wisdom and truth that was inherent in them. "That's it. Just do it." That is how I was taught. I could teach that too.

I concentrated on training the trainers—teaching the older students how to impart meditation instruction, how to teach, how to grow their centers, how to plan curriculum. I also did many introductory public programs. Teaching in Latin America and Spain wasn't just a question of teaching in another language; it was a question of being open to a shared cultural karma both wise and confused. I taught not just in Spanish and *Portunol* (a mixture of Portugese and Spanish). I spoke Dharma *del pueblo*, Dharma of the people. This was *El Dharma nuestro de cada dia*, everyday Dharma.

There were many poignant moments in the three years I held the Liaison post. But a few stand out as particularly indicative of the nature of Latin and Iberian Dharma. The first time I was asked by the head of a local Vipassana center to teach in Cuba, my immediate reaction was to say "I am not Padmasambhava (who brought Buddhism to Tibet). This land belongs to the Orishas (the Santeria gods) and I am not going to get in their way." I declined. But I nevertheless went to meet an authentic Babalao (a Santeria priest—in this case a black Chinese woman in her mid-sixties) in Regla, across Havana Harbor. I asked her to ask the Orishas if Shambhala could come to Cuba. I gave the Babalao my Shambhala "Ashe" lapel pin. *"Ashe"* is a calligraphy stroke that represents the unconditional confidence of wakefulness in the Shambhala tradition. *"Ache"* is the force and good favor of the Orishas in Cuban Santeria. The Babalao gave me a stone of Chango, who she said was my tutelary deity. It was a meeting of hearts and minds. Months later, the reply from the Babalao arrived: "The Dralas (manifestations of wisdom in Shambhala) are similar to the Orishas in that they both want the well-being of the Cuban people. They can come." I could now assist with the arrangements for a practitioner from the Santiago de Chile Shambhala Center to come to Cuba to teach an introduction to meditation program.

A few years later I did agree to teach a Dharma program in Havana in one of my university research trips there. Unfortunately, the trip coincided with a wave of repression in 1999 that included the jailing of four journalists for "contempt for authority" and general "dangerousness." I realized that the Shambhala language of "warriors" and the possibility of an "enlightened society" was actually a counterrevolutionary discourse. To make matters worse, it was being spoken by an exile in an environment where there was no freedom of assembly. It was confusing for me. It was dangerous for them. I have not gone back to Cuba, either as a professional, or as a practitioner. I do not want to develop negativity towards the Revolution. I do plan to return once the government changes and start a Dharma retreat center—if my Dharma teachers, the Cuban government, the Orishas, and the Dralas give the green light.

In 2000, I went to Isla Negra in Chile, to visit Pablo Neruda's oceanfront home. When I looked into his closet, I was taken aback. I felt that I was looking into Trungpa Rinpoche's own closet. So many unique outfits. So many different manifestations of being. Such outrageous regal bearing. Such mischievousness. So much love. So much passion. So many brilliant opportunities to catch wisdom mind. That is when I realized that we would have our own idiosyncratic Iberoamerican Dharma form. Just as Tibetans have a colorful

Bon-influenced Dharma, and the Japanese an aesthetic and stylized Dharma, we Iberoamericans could also find a way to express the brilliant richness of our homes.

We learn from our teachers to trust in our inherent wakefulness and, in this way, see everything that happens in our world as Dharma. If Chile has been the "good cop" guru for me, Spain has been the "bad cop" guru. I got stuck in a very small elevator in Malaga when teaching a seminar on Pema Chödrön's books. *The Wisdom of No Escape* and the need to *Start Where You Are* were abundantly clear at that moment. This is where I finally learned how to use the breath as a medium for taking in confusion and sending out sanity. The intense claustrophobia that I experienced for some time afterwards in closed spaces became the fuel of my Mahamudra practice. On a tour of Spain in 2002, I realized that I could no longer teach the Dharma unless I understood much, much more. Karaoke Dharma would simply not do. The living quality of the lineage transmission would be lost unless those in my generation made it a priority to realize what we had been taught. I have fundamentally spent my spare time on retreat since then. I owe that command to the bluntness and tough love of Spain.

My teacher's life and how he taught his students in the West continue to provide me with the inspiration for giving away what I have received. Chögyam Trungpa Rinpoche disrobed, married, caroused, drank, smoked, spoke English, not for his benefit, but for ours. He walked on the wild side—the side of our neurotic and confused minds—so we could relate to the Dharma as something personal, relevant, au courant. But he never veered from teaching the true and genuine heart of Dharma. He was an extraordinary teacher of an authentic Tibetan tradition driven by a passion for knowing and liberating the minds of his Western students. When I was at seminary in 1973 I asked Rinpoche what was the difference between Buddhas and sentient beings. He said they were the same, except that Buddhas had the memory of the path.

May the memories of the path of this homeless Dharma beginner a long way from Buddhahood be of benefit to all sentient beings.

HOME AMONG THE HOMELESS
Julia Sagebien

You can only teach that which you have learned,
You can only transmit that which you have realized,
You can only transform in others that which you have liberated in
yourself.

Trust your Buddha nature,
Trust that of others.
Teach others to take to heart the guru's instruction in formal practice
and everyday life.

Bringing the Dharma to new lands requires that one be true to form.
To stay true to form is to stay true to the meaning of form.
I have nothing to imitate,
I have much to learn.

I don't have to be a Cuban imitating an American,
who is imitating a Tibetan, and on and on.
I am the Buddha.
We are all the Buddha in the continuity of awakened mind.

Through karmic causes and conditions I was born in a land of brilliant
sensory and emotional displays.
Latin Dharma is color, poetry, food, smells, music, flowers, mountains,
wind, rain, sky, ocean—
And above all—love.
Love of land, love of people, passionate, generous, daring, giving heart.
Devotion to lineage comes naturally,
Discipline and a settled mind are, well, a bit hard.

If we have loving-kindness towards ourselves
we can overcome the self-blame of original sin.
If through compassion we see the emptiness of the display,
we can overcome the blame we put on others.

Our neurotic upheavals are self-liberated through insight,
Boleros are the expression of Bodhicitta,
Without attachment
the feast of the senses can be enjoyed.
Great good fortune to have lost it all in exile,
Great good fortune to realize that I never lost it at all,
Great good fortune to find a teacher in foreign lands
who could show me so,
Great good fortune to share it all with my family
in all my Southern, Northern, Western and Eastern homes.
Refugees find their home among the homeless.

Dharma Has No Color

JAN WILLIS

A<small>T THE CLOSING SESSION</small> of the 2002 African American Buddhist Retreat and Conference held at Spirit Rock Meditation Center, a young black woman asked me, "Was there anything that was *left out* as Buddhism made its way here?" She had prefaced her question by saying that the books she'd read seemed to present a neatly uniform picture of Buddhism coming to the West and she wondered whether this idyllic picture was true, or even, the only story. She was asking me because I was the only "academic" among the fourteen teachers gathered at the conference.

I paused before responding, realizing the true profundity of the question. It seemed clear to me that, in fact, the question contained and suggested many other questions left unspoken. After hesitating, I then gave a somewhat rambling and long-winded answer about the Dharma's being for everyone even though I thought we people of color had a sort of head start given the prominence of Buddhism's discussions of suffering. I hoped that some of what I said might be of use. The young woman was kind-hearted and, nodding as I answered, let me off the hook. In the months since the conference, I have often thought about that question and about the varied implications and unvoiced experiences that may have lain behind it. What I want to do here is attempt a clearer response. This means that I will first attempt to draw out some of the other questions latent within that pregnant one that was uttered.

When the woman asked, "Was there anything that was *left out* when the varied traditions of Buddhism were brought here?" I heard another related question, namely, "Is there anything in the Buddhist traditions in Asia that has *not* been brought here?" In a way, I hear this question as asking, "Have we been given the *whole* picture? Told the whole truth?" I hear it as a question which bears a bit of skepticism as well as of suspicion. I believe that the skepticism at least is well-founded.

It is certainly true that if you walk into any bookstore or library or visit any number of Internet sites of cyber-Dharma, you'll come away with the sense that Buddhism is all about only one thing: *meditation*. But is this all or even most of what Asian Buddhists do? I think that the true answer is: absolutely not. American—or other Western convert—Buddhists like to pick and choose. They like to take this element or practice from this Buddhist tradition, and this other element from this other tradition. This is understandable since most of us in the West live in and with a supermarket mentality and since we, as unique individuals, like to fashion what will be uniquely ours. If we now add to this propensity the fact that most early convert-Buddhists went to Asia in the 1970s to get away from religious traditions they found to be overly devotional and hence stifling, we can understand that their initial desire was to find a so-called pure religious practice that was uncluttered by any elements that smacked of devotionalism. We can imagine them saying, "Just give me the pith without any fluff!" Of course, this demand was, and remains, unrealistic. In Asia, as anywhere else in the world, religion and religious practice comes wrapped in the trappings and paraphernalia of the particular culture. Yet, seemingly unaware of this, those early, counterculture Westerners—myself included—were fed up with the trappings of religion. Encountering and being attracted to Buddhism, we thought we could isolate its essence. And that essence was assuredly meditation. At this point, however, picking and choosing became not just a process of selection but also a process of subtraction. So, many things, in fact, *were* left out.

On the one hand, Buddhist traditions that smacked of the old devotional and worshipful stances from which we were fleeing were the last traditions to reach a large cross-over audience. It has only been recently that non-Asian practioners have heard much about Pure Land or Jodo-Shinshu Buddhism, traditions of Buddhism that extol *tariki*, or reliance upon "other-power" in addition to reliance on "self-power" alone. A form of Buddhist practice that actually enjoins prayer to the Buddhas and rituals of repeating the names of Buddhas appears threatening and un-Buddhist to some newer practioners. But in Asia—even in those seemingly more spare traditions, like Japanese Zen or Thai Vipassana, there are still Buddha statues, and altars, and water bowls, and incense burning, and prayers, and bowing. These practices are different from what we normally think of as purely meditation.

On the other hand, most Asian Buddhists didn't—and still don't—have the time to devote all of their time to meditation. Though we may tend to think that all Buddhists meditate all the time, for most Buddhists in the world, meditation is not the sole or even the main activity. It is a cherished activity, to be sure, but not the only one. For most Asian lay Buddhist followers, the majority of their time must be devoted to the tasks of living. However, even among monastics, meditation is not the sole activity. My teacher, Lama Yeshe, had been a monk at the renowned Sera-je Monastery just outside of Lhasa. One of the three main Gelugpa Sees, Sera housed thousands of monks. But according to Lama Yeshe, only about fifty of the Sera-je monks were revered as great meditators and so were allowed to be absent from group rituals. The great majority of monks busied themselves with the day-to-day chores of running such an institution, whether as cooks, gardeners, teachers, managers, and so forth. The idea that all that Buddhists do is meditate is an invention of Westerners; it does not give a true picture of Buddhism as actually practiced in Asian countries.

Another question behind, or internal to, the one the young woman asked, is this: "Is this a teaching that I can really use?" My answer was and is: Absolutely. The Buddha's teachings of love, compassion, kindness and insight are available to all of us here and now, and all of us, it seems to me, are in clear need of them. They can help us to see the roots of our pain, dissatisfaction, and anguish and they can help us to methodically work to overcome them. Twenty-six hundred years of heart and mind science has come up with some pretty good answers. Even so, unlike most of the world's religious traditions, Buddhism does not ask us to accept uncritically a set of dogmas or principles. Rather, Buddhism calls on us simply to "check-up!" One of the core aspects of Buddhism is, in fact, its call to experience. Urging his followers to "come and see for themselves," the Buddha cautioned them against accepting as fact anything that did not accord with their own experiences.

The most foundational teachings recorded in the Buddha's First Sermon, the Four Noble Truths, are not taught as dogma to be accepted and believed with blind faith. Rather, for each of the Truths, there is a specific action required on our parts which is geared to lead us to our own understanding of the veracity of the Truth. Not until that action has been carried out and tested against our own experience should we embrace it as a guiding principle. We cannot take the Teachings for granted; we have to come and see for ourselves.

The First Noble Truth says that "There is suffering." The specific action enjoined upon us in connection with this truth is that we must *understand* it (that is, suffering). With respect to the Second Noble Truth—that there is a cause of suffering which is, most palpably, desire but also, on a deeper level, ignorance—we are to *eliminate* the cause. With respect to the Third Truth—that there is the cessation of suffering—we are told that we must *realize* that cessation directly, by experiencing it. And, lastly, with respect to the Fourth Noble Truth—that there is a Path leading to the cessation of suffering—we are asked to follow and *cultivate* that path. Of course, all this is easier said than done.

For the time being, I want to concentrate on the First Noble Truth and the specific injunction to understand it. "Understanding" here means more than just grasping the idea intellectually. I have taught many intelligent students over the past three decades. These students certainly grasp the meanings of the Sanskrit term *dukkha* that is usually translated as "suffering." The best students have no trouble in grasping the further Buddhist subdivision of dukkha into three kinds, namely: suffering plain and simple, suffering caused by change, and suffering that is inherent in the cycle of birth and death that is called samsara. Yet, even appreciating the three kinds of suffering is not the same as understanding suffering.

I believe that people of color, because of our experience of the great and wrenching historical traumas of slavery, colonization, and segregation, understand suffering in a way that our white brothers and sisters do not and, moreover, that this understanding is closer to what is meant by the Buddhist injunction. Hence, I believe that—in this regard, and without putting suffering on a scale—we people of color are actually already "one-up" on other convert-Buddhist practitioners. We come to the practice with this deeper understanding. And this understanding, I believe, makes it easier for us to actually "get it" when we're told that we need to understand the Noble Truth of suffering.

Now, there is another question in the one uttered by the young black woman. It is a question that is pressing for people of color who see something of value in Buddhist teachings. That question, simply stated, is this: "In order to practice Buddhism, do I have to abandon the tradition of faith in which I was raised?" Often this question is asked explicitly of me in private moments. Since I have publicly referred to myself as a Baptist-Buddhist, I get the question a lot. I believe that the answer to this question is, most assuredly, "No." Buddhism does not demand blind allegiance from us. Usually, however, our own faith-tradition is not so open.

I once gave a reading at the only women's prison in Connecticut. As I reached the conclusion of my talk, a very tall, slender, and muscular black woman stood up and began waving a pocket-sized Bible in the air. She then yelled out, "I have all the help with overcoming my problems right here, in this book!" I was clearly being challenged. On this one, I had no hesitation. I responded, "I am very happy for you, then. However, I couldn't find the answers there—at least not when I needed them. I needed to know how to love my neighbors when my neighbors—some of them Klan members—didn't care much for me. I liked the sentiment, "Love thy neighbor"; but I didn't know how to put it into practice. I needed another method. And *I* found those methods in Buddhism." She seemed to hear me. The point is that I can use *Buddhist* methods to help me practice *Baptist* ideals. I can use Buddhist meditations to help me to transform negative emotions and perceptions into more positive ones. In a well-known Buddhist parable, the Buddha tells his followers to use his Teachings like a raft. If they are helpful, use them. But, afterwards, you needn't hold on to them or carry them around with you. I'll quote a bit of this parable here, as translated by the Venerable Walpola Rahula. It goes like so:

> "O bhikkhus, a man is on a journey. He comes to a vast stretch of water. On this side the shore is dangerous, but on the other it is safe and without danger. No boat goes to the other shore…nor is there any bridge for crossing over. He says to himself: '…It would be good if I would gather grass, wood, branches and leaves to make a raft, and with the help of the raft cross over safely to the other side, exerting myself with my hands and feet.' He does this and safely crosses to the other shore. Having crossed over to the other side, he thinks: 'This raft was of great help to me. With its aid I have crossed safely over to this side. It would be good if I carry this raft on my head or on my back wherever I go.' What do you think, O bhikkhus, if he acted in this way would that man be acting properly with regard to the raft?"

> "No, Sir" the monks respond.

> "In which way then would he be acting properly with regard to the raft?….Suppose that man should think: 'This raft was a great help to me…It would be good if I beached this raft….or moored it and left it afloat, and then went on my way.' Acting in this way would that man act properly with regard to the raft? In the same manner, O bhikkhus, I have taught a doctrine similar to a raft—it is for crossing over, and not for carrying."[1]

Practicing Buddhist meditation does not require that one abandon one's original faith-tradition. I can find many virtuous ideals in Biblical scriptures but still need to work on developing compassion and fearlessness with specific meditations from the Buddhist traditions that are aimed at helping these qualities to grow and blossom within me. At least so far, this strategy has proven beneficial for me.[2]

Perhaps when the young black woman at the People of Color Retreat was asking her question she was thinking of the very special nature of the retreat we had all just shared and which was fast coming to an end. In this case, the question also entailed the recognition that such retreats were indeed a rarity. To what extent, she may have been pondering, are the teachings of Buddhism truly accessible to me, and to us people of color generally, when we leave these grounds? I have written about this particular issue before. There is little doubt that convert-Buddhism in America is largely a white, and upper middle-class affair. This is so not only because those 1970s counterculture folk who went to Asia and brought back a fervent interest in Buddhism were from this economic background, but also because of the way American Buddhist institutions have been organized and developed here. In short, there are two essential requirements necessary for doing a Buddhist retreat here: money and leisure time. Most working-class people and many people of color do not have a great quantity of either. This situation calls for creative solutions worked out between those white convert-Buddhists and people of color with a sincere interest in Buddhist Dharma.

The Dharma itself is colorless. It is not limited by the gender, race, class, sexual orientation, or church affiliation of the person studying or practicing it. The *Diamond Sutra*, an early Mahayana wisdom text said this like so:

> Those who by my form did see me,
> And those who followed me by my voice,
> Wrong the efforts they engaged in,
> Me those people will not see.[3]

When the Buddha says in this text that those who saw him by his physical form did not see him in truth, an end is posited to questions of discrimination based upon categories like those mentioned above. None of these categories has any bearing on enlightenment. Therefore, the answer to the question of accessibility—like the Buddhist notion of the "two truths," that is, conventional, or relative truth on the one hand, and ultimate truth on the other[4]—is twofold: on the ultimate level, the answer is: Of course, Buddhist Dharma is accessible and available to all sentient beings, without exception and, since every sentient being already possesses Buddha nature, all without exception have the capacity and potential of becoming fully enlightened beings. On the conventional or relative level, however—where we all exist until we are enlightened—we need to work together to insure that diversity is a reality in all Buddhist communities.

A last question—though not a final one—inherent in the query voiced by the young woman might be this: "Is there really value for us in the Buddhist teachings?" I think the answer here is, "Yes, there is much of value." But that is my personal opinion and one that I have verified for myself through trial and experience. I cannot speak in the name of others here. We might, however, for a moment consider the question of value as it was posed by a very distinguished Black intellectual. In a speech delivered in 1923, W. E. B. Du Bois asked us, as a people, to consider the question of value in the following way: "What do we want? What is the thing that we're after? If you suddenly should become full-fledged Americans, if your color faded or the color line...and was miraculously forgotten, what would you want? What would you immediately seek? Would you buy the most powerful of motorcars? Would you buy the most elaborate estate?"[5]

Clearly these are important questions for people of color to ponder. Yet, they are also important questions for everyone who lives and breathes and shares this planet. Buddhists answer the question of what do we want like this: we all wish happiness and we all wish to avoid suffering.[6] It is our most common denominator as living beings. Therefore, if we have heard about a tradition which might offer us genuine help in accomplishing this most basic of goals, wouldn't it be prudent to check it out, to come and see for ourselves?

NOTES

1   The full text of the parable of the raft can be found in the *Majjhima-nikaya* of the Pali Canon. The translation from which I have excerpted the story is that by Walpola Rahula in *What the Buddha Taught*, (New York: Grove Press, 1974), pp. 11-12.

2   Clearly, I am not the only person who holds this opinion. I am reminded, for example, of Sylvia Boorstein's book, *That's Funny, You Don't Look Buddhist: On Being a Faithful Jew and a Passionate Buddhist* (HarperSanFrancisco, 1998). And His Holiness the Dalai Lama often begins his talks today, in various parts of the world, by saying that one need not leave the religious tradition of one's upbringing in order to take advantage of the Buddha's teachings.

3   The *Diamond-cutter sutra* (Skt. *Vajracchedika-sutra*) was composed circa fourth century A. D. This particular translation was done by Edward Conze and appears in his *Buddhist*

Wisdom Books (London: George Allen and Unwin, 1958; reprinted, New York: Harper Torchbooks, 1972), p. 63.

4 The Buddhist theory of the "two truths" is perhaps most thoroughly presented and analyzed by the great Mahayana philosopher and founder of the Madhyamaka School, Nagarjuna (circa 150-250 A.D.). The theory explains that words and language constitute and create a conventional, relative world wherein communication and action takes place among ordinary beings. Yet, the experience and view of an enlightened being ultimately transcends all conventional structures, being unmediated, ultimate and ineffable.

5 The speech, entitled "Criteria of Negro Art" was delivered by Du Bois in Chicago in 1923. This section of the speech is quoted by John Malkin as part of an interview conducted with Charles Johnson and recorded in *Shambhala Sun*, January 2004, p. 84.

6 The Dalai Lama begins many of his lectures with this gentle, but realistic, declaration.

GODDESS OF LOVE

Contributors

LOURDES ARGÜELLES, Ph.D. is Professor of Education at the Claremont Graduate University in Claremont, California. She also works, assisted by a group of her doctoral students, directing several immigration advocacy, technology assistance, and service projects in Latino and African American communities surrounding the university. Her research and writings on educational alternatives and on social inequality and grassroots movements have been published in academic and popular journals around the world. In 2001, she coedited an issue of the Buddhist Peace Fellowship's journal *Turning Wheel* devoted to Buddhism in Latin America and in Latino communities. Her book, *The New Jihad*, cowritten with Jorge Erdely, a Mexican theologian and social activist, was published in 2003 in Spanish by the Mexican Academy for the Scientific Study of Religion. She and her life partner of over sixteen years, Anne Rivero, were recently married in British Columbia, Canada. They practice in the Tibetan and also Thich Nhat Hanh's Zen Buddhist traditions and live in the San Jacinto Mountains with three rescued companion dogs named Karma, Bodhi, and Dorje.

REVEREND HILDA GUTIÉRREZ BALDOQUÍN (RYŪMON ZENJI) is a Soto Zen priest in the lineage of Shunryu Suzuki Roshi. A student of Zenkei Blanche Hartman Sensei at San Francisco Zen Center, she is the founder of the SFZC People of Color Sitting Group and a co-founder of the Buddhist Meditation Group for the LGBTQ community at The Center, also in San Francisco. She leads retreats for People of Color at Dhamma Dena Meditation Center in Northampton, Massachusetts and is a practice leader for the Zen Sangha at Cerro Gordo Temple in Santa Fe, New Mexico. For the past twenty-five years she has worked in the fields of multicultural organizational change and conflict resolution as a consultant, trainer, facilitator, and bilingual/bicultural mediator. Baldoquín was born in Cuba, grew up in Harlem, lived in Miami, Florida and now makes her home in San Francisco, California.

MICHELE BENZAMIN-MIKI is a meditation, martial-arts teacher and artist. She has two fourth-dan black belts, and one fifth-dan black belt in Aikido and Iaido. She has led meditation retreats and workshops in the US and Europe for two decades. She has trained with teachers in both the Vipassana traditions and the Vietnamese Zen tradition of Thich Nhat Hanh. With her partner Caitriona, she is co-founder of Ordinary Dharma in Los Angeles and Manzanita Village Retreat Center in Warner Springs.

REVEREND MERLE KODO BOYD is a priest and Dharma Holder in the lineage of Maezumi Roshi. She studies and trains with Sensei Egyoku Nakao, Abbot and Head Teacher at the Zen Center of Los Angeles. She lives with her husband and daughter in New Jersey.

VIVEKA CHEN is an order member of the Western Buddhist Order (WBO) and Chairwoman and a meditation and Dharma teacher at the San Francisco Buddhist Center (SFBC) of the WBO. She is second-generation Chinese American born and raised in New Jersey who moved to San Francisco in 1991 seeking a diverse, multicultural city to make her chosen home. Although starting out on a model minority trajectory with an Electrical Engineering degree, she happily found her true calling in the path of service. Viveka has been working on social justice issues in the Bay Area's communities of color since 1991, most recently as a consultant helping organizations through strategic conversations. She is currently working to make meditation available and accessible to people of color and activists and for several years has led sits, workshops, and retreats for these groups both at the SFBC and in partnership with other community based organizations. Viveka is a regular contributor to *Dharma Life* Buddhist magazine and has an essay on being a practitioner of color in *Blue Jean Buddha II: Voices of Young Buddhists* (Wisdom Publications, 2004).

BONNIE DURAN, PH.D. is an associate professor of Public Health at the Department of Family and Community Medicine, University of New Mexico School of Medicine. Working with tribal collaboratives, her research includes American Indian and Alaska Native mental health and HIV epidemiology and health services research. Bonnie studies and practices Theravada and Tibetan Buddhism and lives alone in Albuquerque, New Mexico.

EDUARDO DURAN, PH.D. is a clinical psychologist and is presently the director of behavioral health for the Albuquerque Area Indian Health Service. He has taught psychology at Fort Lewis College, the Pacific Graduate School of Pyschology, and the California School of Professional Psychology. His work has been published in many books and anthologies including *Native American Postcolonial Psychology* (New York: SUNY, 1995) and *Buddha in Redface* (Writers Club Press, 2003).

GAYLON FERGUSON took refuge with the Venerable Chögyam Trungpa Rinpoche in 1973. He has led meditation retreats and taught in the Shambhala Buddhist tradition for the past thirty years. He served as Executive Director of Karme Chöling Buddhist Meditation Center (formerly Tail of the Tiger) in the late 1970s, and was the teacher in residence of the Shambhala Meditation Center in Berkeley, California from 1979 to 1983. He was a Fulbright Fellow to Nigeria in 1994 and received his doctorate in anthropology from Stanford University in 1996. Trungpa Rinpoche's successor and Dharma heir, Sakyong Mipham Rinpoche appointed him an *acharya*, a senior teacher in the Shambhala Buddhist lineage in 2000. After teaching cultural anthropology at the University of Washington, he returned to Karme Chöling as teacher in residence in 2001. He has published articles and discussions of meditation in *Shambhala Sun* and *Buddhadharma: The Practitioner's Journal.*

MUSHIM IKEDA-NASH is author of a quarterly column on Buddhism and family practice for *Turning Wheel: The Journal of Socially Engaged Buddhism*, and is a community activist working with issues of diversity. She has been included in documentary films on Asian American women poets (*Between the Lines*) and faith-based activists (*Women of Faith*). Mushim lives in Oakland, California with her husband and son, and is a volunteer literacy tutor in the Oakland public school system. Under the name Patricia Y. Ikeda, she has published poetry in numerous anthologies and journals. With the publication of her volume of poetry, *House of Wood, House of Salt* (Cleveland State University, 1978) she became known as one of the pioneers of Asian American poetry. Under her Buddhist name, Mushim has published essays on Buddhism and childrearing, family life, women, and racism in books and journals such as *Shambhala Sun, Inquiring Mind, Turning Wheel*, and *Innovative Buddhist Women: Swimming against the Stream.*

DR. CHARLES JOHNSON, a 1998 MacArthur Fellow, received the National Book Award for his novel *Middle Passage* in 1990, and is a 2002 recipient of the Academy Award for Literature from the American Academy of Arts and Letters. In 2003, he was elected to membership in the American Academy of Arts and Sciences. A literary critic, screenwriter, philosopher, international lecturer and cartoonist with over 1,000 drawings published, he is the S. Wilson and Grace M. Pollock Endowed Professor of English at the University of Washington in Seattle.

His fiction includes *Dreamer* (1998), *Oxherding Tale* (1982), and *Faith and the Good Thing* (1974) as well as two story collections, *The Sorcerer's Apprentice* (1986) and *Soulcatcher* (2001). Among his many nonfiction books are *King: The Photography of Martin Luther King, Jr.* (coauthored with Bob Adelman, 2000), *Africans in America: America's Journey through Slavery* (coauthored with Patricia Smith, 1998), *Being and Race: Black Writing Since 1970* (1988), *Black Men Speaking* (coedited with John McCluskey, Jr., 1997), and two books of drawings. This piece is an excerpt from his newest book, *Turning the Wheel: Essays on Buddhism and Writing* (New York: Scribner, 2003).

In 1999 Indiana University published a reader of his work, *I Call Myself an Artist: Writings by and about Charles Johnson*. For more information, visit www.oxherdingtale.com or www.siu.edu/~johnson.

DR. MARLENE JONES is a woman of African ancestry who holds a professional appointment in the Social and Cultural Studies Department in the School of Humanities at Dominican University. Her doctorate is in International Multicultural Education. She is a social and community activist, and has worked in diversity and multicultural education for many years. Dr. Jones leads and teaches the People of Color daylong workshops and Residential Retreats and the African American Retreats at Spirit Rock Meditation Center. She is cofounder of the Spirit Rock Meditation Center's Diversity Council and is the current co-chair.

MAXINE HONG KINGSTON was born to Chinese immigrant parents in Stockton, California. Maxine won a scholarship to the University of California, Berkeley and received her bachelor's degree in English in 1962. Soon after she married Earll Kingston, a Berkeley graduate and an actor. She has taught at University of California, Berkeley and the University of Hawaii at Honolulu and is now Senior Lecturer Emerita at University of California, Berkeley. Hong Kingston received a Guggenheim Fellowship in 1981, and has written several books, including *The Woman Warrior, China Men, Tripmaster Monkey: His Fake Book,* and *To Be the Poet.* This piece is an excerpt from her most recent book, *The Fifth Book of Peace.*

EARTHLYN MARSELEAN MANUEL currently sits at the San Francisco Zen Center. She is a writer and visual artist living in northern California. She is the author and illustrator of the *Black Angel Cards: A Soul Revival Guide for Black Women* (Harper San Francisco, 1999) and author of *Seeking Enchantment: A Spiritual Journey of Healing from Oppression* (Kasai River Press, 2002).

KAMALA MASTERS was born in Manila and immigrated to the San Francisco Bay Area when she was two years old with her Filipina mother to join her American father. She lives in Hawaii where she raised four children, and is now blessed with five grandchildren. She is one of the founders and teachers of the Vipassana Metta Foundation on Maui, where she is currently developing Ho'o-malamalama, a sanctuary-hermitage for long term practice. Masters teaches retreats in the Theravada tradition at venues worldwide. Practicing since 1975, her teachers have been the late Anagarika Munindra of India and Sayadaw U Pandita of Burma with whom she continues to practice.

GEORGE T. MUMFORD is a Sports Psychology Consultant, Personal and Organizational Consultant, and Insight Meditation Teacher. As a Sports Psychology Consultant, he is currently working with the Los Angeles Lakers, Boston College Athletic Department, as well as with other athletic organizations and private clients.

Since May 1999, he has taught insight meditation in the Fort Greene neighborhood of Brooklyn, New York. George has been teaching insight meditation in a variety of places (prisons, Harvard University, medical clinics, corporations, etc.) since 1986. He has been working with incarcerated inmates for many years teaching Insight Meditation, Substance Abuse Recovery Training, and chairing meetings as a member of the Hospitals and Institutions committees of both Alcoholics Anonymous and Narcotics Anonymous. He has written for *Tricycle, O Magazine,* and the *Boston Globe* as well as appearing in the PBS series on Mind, Body, and Spirit (Spring 1999).

THICH NHAT HANH, Zen master, poet, and peace and human rights activist, was born in central Vietnam in 1926 and joined the monkhood at the age of sixteen. The Vietnam War confronted the monasteries with the question of whether to adhere to the contemplative life and remain meditating in the monasteries, or to help the villagers suffering under bombings and other devastations of the war. Thich Nhat Hanh was one of those who chose to do both, helping to found the "engaged Buddhism" movement. His life has since been dedicated to the work of inner transformation for the benefit of individuals and society.

Thich Nhat Hanh has written seventy-five books, more than fifty in English. He lives in Plum Village, France in the meditation community he founded, where he teaches, writes, and gardens; and he leads retreats worldwide on the art of mindful living.

SISTER CHAN CHAU NGHIEM (TRUE ADORNMENT WITH JEWEL) is a bhikshuni in the Vietnamese Zen tradition of Thich Nhat Hanh. She is of both African American and European American heritage. Before ordaining, she graduated from Stanford University with a B.A. and M.A. in Anthropology and Social Sciences. She currently lives in Plum Village, France. Her writings have been published in *Friends on the Path* (Parallax Press, 2002) and in the *Mindfulness Bell,* and the Vietnamese newsletter, *Dat Lan.*

JOSÉ LUIS REISSIG was born in Buenos Aires, Argentina in 1926 to parents of Italian and Spanish descent. José went to the U.S. to study from 1946 to 1952, and returned home with a Ph.D. from the California Institute of Technology. He pursued research in molecular biology in Argentina, Chile, Scotland, Denmark, and France, returning home again in 1962 as professor of biology at the University of Buenos Aires. Five years later, he and his family moved to New York, where he carried out research and taught biology at the C. W. Post College of Long Island University for twenty years. He has published over fifty papers and two books.

In 1982, Reissig took a sabbatical in India that became a spiritual pilgrimage. He trained as a teacher of Insight Meditation with Christopher Titmuss. He taught regularly at the Insight Meditation Society in Barre, Massachussets from 1991 to 2002. He has contributed articles to *Tricycle* and the *Mountain Record.* Jose lives currently in Rhinebeck, New York, where he leads the Rhinebeck Insight Meditation Group. He teaches primarily in the Northeast, and is interested in promoting the practice of meditation among Latino communities.

ANNE RIVERO works as a bilingual psychiatric social worker at a Kaiser Permanente mental health clinic in southern California. She works with adult clients, many of whom have abuse and trauma histories, and with recent Latino immigrants. Ms. Rivero has also been active in counseling and working on behalf of gay, lesbian, and transgendered people as well as people living with HIV/AIDS. She lives with her partner of over sixteen years, Lourdes Argüelles, and has published several articles on her work.

JULIA SAGEBIEN was born in Havana, Cuba in 1954. With her parents and sister, she immigrated to Lima, Peru in 1957. She received a B.A. in Psychology and Buddhism from Hampshire College and a Masters in Western and Buddhist Psychology from Naropa University. Sagebien received an M.B.A. from Simmons Graduate School of Management and worked as a marketing manager, advertising executive, or consultant for several companies including Fidelity Investment and Lotus Development. Upon moving to Halifax, Nova Scotia, Canada she began a new career as a university professor in marketing. She obtained a Ph.D. in the area of planning and political economy from the London School of Economics. Her research on economic development made it possible for her to return to Latin America and especially to Cuba where she worked on the crafting of Canadian foreign and commercial policy towards the island. She is a former Senior Fellow for the Canadian Foundation for the Americas. She is now an Associate Professor in the School of Business Administration at Dalhousie University in Halifax. She teaches at undergraduate, graduate, and executive levels. Her research now focuses on issues of Corporate Social Responsibility and sustainable development. Her dog, Trouble (a little white terrier), comes to work with her.

She would like to thank Hilda Gutiérrez Baldoquín for making this book possible and is honored and delighted to have a chance to share a few short passages of her adventures in the Dharma.

RALPH STEELE is adjunct faculty at Spirit Rock Meditation Center, California and Insight Meditation Society, Massachusetts. For the past ten years he has facilitated People of Color and Diversity Meditation Retreats in the U.S. Ralph lives in Santa Fe, New Mexico, with his partner Sabina Schulze. They manage Life Transition Institute, which is dedicated to healing racism through practicing the Dharma and reaching out to under-served populations (www.lifetransitions.com).

SALA STEINBACH is a long-time student of Reb Anderson at Green Gulch/San Francisco Zen Center. She has worked as a nurse-midwife for twenty years, bringing over 2,000 babies into the world. She continues her work of supporting people during the biggest of life's transitions, birthing and dying. She lives in Muir Beach, California with her husband, her best friend, and an occasional racoon.

REVEREND KENNETH KENSHIN TANAKA grew up in the San Francisco Bay Area, and attended the Mountain View Buddhist Temple from youth. He was active in the Young Buddhist Asscociation of the Buddhist Churches of America, serving as president of its national organization in the early seventies. Upon developing greater interest in Buddhism in college, he pursued graduate studies at the Institute of Buddhist Studies (IBS) in Berkeley, Tokyo University, and University of California, Berkeley, where he earned a Ph.D. in Buddhist Studies. He also became a Theravada novice monk for a short period in 1970 in Thailand. Professionally, he has served on the faculty of the IBS and as a resident priest of the Southern Alameda County Buddhist Church. He is currently a Professor of Buddhist Studies at Musashino University in Tokyo, Japan.

ALICE WALKER, winner of the Pulitzer Prize and the American Book Award for *The Color Purple*, is internationally honored as an essential writer of our time. Among her twenty-six published volumes, she has authored seven novels, three collections of short stories, three collections of essays, seven volumes of poetry and three books for children. An activist and social visionary, Ms. Walker has been a participant in most of the major movements for planetary change: among them, the Human and Civil Rights movement in the South, the Hands Off Cuba Movement, the Women's Movement, The Native American and Indigenous Rights Movement, the Free South Africa Movement, the Environmental and Animal Rights Movement, and the Peace Movement. Her advocacy on behalf of the dispossessed has, in the words of her biographer, Evelyn C. White, "spanned the globe."

Her most recent works include the novel *Now Is The Time To Open Your Heart* (April 2004); *Absolute Trust In The Goodness Of The Earth,* new poems published by Random House in March 2003, and *A Poem Traveled Down My Arm,* a book of poems and drawings, published in fall 2003. Two children's books: *Why War Is Never A Good Idea* and *There Is a Flower at the Tip of My Nose Smelling Me* will be forthcoming. Ms. Walker was born in Eatonton,

Georgia, attended Spelman College in Atlanta, and is a graduate of Sarah Lawrence College. She is the mother of a daughter and lives in Northern California.

JAN WILLIS, PH.D. is Professor of Religion and Walter A. Crowell Professor of the Social Sciences at Wesleyan University in Middletown, Connecticut. She has studied with Tibetan Buddhists in India, Nepal, Switzerland, and the United States for more than three decades, and has taught courses in Buddhism for over twenty-five years. She is the author of *The Diamond Light: An Introduction to Tibetan Buddhist Meditation* (1972), *On Knowing Reality: The Tattvartha Chapter of Asanga's Bodhisattvabhumi* (1979), *Enlightened Beings: Life Stories from the Ganden Oral Tradition* (1995); and the editor of *Feminine Ground: Essays on Women and Tibet* (1989). One of the earliest American scholar-practitioners of Tibetan Buddhism, Professor Willis has published numerous essays and articles on Buddhist meditation, hagiography, women and Buddhism, and Buddhism and race. Her most recent publication is the memoir, *Dreaming Me: An African American Woman's Spiritual Journey*, published by Riverhead Books. In December of 2000, *Time* Magazine named Willis one of six "spiritual innovators for the new millennium." In 2003, Professor Willis was a recipient of Wesleyan University's Binswanger Prize for Excellence in Teaching.

LARRY YANG, M.F.A., M.S.W., L.C.S.W., is a psychotherapist and a consultant in cultural competency who gives workshops, presentations, and trainings in diversity and multicultural issues. He was most recently Program Coordinator for Diversity and Multicultural Services in the Department of Psychiatry of University of California at San Francisco and San Francisco General Hospital. Born to and raised by immigrant parents from Shanghai, Larry has explored the identity issues of culture, race, and the experience of difference for most of his life. He has been a National Park Ranger in the desert southwest and northern California, a trained forest fire fighter, and an award-winning graphic designer with posters in the Metropolitan Museum of Fine Art and Museum of Modern Art in New York.

Larry is a long-time practitioner in the Theravada Buddhist tradition and explores how to use contemplative practices to enhance effectiveness in social justice and activism. Larry's article, "Directing the Mind towards Practices in

Diversity" was included in *Friends on the Path: Living Spiritual Communities* (Parallax Press, 2002). His essay "Family Tree Practice" is part of *Will Yoga and Meditation Really Change My Life*, edited by Stephen Cope (Storey Press). Larry is a coeditor of *Making the Invisible Visible: Healing Racism in Our Buddhist Communities*, a booklet developed for building inclusive communities within spiritual practice. Larry leads daylong and weekend meditation retreats with themes for People of Color, diverse communities, men's work, and people in recovery from addiction. He co-leads a meditation group for the LGBT community in San Francisco.

Rosa Zubizarreta was born in Peru to a Peruvian father and a Cuban mother, and immigrated as a child to the United States. She works as an organization development consultant, facilitating creative collaboration in business, government, nonprofit, and community settings. Her background includes education, social work, activism, re-evaluation counseling, and focusing. Her published writings include the essays "Toward a Deeper Unity: Honoring Divergent Perspectives in Difficult Times," "El Latinismo y sus Bellos Colores: Voices of Latina and Latino Buddhists," and "The Joy of Diversity" (with Rita Archibald). She also writes for the Collective Wisdom Initiative (www.collectivewisdominitiative.org).

Acknowledgements

Mafereun Elegua
Moyuba Olofi, Moyuba Olorun, Moyuba Olodumare,
Moyuba Eggun, Moyuba Baba de Ocha, Moyuba Illa de Ocha o Oyubona
Mafereun Yemaya, Maferefun Yenya mi, Mareferun Olokun

Endless sentient beings, in the ten directions, in all realms, have paved
the way for the birth of this anthology:

Mother Earth who gives me sustenance.

Orishas and spirits who walk with me.

Buddhas, Devas, and Ancestors who protect me.

Zenkei Blanche Hartman Sensei who loves and challenges me.

Lou Harman who shows me the way.

SFZC People of Color Sitting Group who sustain my practice.

I give special thanks to:

All the contributors for graciously and generously allowing me to come into
your already full lives and demand more, and more and more.

Charles Johnson for saying, "Anything for the Buddhadharma."

Alice Walker for Cuba, angels, and yes!

Maxine Hong Kingston for generous heart.

Thich Nhat Hanh for giving us you.

Jan Willis for willingness and enthusiasm.

Mayumi Oda for beautiful art.

Ruth Frankenberg for wise counsel and keen insight into matters of book writing and publishing.

Beth Roy for unwavering conviction that writing is something people of color do.

Parallax Press for the commitment to publish this book.

The original working group who met for many months to develop a vision of joining Thich Nhat Hanh and the growing community of western Dharma Practioners of Color: Larry Ward, Travis Masch, Maria Hirano, Natalie Fisk, Mushim Ikeda-Nash, Abbot Ryūshin Paul Haller, Shosan Victoria Austin, Lee Lipp, Ilene Oba, and Larry Yang.

Sister Chan Chau Nghiem and Larry Ward for making the vision come true.

Arinna Weisman and Dhamma Dena Meditation Center for providing support and the space to bring the Dharma to People of Color at the other end of the country.

Michael Diaz for the invitation to create community in New Mexico.

Joan Watts and the Zen Sangha at Cerro Gordo Temple for the generous welcome and offering of a seat from which to share the Dharma in the Southwest.

The Sea Ranch Lodge staff, in particular Gabriel, Candace, Vicki, Diana and Kathy for maintaining my most favorite place in the world. The nurturing and inspiration I received by the sea allowed the words to flow.

And my deepest appreciations to:

La familia Gutiérrez por aceptarme completamente.

Carlos Andrés Gutiérrez Vázquez por ayudar a crearme.

Eugenia Acuña Lillo, Robin Barnett, Terry Berman, Valerie Batts, Judit Moschkovich, Sarah Stearns, Varda Wilensky and Nadine Zenobi for walking with me, staying close and loving me through all the years, no matter what.

Lázaro Jas por compartir nuestra tierra natal, las enseñanzas de Yogananda, mutua hermandad espiritual, apoyo cotidiano, visitas en el pasillo y travesuras sin fin.

Babá Funké Carlos Jiménez, Jr. por el camino.

Carol Jenkins for the practice.

The *VISIONS* family of friends and colleagues for twenty life-changing years.

The hundreds of women and men in the past twenty-five years, who by hiring me, have provided the means to food, shelter, medicine and clothing.

To those who will review this book and give commentary for your time and energy.

And to Rachel Neumann, senior editor at Parallax, for your trust, guidance, respect, humor, and relentless support. You handled this first timer with silk gloves. Little did I know when we met, and you were just a girl, that it would be you, assisting me, with this birth. Nine bows.

Ache Baba Elegua

PARALLAX
P
PRESS

Parallax Press publishes books on engaged Buddhism and the practice of mindfulness by Thich Nhat Hanh and other authors. As a division of the Unified Buddhist Church, we are committed to making these teachings accessible to everyone
and preserving them for future generations. We believe that, in doing so, we help
alleviate suffering and create a more peaceful world. All of Thich Nhat Hanh's
work is available at our on-line store and in our free catalog. For a copy of the catalog, please contact:

Parallax Press
P.O. Box 7355
Berkeley, CA 94707
www.parallax.org
Tel: (510) 525-0101

Monastics and laypeople practice the art of mindful living in the tradition of Thich
Nhat Hanh at retreat communities in France and the United States. Individuals,
couples, and families are invited to join these communities for a Day of Mindfulness and longer practice periods. For information, please visit www.plumvillage.org
or contact:

Plum Village
13 Martineau
33580 Dieulivol, France
info@plumvillage.org

Green Mountain Dharma Center
P.O. Box 182
Hartland Four Corners, VT 05049
mfmaster@vermontel.net
Tel: (802) 436-1103

Deer Park Monastery
2499 Melru Lane
Escondido, CA 92026
deerpark@plumvillage.org
Tel: (760) 291-1003

For a worldwide directory of Sanghas practicing in the tradition
of Thich Nhat Hanh, please visit www.iamhome.org.